FORT WORTH LIBRARY
W9-AKG-216

TERMINAL LANCE ULTIMATE OMNIBUS

Also by Maximilian Uriarte

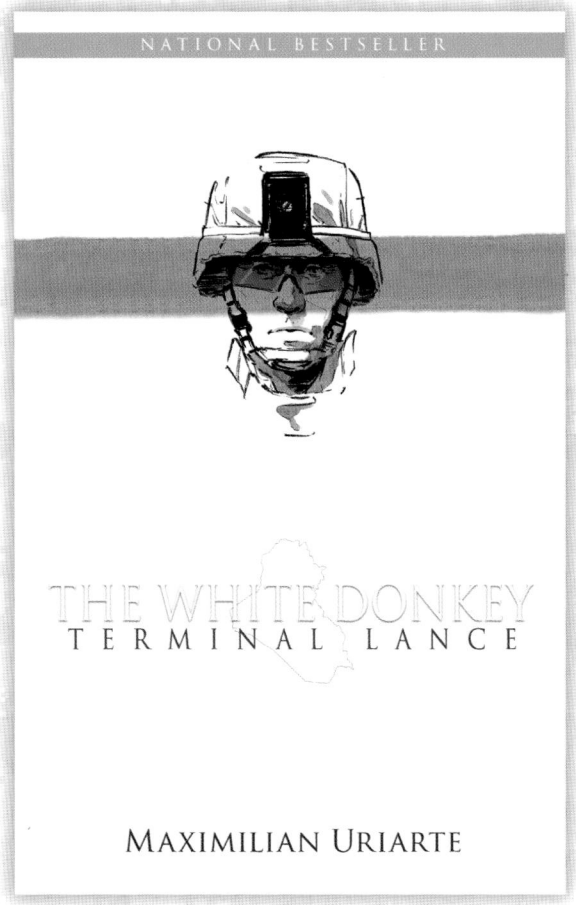

That's where it comes from.
I thought it was voluntary, Staff Sergeant.
Well, it's "voluntary" in the sense that I'm telling you to give it to me, and you have to volunteer to do it.
So yeah, it's "voluntary".
Touche...
LANCE #237 "Obvious Observations"
You know how you always see pictures of like... Recon Marines or SEALs all soaking wet on the beach or coming out of a river or something?
Yeah?
And you stop, and you go "Man... that looks so fucking badass."
That's the fuckin dumbest shit eve
TERMINAL LANCE #244 "Have You?"
HAVE YOU EVER YELLED SO HARD
Created by Maximilian Uriarte ©
TERMINAL LANCE #289 "Size Matters"
So... you guys do realize that blouses come in different sizes, right...?
What do you mean, Lance Corporal?
Well, what sizes are you wearing?
Medium-Reg.
Medium-Reg.
Medium-Reg.
TERMINAL LANCE #206 "MILES Gear"
BEEP
BEEP
BEEP
BEEP
BEEP
I don't know who "Miles" is...
...But he's a fucking assh
TERMINAL LANCE #445 "Always Room For One
I dunno, I just don't like being called a dog.
You know... I brought the WAG bag for you...
TERMINAL LANCE #389 "Lance Corporal Time"
Abe, listen up...
I need you and Garcia at the Motor Pool at 1400 to pick up a high back.
I don't...
...What does
in Lance Corporal...
I need you at the Motor Pool at two jacks past Afternoon Chow.
Hey duc
*SIG
Fuck my li

TERMINAL LANCE ULTIMATE OMNIBUS

Created by

Maximilian Uriarte

Little, Brown and Company
New York Boston London

The characters and events in this book are fictitious. Any similarity to real persons, living or dead, is coincidental and not intended by the author.

Copyright © 2018 by Maximilian Uriarte

Hachette Book Group supports the right to free expression and the value of copyright. The purpose of copyright is to encourage writers and artists to produce the creative works that enrich our culture.

The scanning, uploading, and distribution of this book without permission is a theft of the author's intellectual property. If you would like permission to use material from the book (other than for review purposes), please contact permissions@hbgusa.com. Thank you for your support of the author's rights.

Little, Brown and Company
Hachette Book Group
1290 Avenue of the Americas, New York, NY 10104
littlebrown.com

First Edition: April 2018

Little, Brown and Company is a division of Hachette Book Group, Inc. The Little, Brown name and logo are trademarks of Hachette Book Group, Inc.

The publisher is not responsible for websites (or their content) that are not owned by the publisher.

The Hachette Speakers Bureau provides a wide range of authors for speaking events. To find out more, go to hachettespeakersbureau.com or call (866) 376-6591.

All strips were previously published on terminallance.com or in the *Marine Corps Times*.

Interior book design by Jason Snyder

ISBN 978-0-316-41224-7
LCCN 2017958898

10 9 8 7 6 5 4 3 2 1

WOR

Printed in the United States of America

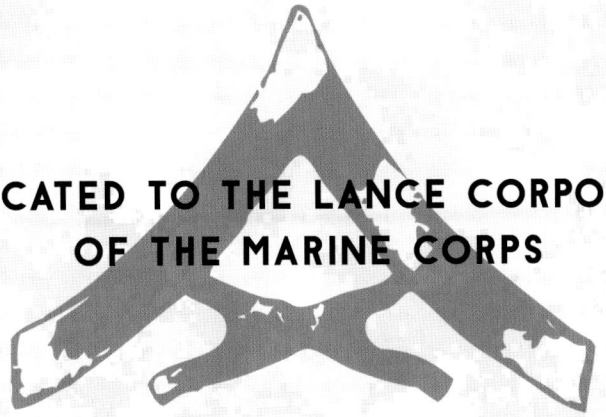

DEDICATED TO THE LANCE CORPORALS
OF THE MARINE CORPS

Foreword from Paul Szoldra

Duffel Blog creator

There must be something in the water in Hawaii.

Back in 2003, I walked off a plane onto the island of Oahu and headed to the Kaneohe Marine Corps base where I had been assigned with 3rd Battalion, 3rd Marines. I was stationed there for three years.

A short time after I left, a Marine I had never met did the same. His name was Maximilian Uriarte, and, like me, he was always questioning the things around him. "Why are we doing it this way?" he probably asked his fellow Marines.

This doesn't make any sense, he and I would think, while standing outside in formation for hours on end waiting for the commanding officer to show up.

But soon Max progressed from being a minor annoyance to his platoon sergeant to becoming the creator of the incredibly successful *Terminal Lance* comic strip. For Max, it wasn't enough to talk about the trials and tribulations of infantry life to just the fellow Marines in his platoon.

He had to do something. He had to build something new that would unite all Marines in their shared experiences, and give them a hearty laugh in the process.

And build it, he did.

As for me, well, I later created the military satire site known as Duffel Blog, for much the same reasons as Max. I had things I wanted to say and that was the platform that did it. And Max's creation is directly responsible for my own. His courage, dedication, and hilarious comics inspired me to go down a similar path, and for that, I'll forever be grateful.

I never had the pleasure of serving with Max, since we both just missed each other in our paths to Hawaii. But thankfully, we met after I moved to the San Francisco Bay Area in 2013. I recall our first meeting as being slightly awkward. We walked around Union Square, two internet friends, talking about what we were up to and chatting about our time in the Marines.

But that awkwardness was quickly dashed as I realized how alike we were. We had similar outlooks on life, agreed on a number of contentious issues, and most strikingly, did not have enough time in the world for all the ideas we had in our heads. That's the most amazing thing about Max.

He has more ideas for new projects than he can count. He'll never be satisfied with just *Terminal Lance,* which dwarfs all other military comics and counts top officers at Headquarters Marine Corps among its readership.

Put simply, Max's drive to create new and even more exciting things is what makes him Max.

And the crazy thing is that he instinctively knows what will work, and he hits home runs just about every time. Whether that's a new strip idea, or completely blowing past his goal on Kickstarter for his *New York Times*–bestselling book, *The White Donkey,* Max's drive should be an inspiration to all Marines, veterans, and civilians alike.

Max and I are now real-life friends. He sometimes texts me something he's working on, or asks for my advice regarding an upcoming project. He dutifully listens to my advice and then usually takes the opposite approach, so much so that I now laughingly tell him, "Well, that's what I think, but I know you're not going to do that."

And yet, that never offends me. Because I know Max. He has blazed his own trail for so long without my advice that he already knows the way.

With this book of the complete *Terminal Lance,* you'll see rather quickly why Max has been so successful. He speaks to the issues of Marines with authenticity and biting humor, because he has been there right alongside them.

He loves the Marine Lance Corporal, and he has never forgotten to focus singularly on that person with everything he creates. And I'm thankful that, even with the strip's Lance Corporal focus, a former sergeant like me can get the humor and enjoy it all the same.

But, I wonder as I write this, about seven years after *Terminal Lance* was born, what will come next and credit its inspiration to Max?

Hopefully nothing has changed with the water in Hawaii.

Author's Note

When I created* Terminal Lance *back in 2010, I never could have foreseen what it would become over the years. What began as a humble three-panel comic strip and a rambling blog soon became a staple of Marine Corps culture.

The strip, which was once considered taboo by the military establishment, has since been embraced by Marines stationed in every clime and place from every rank and rate. Now, it is hard to imagine a Corps before the age of social media and before the biting critique that this comic presented. Few people were willing to publicly go against the grain of Marine Corps culture, and the few outlets and comic strips that existed seemed like extensions of a self-indulgent Public Affairs office rather than something that truly challenged the Marines' own image.

It might not seem like it now, but at the time of its original publication, *Terminal Lance* was quite subversive. Marines are prideful people and are generally unwelcoming of anything that challenges that pride.

But I'm proud to say that the strip quickly grew in popularity. I suppose it's hard to be mad at something when you know it's true, and it's doubly difficult when that something makes you laugh.

With that said, *Terminal Lance* is a product of its time, and the last seven years have seen enormous social change, both in the military and in the country as a whole.

For example, in late 2010, President Obama repealed the long-standing "Don't Ask, Don't Tell" policy that expelled many service members based on their sexual orientation. For the first time in American history, openly gay men and women were allowed to serve in the United States Armed Forces without fear.

Terminal Lance has found itself in the unique position to speak directly to a large population of active-duty service members. For this reason, I have tried my best to provide a comforting voice in the face of rapid change. In the case of the DADT repeal, I did a comic strip (*Terminal Lance* #34 "It's Already Gay") pointing out how absurd it is to be upset at the new order when being in the Marine Corps is already extremely gay in itself.

It is because of strips like these that *Terminal Lance* has earned itself a reputation for being one of the few military voices that has been outspoken in its support of social progress.

With that said, *Terminal Lance* is still a product of its time, and I started this comic at the age of twenty-two. My own viewpoints on varying subjects have shifted over time, with the times. Some of the comics in this collection are perhaps outdated in their humor, language, artwork, or their political stance, but they are presented here as they were created. It is with this knowledge that I hope the comics are appreciated for what they are:

The examination and characterization of the often absurd experience of being a United States Marine infantryman.

PART 1
REGULAR STRIPS

1 "How Nicknames Are Born"

Good morning Marines and anyone else who decides to read this!

So this was the first post, the first comic, the launch of *Terminal Lance* officially. This comic was inspired by my experiences with the crazy nicknames that get invented around here. We've all seen it happen, standing around in a circle talking—one sentence leads to the next, one connection to another, and suddenly you have a nickname for someone that has nothing to do with what you were originally talking about.

One example I can think of specifically is my friend Bill. My section leader at the time decided that Bill looked like the character Bill from *King of the Hill*, so he declared him "Bill," even though his real name has absolutely no similarity.

I suppose I was always lucky, as my last name was too hard for my seniors to pronounce so they started calling me by my first name—Max. And thus, I became known as my actual name.

2 "SNCO Syndrome"

I find the many dialects of the Marine Corps to be interesting, or at least entertaining. It's strange how once someone goes into boot camp and gets shat out the other side, his entire vocabulary is often reduced to a bunch of nonsensical grunts and half-phrases. Some of these people continue to talk like this for years, and their vocabularies certainly suffer for it. I refer to this as "SNCO Syndrome." (Staff Non-Commissioned Officer.) Keep in mind that not all Staff NCO's suffer from this.

Some, however, retain this mode of thought and speech for the rest of their lives. This comic is actually inspired by a true story. I had a Master Guns (Master Gunnery Sergeant) who would literally say "Cleared Hot!" in place of most of his vocabulary. Sometimes it made sense, most of the time it didn't. I know how it affected the work environment, which is to say, not really at all. However, I can't imagine that, were the man to return home and continue yelling "Cleared Hot!" at the most inappropriate times, it would end well. These things carry on all over the Corps, though; my recruiter used to end every sentence and answer every question with "Good to Go." Other words permeate the barracks and chow halls of the Marine Corps, such as "Hello, Roger," and the almost always inappropriate "Kill," or its extended version: "Kill Bodies." I think what bothers me the most about "Kill" as a response is that it's never the people who've actually killed someone that use it.

Whatever the case, I think all Marines—SNCO's and motivated junior enlisted—could stand to expand their vocabularies. If you're the kind of person that answers a question with "Semper Fi," you probably need to be on medication. Still, whether you love it or hate it, Marine-speak is universally understood by Marines alike.

3 "Looking Professional"

I always found the rules surrounding what we are allowed to do while in uniform sort of silly. We can't have things in our pockets and we can't carry anything in our right hand. Technically, we can't even hold the hand of our loved ones while in uniform. For an organization that prides itself on practicality and adaptability in combat, the military practices none of that regarding the wearing of service uniforms.

Today's service uniforms are really nothing more than modernized versions of the ones that the Marines of old used to wear. Back then, however, I don't think anyone cared if you used your pockets to store items, as that is why pockets exist. Yes, I am stating this as a fact: Pockets exist to store items on your person. This concept is extremely hard for some of the more hardcore regulation-thumpers to grasp. The idea that you could honestly get in trouble for putting your wallet in your back pocket is completely absurd to anyone outside of the service.

This happens all the time: We get corrected for doing something that would seem practical enough in your uniform. Not just the Service Alphas, Bravos, and Chucks—but in cammies as well. Have you ever tried to put your hands in your pocket on a cold field op? Or tried to wear a backpack or some other carry-able storage device using the straps provided only to be yelled at by some random, butt-hurt Staff NCO? Of course, you have! But we're all used to it. Regulations are regulations, and some people truly pride themselves on their ability to angrily enforce them.

TERMINAL LANCE #4 "Modern Warfare"
...So I was in the prone killing motherfuckers like it was cool. I killed so many I had to use my M9!
...?
Damn, that's pretty badass.
Wow man, that's a pretty intense story, you just get back from Afghanistan?
Wha...?
...Huh?
What? Fuck no, we're talking about Modern Warfare 2, you idiot.
What a retard!

TERMINAL LANCE #5 "Race Card"
Hey Childs, go take those tires over to the motor pool.
Oh hell no, Staff Sergeant. I'm not touching no racist-ass tires!
What the hell? How can tires possibly be racist?
Have you ever SEEN the Michelin Man?
How can a man made out of tires be white?! How many white tires have you ever seen?!

6 "Jambo!" (If you went to Iraq, you'll get it.)

The Ugandan guards that protect the chow halls and posts around Iraq's major bases always brought joy to me. I remember my days in the turret fondly, riding past the guard posts and yelling "Jambo!" from my hole atop the MRAP as we cruised around Camp Fallujah. I was always reciprocated with an even more enthusiastic reply of "JAAAAM-BOOOO SIR!" from the Ugandans.

For some reason the word "Jambo" gets them going pretty good. I haven't made the journey to Afghanistan, so I'm not sure if these guys are there. If they are, and you happen to be there now, make sure you give them a good Jambo next time you see them. If you happen to be in Iraq, and pass by some Ugandan guards, definitely give them a hefty Jambo.

8 "The Many Uses of a Glow Belt"

This strip is based on a true story. During my first deployment in '07, the ISF (Iraqi Security Forces) guys didn't have any uniforms. These were men who wanted to stand up for their neighborhoods and regions. The US Military would pay them to stand around at checkpoints and defend their locale. There were no uniforms then, however, so we gave them glow belts.

I remember my first few convoys, seeing these seemingly shady guys and having no idea whether we could trust them. A lot of Marines had trouble trusting the local forces because we didn't always know where they came from. While we were there, there was a lot of chatter that the IP's (Iraqi Police) were going to turn on us. We were on high alert just in case.

I recall one story from this time of friction between the IP's and the Coalition forces quite fondly. I was part of a PSD platoon during my first deployment. I was the lead turret gunner of an MRAP behind the M2 .50 Cal. We would often escort our company commander to the local Iraqi Police chief's headquarters and would sit outside during their long meetings. During one of our trips, I was sitting in the turret posted on security around the building as usual. Suddenly, I heard a three-round burst coming from the inside. Naturally, given the level of mistrust that existed between us and the Iraqi police, I assumed it was time—the Iraqi Police had turned on us. I sprung from my strap and immediately rotated my gun to the house, ready to rock and roll on the Deuce.

To my surprise, no one in the compound was firing or on high alert. I saw an Iraqi behind a PKC machine gun and took aim at him, but he put his hands up and the Iraqi Police and Marines started waving me down before I started firing. It was passed over the 'net that apparently one of the IP's was fucking around a bit too much on the PKC and had a misfire. I wanted to punch him, but I think I got my vengeance on his pants—as the look on his face when he saw the barrel of my .50 on him could only be described as that of someone shitting himself.

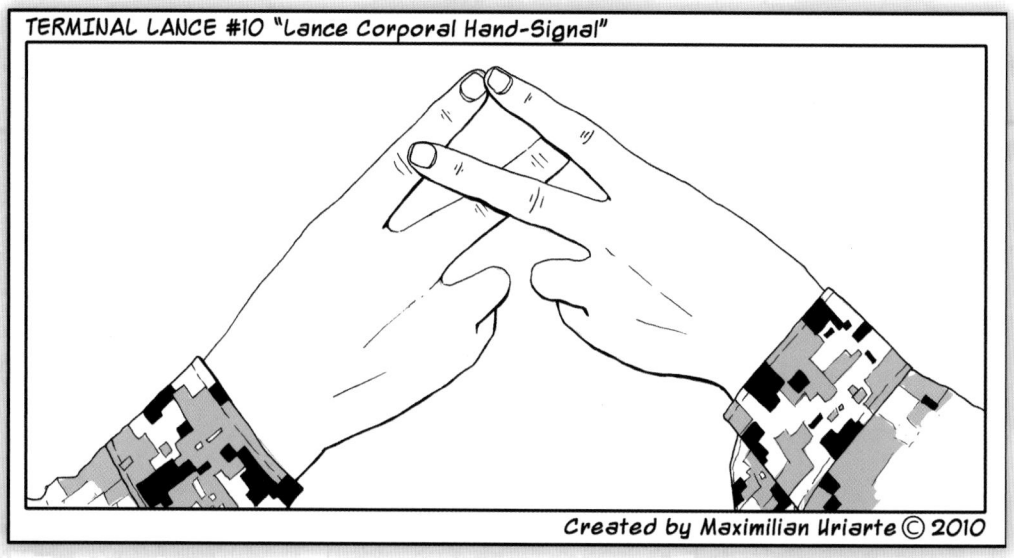

10 "Lance Corporal Hand-Signal"

Throw it up, gents! Represent your true colors, with the Lance Corporal hand signal. I can't actually take credit for the hand signal; my aforementioned friend Bill created it during our first deployment.

The Lance Corporal in the infantry goes a long way. It is generally recognized within our ranks that being a Lance virtually means nothing to us. We have a full understanding of how broken the cutting score system is and how ridiculous promotions are. And the best of us are unwilling to suck enough dick to get promoted.

If Sergeants are the backbone of the Marine Corps, then Lance Corporals are the extremities, ultimately responsible for performing the tasks to keep the Corps alive. Unfortunately for the infantry, Lance Corporals have to be more than just extremities. I have seen Lances fill billets they shouldn't have to, and do it admirably. For instance, the Section Leader billet of an Assaultman section is supposed to be a Staff Sergeant. Obviously, that doesn't happen in real life. But couldn't it at least be a Sergeant? Nope, that usually doesn't happen either. For my first couple years in the Marines, my section leader was a Lance Corporal, until he was rightfully meritoriously promoted to Corporal. After he left, we had another Lance Corporal take his place until he was again promoted to Corporal.

So if Lances can fill the shoes of Staff NCO's and NCO's, why shouldn't we be proud to be one? I say we take the shame away from being a one-chevron, cross-rifle rocking monkey and take pride in it! Throw up that hand signal and let the world know that with a promotion system as fucked as ours, there's no point in giving a shit! Ever seen a Corporal or Sergeant with fewer ribbons than you? I have, and it pisses me off every time.

I'm not a Lance because I got in trouble, or I didn't do my job. I never claimed to be God's gift to the Marine Corps, but I performed my job just fine. I'm the result of a promotion system that is flat-out broken. The cutting score requirement for my MOS (Military Occupational Specialty) was always either absurdly high or simply closed entirely.

So like I said, throw that shit up.

11 "Where the Big Bucks Are"

This strip may hit a bit too close to home for some. But I'll be honest: Marriage in the Marine Corps is more of a problem than a blessing. Too often, especially in the infantry, Marines get married as an answer to financial problems. The problem lies within the foundation of the system itself. Where in the civilian world would you get paid to be married? Probably nowhere, but the military unwittingly encourages it with gratuitous BAH (Base Allowance for Housing) payments or potentially even a rent-free two-bedroom house in one of the base housing blocks. When living in the barracks is such a shit show, tying the knot can be an easy escape for an enterprising Lance Corporal.

While there are plenty of hoops to jump through when it comes time to tie the knot, none of them truly work as a deterrent against a marriage. The result is an 80 percent divorce rate brought on by Marines who just don't understand the consequences of what they're getting themselves into. We shouldn't encourage Marines to get married at such a young age. Whatever the solution, the system needs to be fixed.

Divorce rates and the resultant alimonies truly are a rampant problem in the Marines, and probably the military as a whole. Single Marines need to stop being treated worse, stop getting fucked with 24/7, maybe even have the option of receiving BAH. Little things like this will go a long way in fighting young marriage—and divorce—rates.

TERMINAL LANCE #12 "Tom Clancy Is Full of Shit"

Created by Maximilian Uriarte © 2010

TERMINAL LANCE #13 "Salty Cammies"

Created by Maximilian Uriarte © 2010

TERMINAL LANCE #14 "The Mr. E Mystery 1"

Created by Maximilian Uriarte © 2010

TERMINAL LANCE #15 "SPECIAL EDITION"

Well here you are again, another dumb grunt stuck in Iraq. You said you wanted it, you told your recruiter you knew it was going to suck, you didn't care. You were right, it did suck, but it certainly wasn't the kind of suck you thought it would be.

You spend as much time listening to First Sergeant chew your platoon's ass as you do standing post. You'd give a shit if you thought you had a chance in hell of picking up, but your chain of command has its head stuck so far up its ass it's more concerned with throwing NJP's at you and your Marines than seeing you succeed. To them you're just another pissed-off grunt.

But fuck it, you stopped giving a shit after your first deployment. You didn't just drop your pack, you cut the motherfucker off and threw it off a cliff harder than that retard threw that puppy.

So who gives a shit? No one here, for sure. So fuck it, embrace it, count the days til your EAS and live it up while you can. You *are* just another pissed-off grunt. You ***are*** the meaning of a ***Terminal Lance.***

Created by Maximilian Uriarte © 2010

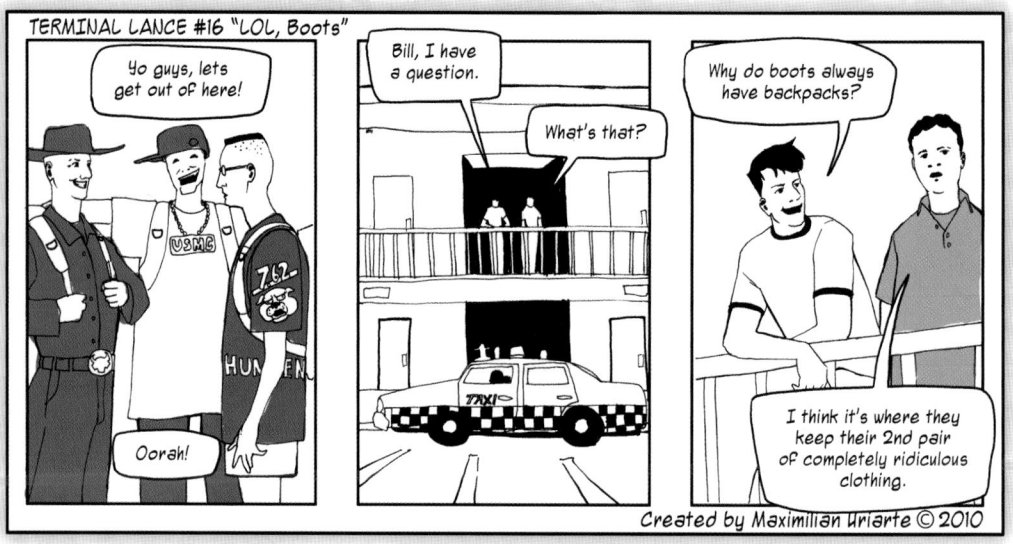
TERMINAL LANCE #16 "LOL, Boots"
Yo guys, lets get out of here!
Oorah!
Bill, I have a question.
What's that?
Why do boots always have backpacks?
I think it's where they keep their 2nd pair of completely ridiculous clothing.
Created by Maximilian Uriarte © 2010

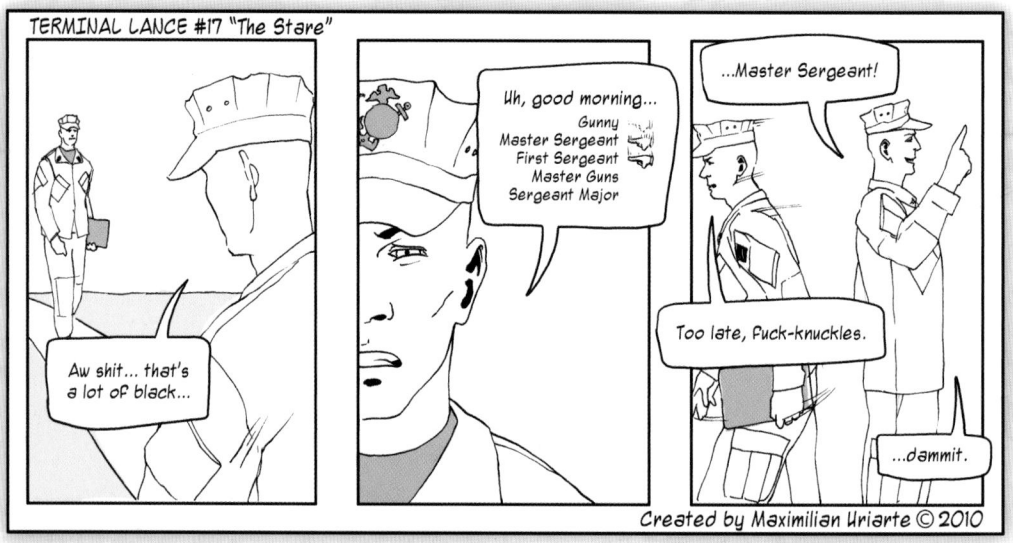
TERMINAL LANCE #17 "The Stare"
Aw shit... that's a lot of black...
Uh, good morning...
Gunny
Master Sergeant
First Sergeant
Master Guns
Sergeant Major
...Master Sergeant!
Too late, Fuck-knuckles.
...dammit.
Created by Maximilian Uriarte © 2010

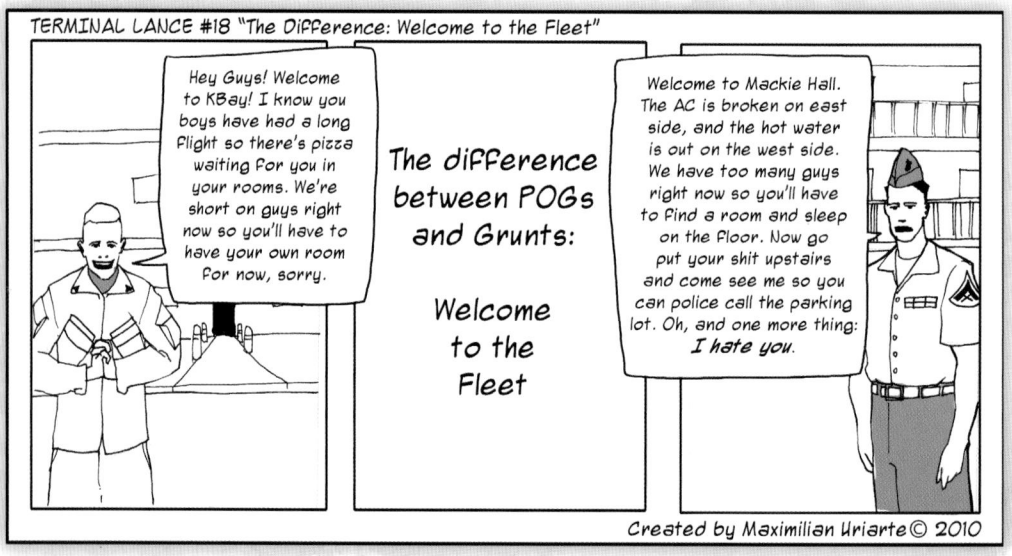
TERMINAL LANCE #18 "The Difference: Welcome to the Fleet"
Hey Guys! Welcome to KBay! I know you boys have had a long flight so there's pizza waiting for you in your rooms. We're short on guys right now so you'll have to have your own room for now, sorry.
The difference between POGs and Grunts:
Welcome to the Fleet
Welcome to Mackie Hall. The AC is broken on east side, and the hot water is out on the west side. We have too many guys right now so you'll have to find a room and sleep on the floor. Now go put your shit upstairs and come see me so you can police call the parking lot. Oh, and one more thing: I hate you.
Created by Maximilian Uriarte © 2010

20 "The Green Weenie Strikes Again!"

This comic was inspired by what transpired at my final physical. Over the years in an infantry battalion, you really don't get to go to BAS (Base Aid Station) enough. Well, those of us that are worth a damn don't. There's definitely a stigma associated with going to medical while you're in the infantry. To go to medical is to be weak, and as a result most grunts end up with all kinds of improperly treated problems by the time their final physicals roll around and have no real excuse for it.

All the medical problems I'd ever had came to light during my final physical, and the good doctor was noticeably annoyed. Granted, she was an H&S Bn. doctor and probably doesn't see too many grunts, but I can imagine her frustration at my helplessness. She took about four pages of notes while I explained all my problems, including the fact that I didn't have my medical record because my old unit decided to take it with them to Twentynine Palms despite the fact that I had moved over to the base Combat Camera shop. Oh, the green weenie strikes hard, and it strikes fast.

This ultimately led to my getting about seventeen X-rays done on my back and rib cage, as well as about four follow-up appointments.

This story may not seem like it has much to do with the strip, but getting "fucked on a daily basis" is precisely what it's like to be in the infantry. The medical record thing is just one of the many nuances of being in the grunts. The doctor was dumbfounded by the lack of recording and procedure followed by my old unit's BAS. I never thought anything of it; I assumed that's just how the Marine Corps was. But I soon discovered that medical care outside of the infantry is actually quite up to par. The clinic I went to was not a shady, cleared-out barracks-turned-BAS, but an actual clinic. The green weenie may be taking its toll on your rectum behind the scenes and you may not even know it, because you've never been exposed to the other side.

Needless to say, grunts get fucked on a daily basis for a number of other reasons. Mass punishment is a common problem, as it usually accomplishes nothing. The same people always make the same stupid decisions, and it especially doesn't work in a weapons platoon. Here's why: Three different MOS (Military Occupational Specialty), three completely different kinds of people. The allure of machine guns, mortars, or rockets appeal to very different people. These three different personality types cannot be expected to act the same, and they often clash. In my experience, the brutes in Machine Guns tend to fuck it up the most, and "skatin' Assault" and Mortars end up paying for it as well.

In addition, grunts typically don't get half of the benefits or the benefits even explained to them that the POG's of the Corps do. You have no idea how many times I've said, ". . . what is that?" when someone around the ComCam shop has mentioned some Marine Corps order that everyone seems to know but me. It's an unfair dichotomy, to be sure. I do feel, however, that the grunt path is the true path of the Marine Corps experience.

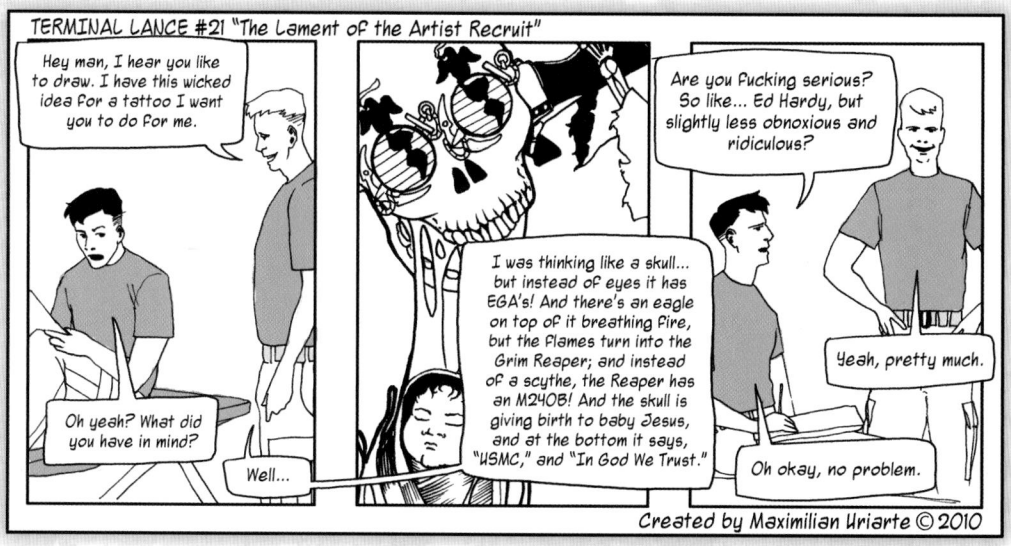

USMC
IN GOD WE TRUST

TERMINAL LANCE #22 "Why He's Always Late"

Created by Maximilian Uriarte © 2010

TERMINAL LANCE #23 "Literally"

Created by Maximilian Uriarte © 2010

24 "It's Worth It"

This is a true story. Well, I dunno if Bill actually did any maniacal laughing at the time, but this is based on true events much in the same way Hollywood makes movies "based on true events."

Wisdom teeth are one of those things that are probably better pulled out while you're active duty and have that ever-so-popular "free medical." After all, they do get you out of work and if you're of the Oh-Three type, maybe even a field op. While they are completely miserable, field ops do have value. The field is where the heart of the Marine Corps is. In a strange way, the field is where things make sense. There's no outside world to worry about in the field, and it brings Marines close, especially because we all hate it. The field is a place of bonding. As one of my seniors explained to me on my first deployment, Marines come closer together when they have the common enemy of the Marine Corps to bitch about. Thus putting Marines through misery on a daily basis makes them much closer in the long run.

Strip a platoon or company of all their material worries, and all they have left is each other.

Going back to the comic, though; before the 2008 recession hit America, getting Marines to join was a problem. Recruitment was low and retention even lower, so Marines were being offered bonuses of up to $90,000 to re-up—a hefty offer to say the least. Maybe—now this is just a thought—retention would be easier to attain if Marines didn't prefer to have brutal oral surgery performed instead of doing their job.

TERMINAL LANCE #25 "Deployments Are Just like Final Fantasy Games"

You get put on bases just like small villages. There's an Item Shop that sells potions and gear; i.e., Rip Its and Spec-Ops merchandise.

You gain levels and experience through combat, and as you get more experience you upgrade your gear and weapons...

Created by Maximilian Uriarte © 2010

TERMINAL LANCE #26 "Did Anyone Actually Read It?"

Created by Maximilian Uriarte © 2010

TERMINAL LANCE #27 "Challenge Coins: Not a Grunt Thing"

Created by Maximilian Uriarte © 2010

TERMINAL LANCE #28 "False Advertising"

Created by Maximilian Uriarte © 2010

TERMINAL LANCE #29 "Why BAS Sucks"

Created by Maximilian Uriarte © 2010

TERMINAL LANCE #30 "The Lance Corporal Food Pyramid"

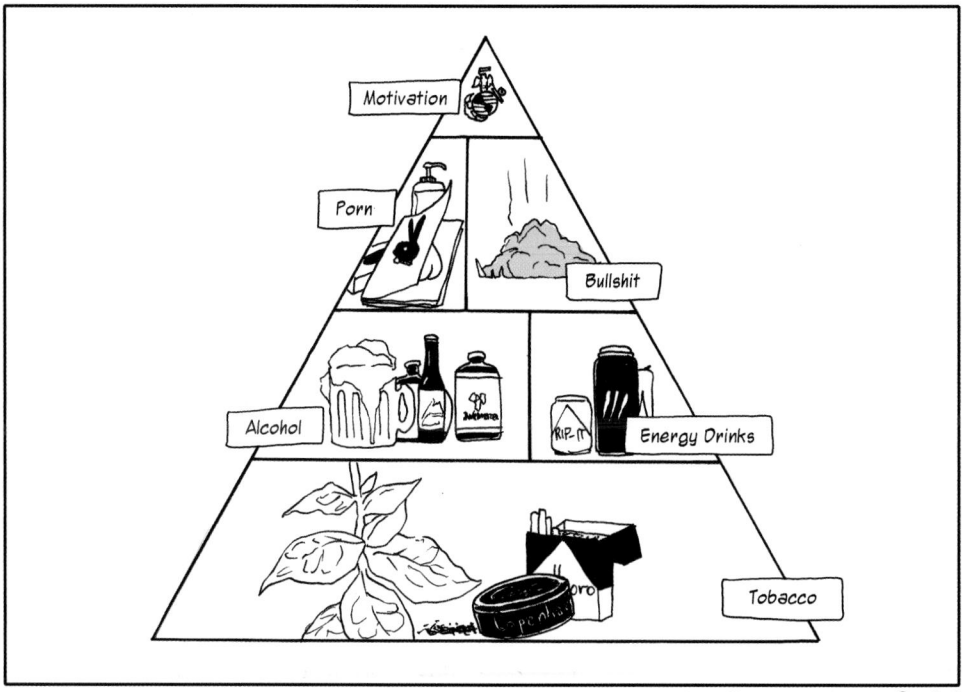

Created by Maximilian Uriarte © 2010

TERMINAL LANCE #31 "Shitter Graffiti Is an Art... of Dicks"

Created by Maximilian Uriarte © 2010

TERMINAL LANCE #32 "The Quest to Check Out"

Created by Maximilian Uriarte © 2010

TERMINAL LANCE #33 "They've Never Been Cool"

Created by Maximilian Uriarte © 2010

34 "It's Already Gay"

The issue of gays in the military has always been a tough subject, and I'll leave my opinion out of this. As the strip suggests though, it is quite ironic that so many Marines are against gays and lesbians serving in the military, but are guilty of doing gayer shit than the average gay man on a daily basis. The "oil check" was something I never really thought was appropriate, in any situation—yet it had its heyday in my old platoon for a good couple of weeks.

There's always some new practical, physical joke that spreads around and lasts for a week or two. Usually it involves some form of homoerotic behavior like fingering another man's asshole or showing someone your balls. I suppose when you're stuck in shitty situations on a near constant basis away from civilization, a group of young men will inevitably resort to using their own bodies to find humor.

MAX NOTE 2017: This strip was released before the repeal of "Don't Ask, Don't Tell," when gays and lesbians were not permitted to serve openly in any military branch. The goal of this strip was to point out the absurdity of the anti-gay vitriol of the time, considering the fact that joining the Marine Corps is by far the gayest thing any straight man can possibly do.

The gayest.

As you'd expect, once the repeal actually happened, absolutely nothing was different—proving that disallowing gays to openly serve in the military was a stupid rule to begin with that cost many otherwise great service members their careers.

TERMINAL LANCE #35 "How Things Have Changed"

Company Office: 1970

For mailing home 2 lbs of C4, a kilo of pot, going UA for 2 months in Thailand, and telling the Sergeant Major to go fuck himself: 30 days suspended bust.

...oh, by the way, great job keeping your squad together during that ambush yesterday.

Company Office: 2010

For being five minutes late to formation, and giving the Sergeant Major attitude, reduction to PFC and 30 days restriction.

...oh, by the way, great job keeping your squad together during that ambush yesterday.

Created by Michael Fay © 2010

TERMINAL LANCE #36 "The Closet Motivator"

Man... I fucking hate this place. I'm so excited to go on leave next week.

Oh yeah? Where are you going?

Just back home: Little Rock, Arkansas.

That's awesome. I bet it'll be great being away from the Marine Corps for a few weeks. Sleeping in every day and giving the Corps a good ol' fuck you daily huh?

My thoughts exactly...

0600, ONE WEEK LATER: LITTLE ROCK, ARKANSAS

Oorah!?

USMC

SEMPER FI!

Did someone say Marine???

Created by Maximilian Uriarte © 2010

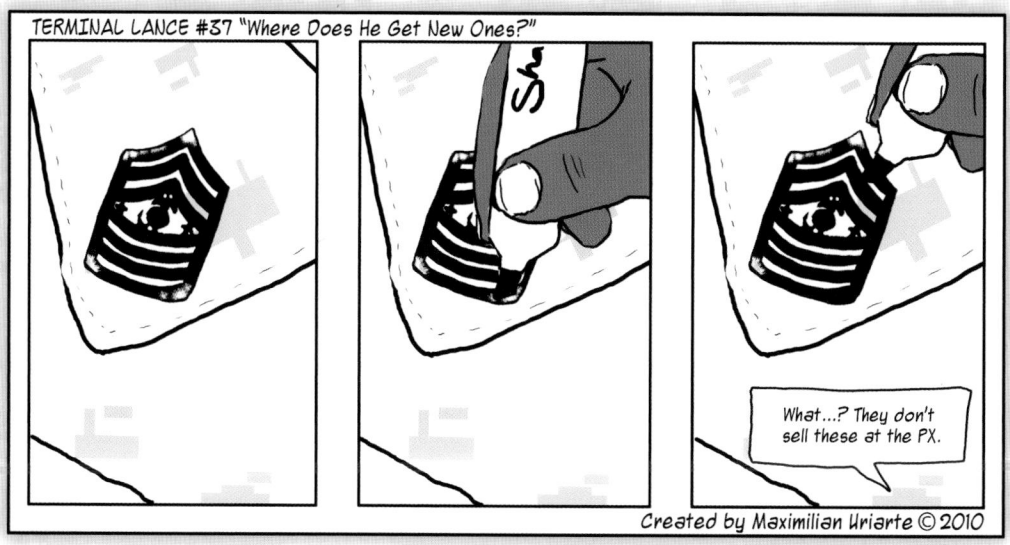
TERMINAL LANCE #37 "Where Does He Get New Ones?"
What...? They don't sell these at the PX.
Created by Maximilian Uriarte © 2010

TERMINAL LANCE #38 "Personal Financial Management"
That's a pretty sick car man. It must've been expensive...
Now it's all good...
...I got a great rate from a loan shark out in town.
Oh yeah? That's pretty cool.
Yeah the APR is only 45.9%!
Uh... dude? That's pretty steep.
Haha, you idiot. It's okay, I'm already paying it off with my new credit cards!
Created by Maximilian Uriarte © 2010

TERMINAL LANCE #39 "A New Staff NCO is Born"
Hey man, how's your re-enlistment package going?
Not that great, they won't let me re-enlist because I wasn't able to pick up, even though our MOS has been closed for the last 6 months.
That's stupid. You're the only person here who actually enjoys this place.
Yeah well, what can I do?
What about you? I thought you hated this place? Why would you re-up? Didn't you get a DUI last month?
Yup! I think they forgot though. I figure I got nothing better going for me and my morbidly obese wife is about to shit out another baby, I may as well re-up till they kick me out or start throwing rockers at me.
Brilliant...
Created by Maximilian Uriarte © 2010

40 "Rip It®: A Documentary"

Rip It® is a registered trademark of Sundance Beverage Company.

I'll just get straight to the point on this one: Marines love Rip Its.

For those of you that have never been to Iraq, a Rip It is an energy drink that they hand out to the Marines and soldiers overseas. They're like delectable cans of liquid candy. Marines will raid the chow halls when they get the chance and shove as many as they can fit in their cargo pockets, shove 'em in their trucks or keep a reserve in their cans. A good Marine can take about eight out of the chow hall on a good run, and boy do they.

Energy drinks are big in the Marine Corps. I did this strip on Rip Its because it is really as much Iraq humor as it is Marine humor. However, back in garrison—where the world is readily available—Monsters and Rock Stars are just as prevalent. I have yet to see the short cans stateside, though I wouldn't be too shocked to find them.

In any case, the Citrus X ones were fantastic. Many long nights in the turret were kept fueled by those sweet little cans of delicious. The initial idea for this strip was actually a live-action documentary I was going to make on my second deployment, given that I worked with ComCam every day and I had access to high-quality camera equipment. However, that idea passed by and has been reborn here in three panels.

TERMINAL LANCE #41 "Standing Post: Stages of Boredom"
Stage 1: Conversation
I'm gonna fuck everything when I get home.
Yup.
I'll have to start freebasing penicillin. Like... some kind of sexual cocaine addict.
Stage 2: Song
You are... my Fiiiire.
My one... desiiiiire.
Believe me when I say...
I WANT IT THAAAT WAY!
Stage 3: Genital Mutilation
Dude, watch me light my pubes on fire!
HAHAHAHAHA! You're the fucking man, dude!
Created by Maximilian Uriarte © 2010

TERMINAL LANCE #42 "Calling Home"
OPSEC!
RING RING
Hello?
Hey babe, it's me. How's everything?
YOU BITCH!
OPSEC!
Honey?
Honey? Hello?
I'MA FUCKING KILL YOU AND HIM WHEN I COME HOME!
Oooh yeah...
Girl, when I come home I'm gonna fuck you in half. What are you wearing? Mmmm...
Hey babe... I think I'll just call you later. The guy to my left is going to kill someone, and I think the one on my right is beating off.
Created by Maximilian Uriarte © 2010

TERMINAL LANCE #43 "Really, No One Does"
Hey there, Marine! Get your hands out of your pockets!
What? Who are you?
I'm the First Sergeant's wife, devil dog!
AHAHA
HAHA
HAHA
HA
HAHA
HAHA
HA
HAHA...
Ahehe
SNORT
Nobody cares.
Created by Maximilian Uriarte © 2010

TERMINAL LANCE #44 "Smear the Gear Queer"
Hey dude, what's up?
SIGH
Fuck my life...
Ugh... Not much man, how about you?
Got some new gear...
Yeah... I can see that.
...
...
...yup.
...This is your first time outside the wire, huh?
...why do you ask?
Created by Maximilian Uriarte © 2010

TERMINAL LANCE #45 "Vacations Don't Count"
Gunny, I gotta ask... The war has been going on for like 7 years now, how have you not deployed yet?
Well I just got out of recruiting duty...
But really, boy--I've been on 7 deployments! I've been to Thailand, Germany, Japan, the Phillipines an
Right, right, right...
That's cool and all, but I mean...
You have yet to go on any REAL deployments.
...
Created by Maximilian Uriarte © 2010

TERMINAL LANCE #46 "Educated Leadership"
Lieutenant James, sir, what was your major in college, anyway?
I was an English major, Lance Corporal!
So basically... you did nothing?
Hey now! I'll have you know that I was an honor roll student!
Lieutenant James, 2 Years Earlier Oregon State University
AWESOME!
It is an honor for me to roll this blunt!
Created by Maximilian Uriarte © 2010

TERMINAL LANCE #47 "Race Card 2"
...the Marines killed many Viet Cong, I can't remember the exact number... Do you happen to know, Nguyen?
...WTF?
...I guess cause I'm Vietnamese I'm supposed to know... right, sir?
Is that what you see when you look at me, sir? Some buck-toothed "Charlie" in a rice-paddy hat?
I... um...
...I don't know what you're talking about...
Created by Maximilian Uriarte © 2010

TERMINAL LANCE #48 "Airport Soldier Envy"
Douchebag...
Huh?
Nothing...
...
Fuck-stick...
Created by Maximilian Uriarte © 2010

TERMINAL LANCE #49 "Myths and Legends"
Hey dude, I want you to meet my girlfriend...
Her name is...
...Susie Rottencrotch. I think it's French...
Hey there, sexy-pants.
My God...
...She does exist...
Created by Maximilian Uriarte © 2010

50 "I'm Putting You Up For One"

For my beloved readers that are not in the loop, "NAM" stands for "Navy/Marine Corps Achievement Medal," and is awarded to people who go above and beyond their normal duties assigned to them. However, the medal somehow always seems to find its way onto the chests of those closest to Headquarters or H&S Company. Even though the guys on the ground are out there every day, risking life and limb, they are usually the last people to receive the award.

Despite the comic, I refuse to believe that the average grunt deserves a NAM every day he's outside the wire. However, I also refuse to believe the company clerk, police sergeant, intel guy, etc., rates the award every time he does his job. I'm not saying I've never agreed with the awarding of it to the less salty population, but I think the system is fairly slanted in their favor.

Take a Headquarters platoon for example: every day they are in the company office, under close supervision to the top-ranking members of the company. How often does the Company First Sergeant or the Commanding Officer see Lance Corporal Dipshit offer a child some water or some of his own food outside the wire? How often does even the platoon commander see it? If you're a good squad leader, hopefully never—because no squad leader wants to have to deal with an "LT" or an "Echo-8" on any sort of a daily basis. Unfortunately, it takes something much greater for the average grunt to earn the medal than just . . . doing what he's asked to do—which isn't always the case for the other side.

TERMINAL LANCE #51 "0351's: Underused, Never Appreciated"
So what the fuck are you supposed to be again?
I'm an 0351, Assaultman.
K... that's like a TOW-gunner or some shit right?
No actually, it's mostly SMAW gunning, but all of us are trained in demolitions and urban-combat breaching as well.
Awesome dude, take this .50 cal and go mount it on the turret. You're my new gunner. Tell one of your 0331 buddies to get you up to speed on it.
Um... okay...
Created by Maximilian Uriarte © 2010

TERMINAL LANCE #52 "Fucked Again..."
Dammit! IPAC messed up my paycheck again!
NAVY FED
Acct Bal: $00.50
Hahaha!
Fucked again... that green weenie sure is relentless, isn't it?
Yeah dude, totally...
Not nearly as bad as they fucked me, though.
Aren't you the guy getting kicked out for like 4 DUI's and 3 other NJP's?
Yup! Bastards didn't even give me a chance... now I'll be unemployed here in a few weeks with a wife and 3 kids.
I think you fucked yourself on that one, buddy.
Created by Maximilian Uriarte © 2010

53 "Reservists and Centipedes"

I don't typically try to sell my punch lines on pop-culture references. However, I recently saw *The Human Centipede* and was so excited I had to find a way to put it into a strip. The point of the strip was easy to make within three panels. Active-duty Marines hate reservists—those assholes found a way to be in the Marines but still be at home all the time and not have to deal with the bullshit every day.

I remember graduation day at SOI. Everyone was in their Bravos, getting ready to head to the airport to continue their Marine Corps journey. Well, at least some of us were . . . half of the company just went to the airport to fly home, never to be seen again by the active-duty guys heading to their duty stations to be hazed by hungover Lance Corporals at 0100 in the morning. The split is abrupt and deceptive. Marines that have been your friends and allies against the common evil of Marine-dom are sent back to their homes, back to their civilian friends and family, and back to their lives. Active duty never gets that luxury. We only go home on leave blocks and the rest of the time, we deal with the brunt of hazing and weekly field ops.

TERMINAL LANCE #55 "Chucks Don't Lie"

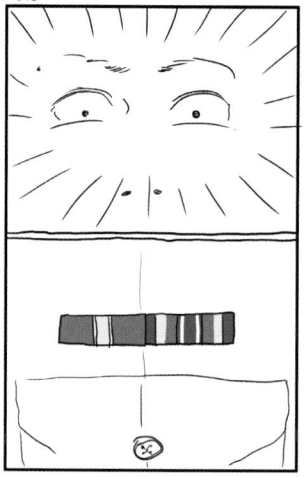

Created by Maximilian Uriarte © 2010

TERMINAL LANCE #56 "Myths and Legends II: The Dependapotamus"

Created by Maximilian Uriarte © 2010

TERMINAL LANCE #57 "Field Day Will Never Mean the Same Thing"

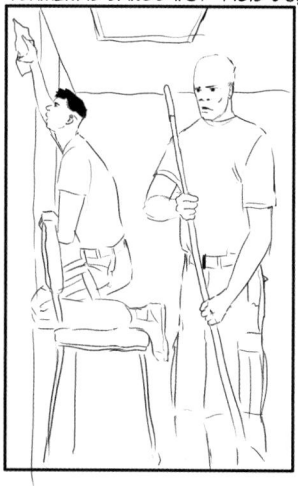

Created by Maximilian Uriarte © 2010

TERMINAL LANCE #58 "Six Bucks Is Already Enough"

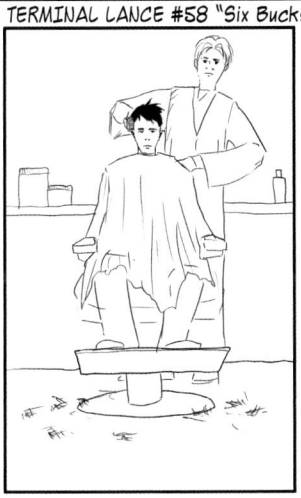

Created by Maximilian Uriarte ©2010

TERMINAL LANCE #59 "Knife-Hand Anger Gauge"

Created by Maximilian Uriarte ©2010

TERMINAL LANCE #60 "Optimism"

Created by Maximilian Uriarte ©2010

TERMINAL LANCE #61 "Why He's Always Late II"
Whoa that's a full rainbow... all the way. Whoaaa... double rainbow all the way across the sky... Oooooh my God...
Oh my God, oh my God... OH MY GOD! WOOOOOOOOOOOOOOOOOOOOO! OH MY GOD! DOUBLE RAINBOW ALL THE WAY!!! What does it mean???
Oh my God so intense!
Captain?! Sir?
Sir, the company is waiting for you. First Sergeant is getting pissed.
GOD DAMMIT MARINE! Can't you see I'm fucking busy?!
Created by Maximilian Uriarte © 2010

TERMINAL LANCE #62 "Why We Hate CIF"
Derr... Hello! Welcome to C...CIF!
Hey... uh I need to turn in my gear. The only thing I don't have are those stupid black leather glove shells that no one uses.
Okaaaaay! You'll have to fill out a missing gear statement, give it to your chain of command, have your battalion commander sign it, then take it to IPAC and they'll take it out of your p... pay.
Um... well I can just give you $30 now. I don't really have time for all of that.
I'm s...sorry sir. I can't count past t...ten, so I c...can't take that monies.
Well that's just retarde... I mean... stupid... I mean... Ah fuck it, that's fucking retarded.
Created by Maximilian Uriarte © 2010

63 "Life After EAS: First Week of School"

With this strip, I decided that instead of making fun of the Marine Corps I would make fun of myself. I doubt I'm the only one that's ever had this problem, but I noticed that after I got out of the Marines and back into school, I found myself really wanting to tell people about what I did—whether they asked to hear about it or not. Though this is obviously an exaggeration, I did find it very difficult to keep my experiences to myself.

A tour through the Marine Corps is such a unique, odd, and life-changing experience that it's hard to ignore it once you're out. It's like some kind of duty afterward, some need to make sure that people know you've seen the world, to explode into a shouted "OMG I WAS IN THE MARINE CORPS I DID THIS" every time the opportunity arises.

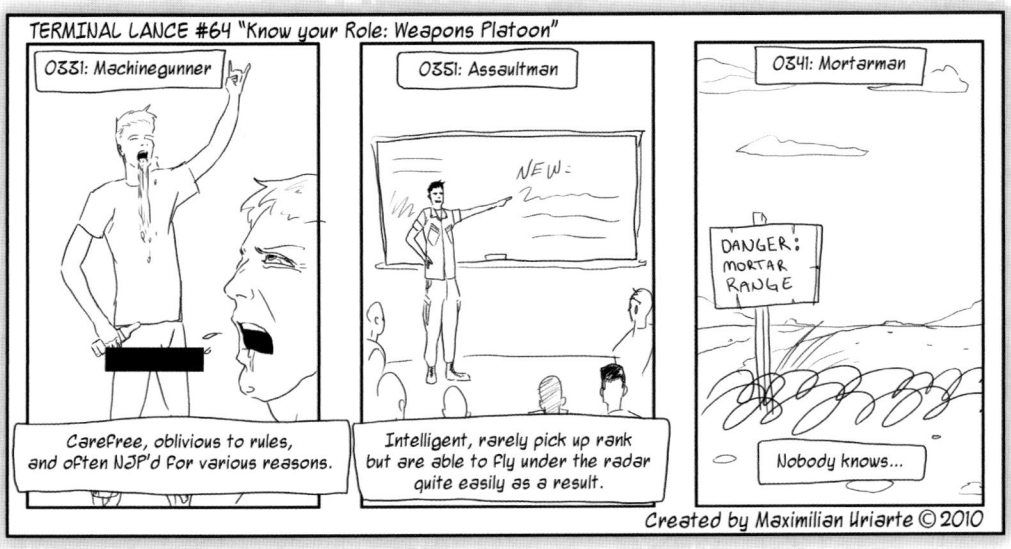

TERMINAL LANCE #65 "LOL, Boots II"

Created by Maximilian Uriarte © 2010

TERMINAL LANCE #66 "Infidelity amongst Infidels"

Created by Maximilian Uriarte © 2010

TERMINAL LANCE #67 "Hypocritical Malingerers"

Created by Maximilian Uriarte © 2010

TERMINAL LANCE #68 "Fuckin' What?"
All right fuckheads, fuckin' listen the fuck up now.
We're fuckin' gonna go fuckin' down to this fuckin' dude's fuckin' house and... fuckin'... we'll fuckin' knock and talk with this fuckin' guy. Fuckin' nothin' crazy... fuckin' should fuckin' be an easy fuckin' day.
Fuckin' anyone got any fuckin' questions?
Yeah... fuckin' go ahead, dick-shitter.
Yeah just to clarify... I think I got everything but...
...who exactly are we fucking...?
Created by Maximilian Uriarte © 2010

TERMINAL LANCE #69 "My Own Personal Hell"
My own personal hell...
FUUUUUUUUUUUUUUUUUUUUUUUUUUUUUUUUUUUUUUUCK!!!
Standing in a never-ending line at the Armory.
Created by Maximilian Uriarte © 2010

TERMINAL LANCE #70 "Addicted to Fail"
Hey man, do you have any dip?
What the fuck?
Dude, you've known about this field op for 2 weeks. You'd have to be a complete idiot to forget to bring dip...
Hey Marines!
Yes, Staff Sergeant?
Either of you boys got any dip on ya...?
Created by Maximilian Uriarte © 2010

TERMINAL LANCE #71 "Deployment Goggles"
Average Female Marine:
5 Months into Your Deployment Later...
Average Female Marine:
Created by Maximilian Uriarte © 2010

TERMINAL LANCE #72 "Happy Birthday, MotherFucker!"
Hey dude, what's going on?
Nothin' much man, today is actually my birthday...
What...?
Oh hell no...
Fuck no...
Who... said... birthday?
RUUUUUN
GET HIM!!!
HOLD HIM DOWN!!!
COME HERE BIRTHDAY BOY!!!
Created by Maximilian Uriarte © 2010

TERMINAL LANCE #73 "Life After EAS: Irony"
Fucking password...
MARINE O
mauriarte
CPL MAXIMILIAN A. URIARTE
Wait what the fuck...? ..Corporal?
So they finally promote me 3 months after my EAS. I guess the Marine Corps just had to get in one last "Fuck you."
Created by Maximilian Uriarte © 2010

74 "No Preference"

In terms of religious experience, boot camp is probably one of the most intense places that hopeful Marines can find themselves. For a number of reasons, recruits tend to undergo a kind of extreme religious epiphany as soon as they step on those yellow footprints. Gone are their old ways of sinful heathenism. Now they are acolytes of God, warriors of the Lord himself . . . that is, until they discover that epic amounts of alcohol can replace their voids of faith on the weekends once they hit the fleet.

I vividly recall the numbers of recruits that attended the church masses. Many even underwent baptism in front of an applauding audience of like-minded recruits. As in "the real world," religion in the Marines tends to only belong where it's needed. During the stressful culture shock of recruit training, Marine recruits find solace in faith otherwise left alone. I succumbed to this endeavor as well, though my Jewish background led me to synagogue on Fridays instead of church on Sundays—which actually worked out great, because I still got to chill out alone in the squad bay on Sundays while everyone else was at church.

But, for many, the culture of fleethood soon replaces this newfound religion. The average Lance Corporal is more likely to attend the omelet line at the chow hall on a Sunday than he is church. Some Marines remain devout, but, for many others, their sudden interest in religion is temporary and is relegated to the Depot.

TERMINAL LANCE #75 "They Will Hate"
Hey there, Master Sergeant!
Huh?
I know you've been in long enough to know you're supposed to salute officers!
You're right, Lieutenant...
...I have been in long enough to know that. I've been in for seventeen years, in fact. You've been in this gun club for about five minutes. Howabout you salute me, you silly boy.
WTF?
HATERS GONNA HATE!
Created by Maximilian Uriarte © 2010

TERMINAL LANCE #76 "LOL, Boots III"
I just... I just think the "high and tight" is a good haircut... It's clean and it's easy to maintain...
Created by Maximilian Uriarte © 2010

TERMINAL LANCE #77 "Selling Out"
...save you 15 percent or more on car insurance? Does a former Drill Sergeant make a terrible therapist?
Man... poor Gunny Ermey. That must really suck having to sell out like that. A fucking "Drill Sergeant?"
He must be hating life having to do these shitty commercials...
Ha
Ha
Ha
Ha
Ha
Ha
...Poor guy...
Created by Maximilian Uriarte © 2010

79 "All That Salt"

I dunno what it is about the Marine Corps. Have you ever noticed how common it is to see Marines barely in their middle age looking like geriatrics? In reality, it is simply a result of a lifetime of physical abuse to the body. All those flak runs, hikes, deployments, hardcore PT sessions, and binge drinking add up over the years. The first time I returned from Iraq, I looked like I had aged several years in the span of seven months. Physical and emotional strain on a daily basis are not good for the human body and those decrepit SNCO's and officers that just barely turned forty are the result. I'm not saying it necessarily happens to everyone. In fact, I would be willing to bet that those who spend their whole careers in the infantry are much more likely to develop this rapid aging syndrome.

As for Marine Corps balls, well they're usually one of two things: an extremely boring cesspool of uniforms and overpriced food, or an extremely boring cesspool of uniforms and overpriced food interspersed with random drunk outbursts from your company

Gunny and your friends. My last and final Marine Corps ball was the only really fun time I've had at one. Drinking with some unlikely people was an especially good time—as was walking to Wailana in Honolulu for pancakes at two a.m. in a drunken stupor.

Birthday balls have a way of being either miserable or a lot of fun, but as with most things in the Corps—it's only fun if you make it that way.

TERMINAL LANCE #82 "These Colors Don't Run"

Created by Maximilian Uriarte © 2010

TERMINAL LANCE #83 "Too Much Chow Hall"

Created by Maximilian Uriarte © 2010

TERMINAL LANCE #84 "The Jack Shack"

Created by Maximilian Uriarte © 2010

TERMINAL LANCE #85 "Great Things Come in Pairs"
DUDE! DUDE DUDE DUDE!
Huh?
My wife just gave birth! We have two twin boys!
Hey man that's great!
You know... I don't mean to preach, but now that you're a dad you should really consider going to SACO for your drinking problem... So... what are their names?
Jack...
...and Coke!
Ugh...
Created by Maximilian Uriarte © 2010

TERMINAL LANCE #86 "A Better Recruiting Commercial"
Hey there, you ugly son of a bitch...
Are people with vaginas repulsed by you? Are you getting tired of... not getting any...?
Join the Marines and get yourself a pair of Dress Blues! Because no matter how hideous you truly are...
...women just can't resist a Marine in Dress Blues!
I just came!
So join now!*
*terms and conditions apply
Created by Maximilian Uriarte © 2010

TERMINAL LANCE #87 "Special Edition Rank"
Whoa... no way!
Gold rank!? That's fucking awesome!
Oh my god...
For the love of big tits, stop... just fucking stop.
Oh hey Gunny, is something wrong? You should check out the PX, they have these special edition gold ranks.
Please... go with me into my office and shut the door. I don't want to wake up the CO while I yell at you.
Created by Maximilian Uriarte © 2010

TERMINAL LANCE #88 "Shiny Things"
Ah Fuck... Good morning, s--
Whoa, whoa, Marine.
I'm just a Petty Officer. I'm enlisted like you.
But... you have the shinies.
Yeah, it's just how the uniform is, I dunno...
...
WHAT KIND OF BUTT-FUCKING NAVY SORCERY IS THIS?!
DON'T YOU KNOW MARINES ARE TRAINED TO SALUTE SHINY THINGS!? STOP FUCKING WITH MY MIND!
Created by Maximilian Uriarte © 2010

TERMINAL LANCE #89 "TSA: Keeping Americans Safe"
SIR! STOP PLEASE!
I'm gonna need you to remove your jacket and any metal items you have on your person.
Seriously...? You realize Marines fight terrorists right? Like... it's all we do now... Seriously.
Yeah, but I'm gonna be a dick because I always wanted to join but couldn't pass the ASVAB.
Ugh... at least you're honest.
Created by Maximilian Uriarte © 2010

TERMINAL LANCE #90 "The Gift of Giving Part I"
Hey Sir? A bunch of us got together and pitched in for a Christmas present for you...
It's not a dyed-green Clone-a-Willy™ of your dick is it?
Hehe... of course not, Sir...
Okay well I'll take it and put it under my tree.
Yeah... I'm just gonna go re-wrap this first...
Created by Maximilian Uriarte © 2010

TERMINAL LANCE #91 "The Gift of Giving Part II"

Here you go, honey. This one is for you.

Hmm? Oh...

...It's from one of my Marines.

To: LT

From:

My God...

What's wrong honey?

Nothing...

...Do we still have that KY...?

Created by Maximilian Uriarte © 2010

TERMINAL LANCE #92 "The Gift of Giving Part III"

Lance Corporal!

Huh?

Hey there numbnuts!

Oh hey, sir...

The next time you decide to give a Lieutenant a dildo for Christmas, I'll make sure you leave the Marine Corps a Terminal Private instead.

Roger that, sir...

Wait...

What's on this thing...? And why does it smell like shit?!

Created by Maximilian Uriarte © 2010

93 "POG's Impressing the Grunts"

Outside of the infantry (and even in it, some could argue), not all Marine Corps MOS are treated equal. It is a complete fallacy to say that there aren't any cool POG jobs—tank crewman, for example—but there are many non-infantry jobs that one could consider badass. Obviously, there are also many POG jobs that one would not consider badass, which I've exemplified here with IPAC. Though, frankly, I think the lamest POG job I've ever heard of is the 1171 Water Tech. When I first heard a Marine say to others, "They call us water dogs!" I literally shuddered in disbelief that the Marines could possibly have a job that lame.

Sorry, 1171's, but it's not the first time I've made fun of you.

TERMINAL LANCE #95 "The Truth About Tray-Rat Sausages"
Ya know...
I'm cool with the bagged eggs and shitty coffee...
...but I can never bring myself to eat one of these sausages...
...where the hell do they find them?
GRUNT SAUSAGES
Created by Maximilian Uriarte © 2011

TERMINAL LANCE #96 "Not Survivormen"
Hey there, I'm Les Stroud: Survivorman. Today I have a special guest, a Lance Corporal in the US Marines. He's an Iraq veteran and he's gonna be surviving with me this week out here in the wilderness.
So, Lance Corporal, why don't you go get a fire started while I go hunt something to eat?
Sure. You got the matches?
There are no matches...
Oh... yeah... we're not really trained for that sort of thing...
Okay well you go hunt for food and I'll get the fire going. Sound good?
Sure. Where's our rifle?
There is no rifle...
Hehe... Yeah... about that...
Created by Maximilian Uriarte © 2011

TERMINAL LANCE #97 "Too Soon?"
PET STORE
Hey there! Welcome to my pet store, how can I help you?
I need a good puppy...
That's a pure-bred German Shepherd. That's as "good" as puppies get, mister.
Right... but how far do you think I could throw it...?
Um...
Haha, I'm just kidding...
Created by Maximilian Uriarte © 2011

TERMINAL LANCE #98 "Unexpected Guest"
Hey there, Devil Dog!
Oh God...
Get yer hands outa yer damn pockets!
Aye, First Sergeant...
You think my hands aren't cold? Of course they are! It's called discipline, Marine! You think Chesty would put his hands in his pockets?!
Gentlemen...
WTF???
I am the ghost of Chesty Puller. For the record, I wouldn't give a Puuuuuuuuuck what you do with your Fucking hands. Who cares about something so Fucking stupid?
Created by Maximilian Uriarte © 2011

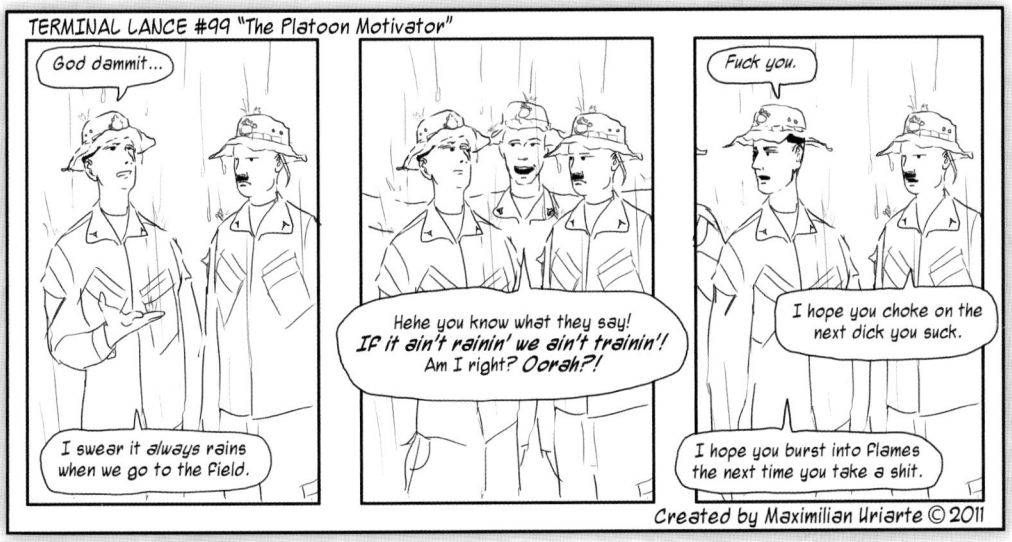
TERMINAL LANCE #99 "The Platoon Motivator"
God dammit...
I swear it always rains when we go to the field.
Hehe you know what they say! If it ain't rainin' we ain't trainin'! Am I right? Oorah?!
Fuck you.
I hope you choke on the next dick you suck.
I hope you burst into flames the next time you take a shit.
Created by Maximilian Uriarte © 2011

TERMINAL LANCE #100 "Unexpected Success"
Hey Master Guns, I guess that "Terminal Lance" thing that came out last year is up to its hundredth strip.
Wha...?
He's even got stuff in the Marine Corps Times...
NOT... CLEARED... HOT...
DOGGON'... DEVIL... DOG...
Master Guns?!
I think he just had a brain aneurysm...
Created by Maximilian Uriarte © 2011

TERMINAL LANCE #101 "The Facebook Poseur"
MEANWHILE BACK HOME...
OMG he's so hawt!
He's a Marine, they're badass! He must be in Iraq or something...
But really...
Hey, you dumb boot! Get back on the line so we can start the tables!
Created by Maximilian Uriarte © 2011

TERMINAL LANCE #102 "Gong Xi Fa Cai"
Hey, Garcia! KUNG HEI FAT CHOY!
What the fuck does that mean?
It means Happy Chinese New Year! It's the Chinese New Year...
Oh... we get a ninety-six for that?
No...
Then who cares?
Created by Maximilian Uriarte © 2011

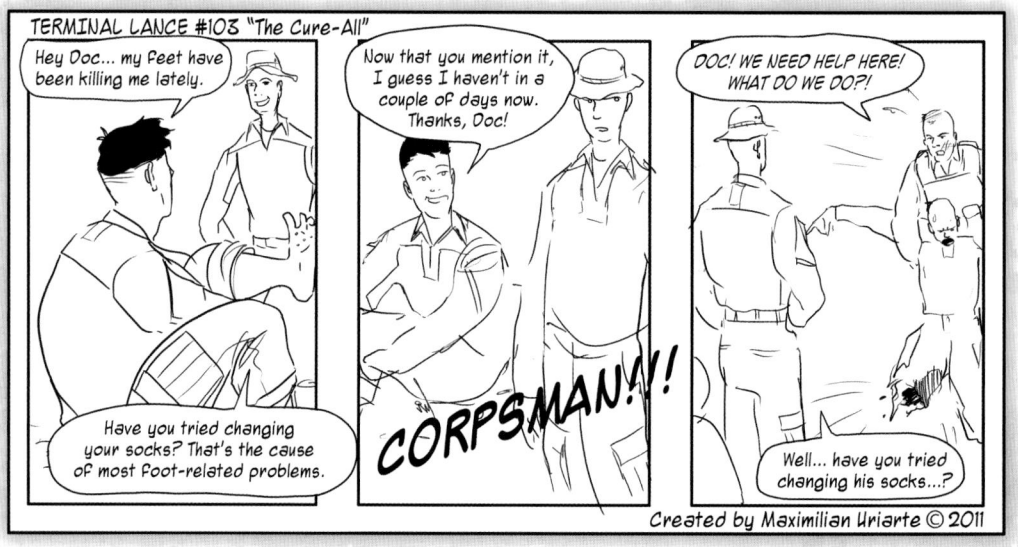
TERMINAL LANCE #103 "The Cure-All"
Hey Doc... my feet have been killing me lately.
Have you tried changing your socks? That's the cause of most foot-related problems.
Now that you mention it, I guess I haven't in a couple of days now. Thanks, Doc!
CORPSMAN!!!
DOC! WE NEED HELP HERE! WHAT DO WE DO?!
Well... have you tried changing his socks...?
Created by Maximilian Uriarte © 2011

TERMINAL LANCE #104 "The Prophecy Fulfilled"
Man this is such bullshit, I can't believe this asshole is getting promoted before me. I've been in the fleet longer than him!
GGHH...
HE'S TURNING! GET THOSE CORPORAL CHEVRONS OFF HIM BEFORE ITS TOO LATE!
RHAAAAAAAAAAAA!
DAMMIT!
It's too late! He's turned into... a giant douchebag...
Created by Maximilian Uriarte © 2011

TERMINAL LANCE #105 "My Valentine"
Ugh, you know I was really hoping to spend Valentine's Day with my girlfriend this year.
But nope, gotta go to the field. Every fucking time.
Hey, you know if the Marine Corps wanted you to have a girlfriend they would've issued you one!
Are you fucking serious...?
I guess they don't want me to have half the shit on the gear list either huh? I had to pay for most of this stupid shit myself!
Seriously, a fucking rape whistle? REALLY?!
Created by Maximilian Uriarte © 2011

TERMINAL LANCE #106 "The Water Dog"
Hey there, sweetheart.
Hi...
How's that water taste?
I dunno... like water?
I bet it's the best fucking water you've ever had. Wanna know why?
Not really...
Cause I'm an 1171, mother-fucking WATER DOG, babe. That's why.
I personally made sure your water was especially delicious today.
Oh, you're welcome.
Jesus Christ, you're such a fucking POG.
Created by Maximilian Uriarte © 2011

TERMINAL LANCE #107 "Treasured Belongings"

Created by Maximilian Uriarte © 2011

TERMINAL LANCE #108 "Disturbing Revelations"

Created by Maximilian Uriarte © 2011

TERMINAL LANCE #109 "Curious Dining"

Created by Maximilian Uriarte © 2011

110 "Boot Camp: The Swarm"

Drill Instructors have a kind of magical quality about them. The animated characters that run around yelling at recruits all day have a certain kinship and likeness to many of my favorite Saturday morning cartoons. I'm fairly certain I once saw a DI pull a large wooden mallet from behind his back and smack a recruit in the face with it.

But really, DI's are always fun to laugh at. Their exaggerated movements, gestures, and voices create someone that is more character than human. Love DI's or hate them, I guarantee that every Marine has done a DI impression at some point in his or her life. The trademark frog voice and knife-hands are as unforgettable afterward as they are feared in recruit training.

I've been out for a while now, and knife-hands still get me every time. Seriously . . . *knife-hands?* Possibly the most absurd and uniquely Marine Corps thing anyone's ever shouted at me with the raging passion of a thousand hungry baboons is simply, "KNIFE HAAAAAAAANDS!"

TERMINAL LANCE #112 "Crossed Choices"

Created by Maximilian Uriarte © 2011

TERMINAL LANCE #113 "Battle: LA"

Created by Maximilian Uriarte © 2011

TERMINAL LANCE #114 "Myths and Legends IV"

Created by Maximilian Uriarte © 2011

TERMINAL LANCE #115 "Welcome Back"
Hehehe... Welcome back from leave, boys.
Stand by, gents. The CO's got a little surprise for you all...
Is it a piss test?
A piss test?
A urinalysis?
...is it a piss test?
Piss test, Staff Sergeant?
Do I gotta drip my dick in a cup, Staff Sergeant...?
...
...it's a piss test.
Yeah, huge surprise, Staff Sergeant...
Created by Maximilian Uriarte © 2011

TERMINAL LANCE #116 "Ruffles"
Hey Abe, meet my cousin. He's in the Air Force.
Oh an Airman huh? That's cool dude...
So how's th...
YEAH WELL I'VE SEEN MORE ACTION THAN MOST MARINES I TALK TO. I WAS A MEDIC, YOUR CORPSMEN CAME TO ME FOR HELP. JUST SAYIN' BRO.
Uh... that's cool bro. Hey, let me get that chip off your shoulder...
Created by Maximilian Uriarte © 2011

TERMINAL LANCE #117 "Pay Freeze Woes"
A fucking pay freeze?!
How the hell am I supposed to buy porn and beer this weekend?!
Why don't you just use the porn you already have...?
Oh Garcia, you naive soul...
I *have* to buy new porn every weekend because it supports the economy. The hard working men and women of the American porn industry have bills to pay. My *solid morals* don't allow me to get porn for free online or otherwise. When a woman takes thirty loads in her mouth and rectum, she deserves some kind of compensation for it. I am a *good, morally sound* **American**...
...*unlike you,* apparently.
Created by Maximilian Uriarte © 2011

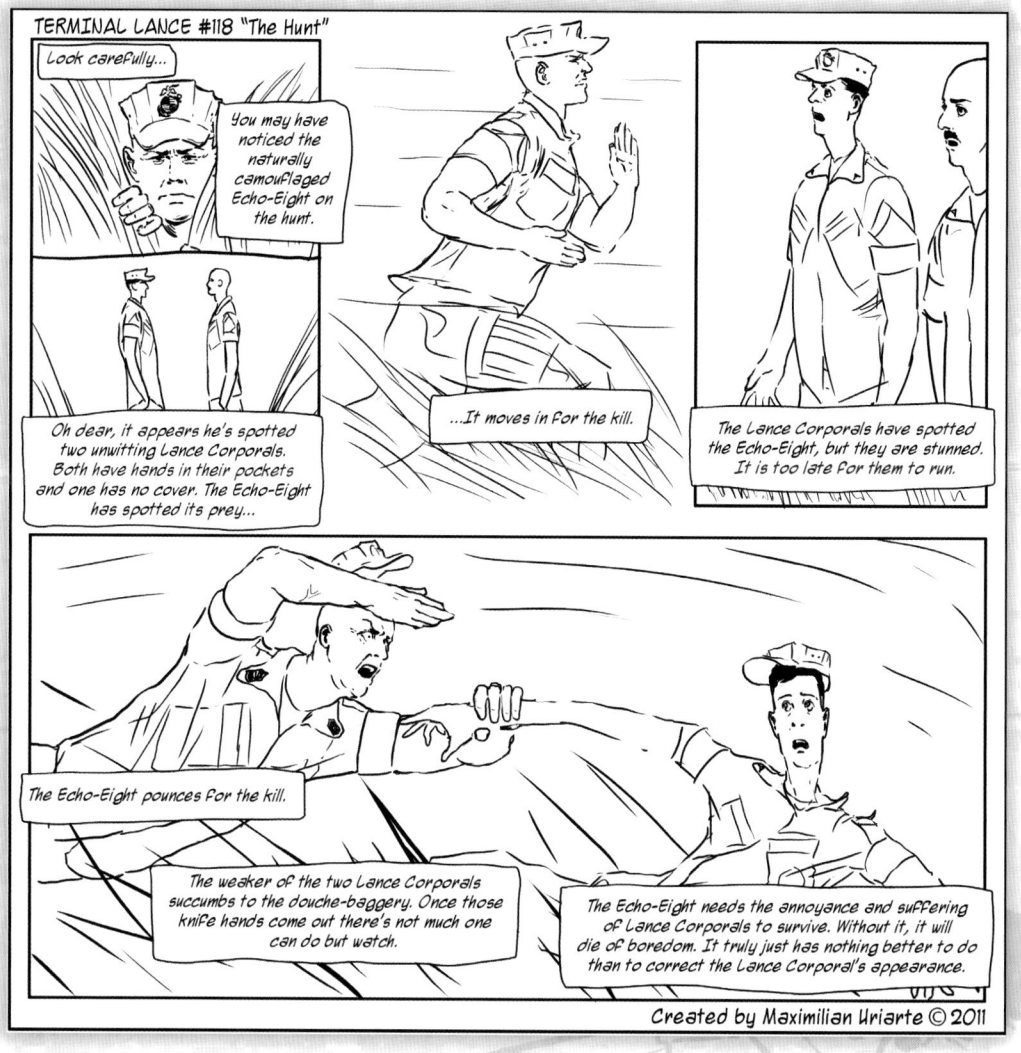
TERMINAL LANCE #118 "The Hunt"
Look carefully...
You may have noticed the naturally camouflaged Echo-Eight on the hunt.
Oh dear, it appears he's spotted two unwitting Lance Corporals. Both have hands in their pockets and one has no cover. The Echo-Eight has spotted its prey...
...It moves in for the kill.
The Lance Corporals have spotted the Echo-Eight, but they are stunned. It is too late for them to run.
The Echo-Eight pounces for the kill.
The weaker of the two Lance Corporals succumbs to the douche-baggery. Once those knife hands come out there's not much one can do but watch.
The Echo-Eight needs the annoyance and suffering of Lance Corporals to survive. Without it, it will die of boredom. It truly just has nothing better to do than to correct the Lance Corporal's appearance.
Created by Maximilian Uriarte © 2011

119 "Boot Camp: The Urinal"

One of the many fond memories I have of boot camp is of the many excursions we had to the men's room. My platoon of roughly fifty Marines was forced to use the "head" all at the same time. There were a total of eight urinals in the main bathroom, with some "shitters" down the hall. It was the only time in my life that I have ever shared a urinal with three other men. Results like you see in this strip were a daily occurrence.

In addition to boning over urine, dropping a deuce became another social activity in boot camp. When you had to do the deed, you would go up to your buddy and ask, "Hey, you wanna go take a shit?" Instead of being met with obvious disgust and confusion, as I'm sure you would be in the "real world," in boot camp, the response will likely be an obliged "Yes, I'd love to take a shit with you."

Well, maybe not so articulate (probably with more "fuckin'"s), but you get the idea.

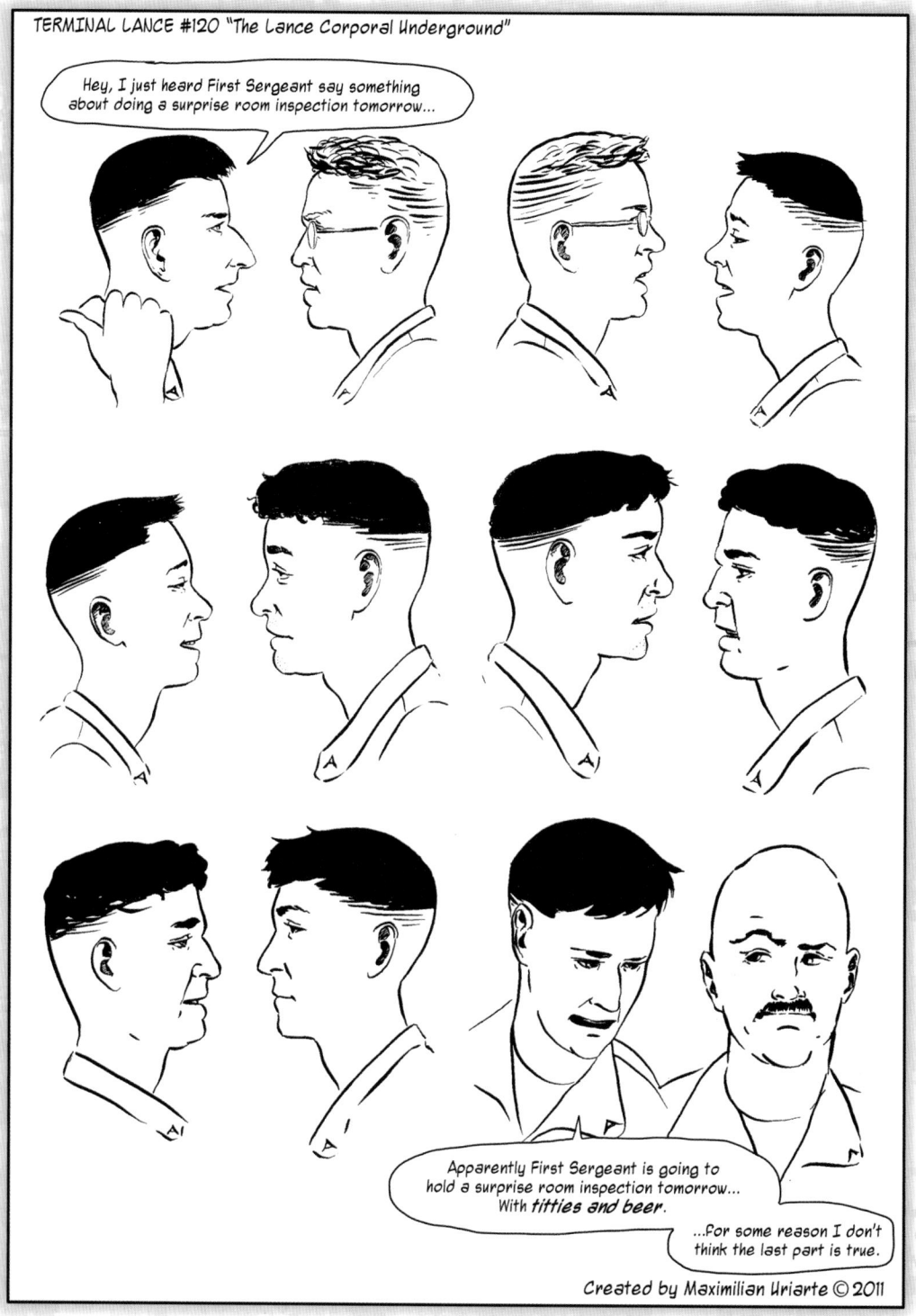
TERMINAL LANCE #120 "The Lance Corporal Underground"
Hey, I just heard First Sergeant say something about doing a surprise room inspection tomorrow...
Apparently First Sergeant is going to hold a surprise room inspection tomorrow... With titties and beer.
...For some reason I don't think the last part is true.
Created by Maximilian Uriarte © 2011

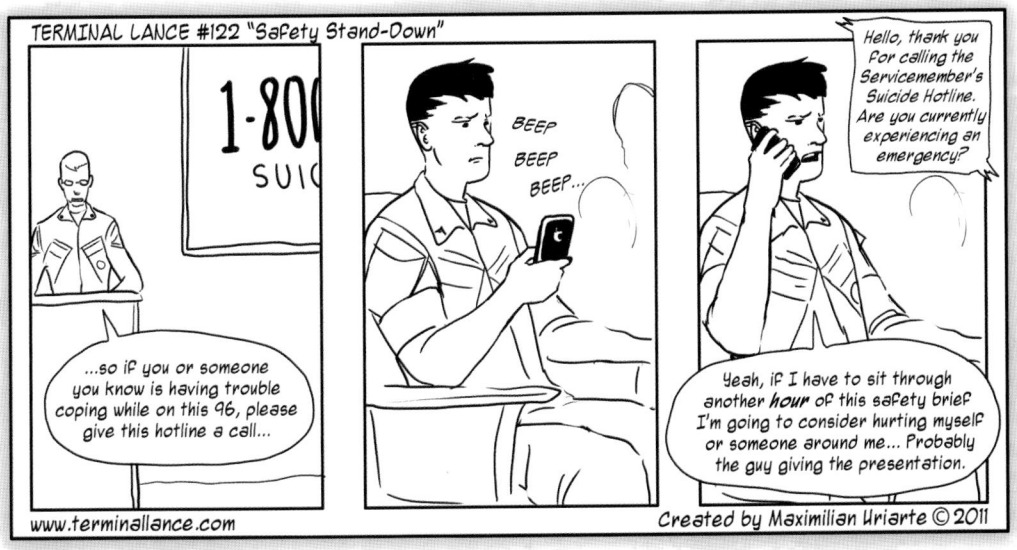

122 "Safety Stand-Down"

I don't want anyone to think I'm making fun of suicide here, just the safety stand-down in a general sense. Everyone who's been on a holiday 96 (what Marines call a four-day weekend) knows the horrendous experience of a safety stand-down. For whatever reason, the Marine Corps' idea of preventing injury to fellow Marines is to make them sit through a mind-numbing six hours of classes prior to letting them enjoy a long weekend. I don't know what statistical evidence there is to support this strategy; I'm sure it exists, but I don't personally feel that six hours of texting-time is an effective way to put a stop to drunk driving or suicide.

Perhaps a more effective way to combat these problems would be to allow these briefs to be done on a more personal level, perhaps at the platoon leadership or even lower. Training NCO's and small-unit leaders to brief Marines on the dangers of everything the Marine Corps hates would probably be more effective than having Marines meander to the base-theater in droves for an apathetic series of briefs on things they already know. Marines—well, anyone really—tend to tune out things performed in this manner anyway. Everyone knows that in education, smaller class sizes are more effective.

TERMINAL LANCE #123 "Shitter Graffiti is an Art... of Dicks II"
Hey man...
Huh?
I bet you $20 you can't take this pen in there with you without drawing a dick on the wall.
Haha, okay. I hope you have cash on you right now, this is the easiest bet I've ever done.
Sure thing, man.
5 minutes later...
Created by Maximilian Uriarte © 2011

TERMINAL LANCE #124 "The First Night Back"
I don't know what you were expecting...
...It's been like 7 months.
Created by Maximilian Uriarte © 2011

TERMINAL LANCE #125 "Barracks Cuts"
Hey man, how's my "line"? Do you think Staff Sergeant will notice?
Naw... you're good.
Created by Maximilian Uriarte © 2011

127 "Incentive"

In real life, your local Career Planner probably won't be trying too hard to get a Lance Corporal to reenlist. However, there was a point in time—around 2008 or 2009—when the Marine Corps was offering $90,000 in cold, hard, dick-twitching cash money to reenlist if you served as a squad leader in combat. Ninety-fucking-grand. Needless to say, many Marines found that to be a fruitful incentive. That's at least two Mustangs and a bottle of Grey Goose.

Abe, on the other hand, isn't so interested in reenlisting. Abe, much like myself, always wondered what kind of ridiculous shit you could get away with when it came to reenlistment incentives. The ridiculous shit you could throw at them would be an endless source of entertainment—one that I missed out on due to the fact that no one wanted an 0351 Lance Coolie to reenlist in mid-2010. Regardless, I wouldn't have, but it would've at least been fun to try and find out.

TERMINAL LANCE #128 "Fresh Meat"

Created by Maximilian Uriarte © 2011

TERMINAL LANCE #129 "Dental Hygiene at the Depot"

Created by Maximilian Uriarte © 2011

TERMINAL LANCE #130 "Just Whip it Out, Already"

Created by Maximilian Uriarte © 2011

131 "Bitch and Moan"

If there's one constant of the Marine Corps, it's that Marines will bitch about pretty much anything. You can give them the world, but something will be wrong with it. When I was stationed in Hawaii, I heard complaints every day. *I can't wait to get off this rock, fuck this place, I hate Hawaii, this island sucks*—it was truly nonstop. All the sun, beaches, warm weather, and beautiful women in the world didn't seem to sway those who were convinced it was the worst place they'd ever been.

Unfortunately, a lot of Marines aren't able to distinguish their raw emotions from their current situation. They're not actually mad at Hawaii, they don't actually hate Hawaii—their misplaced anger is incorrectly directed at the beautiful islands of Aloha. The anguish that comes with being stationed on the islands is a general feeling of discontent toward the military as a whole. To them, the islands become the Marine Corps. The Marines in Hawaii miss their homes and the islands are a new and alien environment to most of them.

Frankly, I loved Hawaii. After all, there are plenty of worse places to be stationed. Take a look at Twentynine Palms—or as I refer to it: *Satan's asshole.* Secluded in the California desert, it is easily the most miserable permanent duty station in the Corps that I've ever been to—and my experiences were limited to a couple of runs through Mojave Viper.

I'm sure the Marines in the desert reading this are going, "WTF? Marines bitch about Hawaii?" Yes. Yes, they do. Every day.

It's true, Marines will bitch about anything.

TERMINAL LANCE #132 "Necropocalypse Part 1"
What... what are you doing...?
I'm packing for the "Necropocalypse."
...what is that?
You know... the zombie apocalypse?
Everyone needs a zombie plan, you know.
Are you serious...?
A bottle of wine, some kerosene, a rope...
A box of condoms?!
What kind of fucked up "zombie plan" do you have?!
Created by Maximilian Uriarte © 2011

TERMINAL LANCE #133 "Literally II"
OKAY ASSHOLE! I TOLD YOU TWO HOURS AGO TO GET ME THAT BATTERY!!!
We can't find it, Gunny!
WELL THEN YOU'D BETTER SHIT ME ONE!!!
Hrrm...
?
HURRRGHHHHHHHHHHHHHH...
Haha! I'm just kidding, you totally thought I was going to though, huh?
You're gross!
...who are you talking to?
Created by Maximilian Uriarte © 2011

TERMINAL LANCE #134 "The First Avenger"
CAPTAIN AMERICA THE FIRST AVENGER
NOW PLAYING
REST ROOM
...yet another thing the Army gets to have that's Fucking awesome that the Marines don't.
Created by Maximilian Uriarte © 2011

135 "Married Marines"

The life of a married Marine is one of perceived luxury, and in many ways, it is luxurious, but at the same time, marriage surely alienates them from the dark, soulless heart of the Lance Corporal Underground: the barracks.

In the infantry word changes, and it changes a lot. It happens like a brush fire in the barracks; one minute you're sitting in your standard-issue chair playing *Call of Duty,* the next minute some other Lance Corporal is peeking his head into your room and saying to you, "Hey, cammies tomorrow instead of PT gear." Without so much as a glance you'll acknowledge it, get your cammies ready for the morning, and be set to go. In this age of modern technical wizardry, it's astonishing that it is still possible for "the word" to not get to those outside the epicenter of Marinedom, yet it happens daily. I suppose in a platoon so large, with word so readily available in the barracks, it just happens that you forget about the guy who lives on the other side of the base with his wife and dog. It could be, of course, a treacherous form of betrayal to spite those luxuries—but he would be none the wiser.

TERMINAL LANCE #136 "Enough is Enough"
Hey can you film me later today?
For what...?
I'm gonna ask a celebrity to the Marine Corps Ball!
Come on man, I know that Sergeant what's-his-face managed to score a date with Mila Kunis, but this shit is really getting out of hand. It was really only funny the first time.
Who are you asking anyway?
Daniel Craig from Casino Royale! Man he is so hot, I hope we fuck. No homo.
That's kind of gay...
No it's not, I said "no homo."
Created by Maximilian Uriarte © 2011

TERMINAL LANCE #137 "Headlines"
MARINE NEWS
BUDGET CUTS!
Marines issued leather jackets to replace body armor! "Whatever" say Lance Corporals, "It looks pretty cool."
ARMY NEWS
BUDGET CUTS!
Soldiers issued slower iPhone 3GS instead of iPhone 4! "This is punishment," say Soldiers.
NAVY NEWS
DADT REPEALED!
Cucumber sales sky-rocket at Naval Commissaries! "Best. Day. Ever." say Sailors.
AIR FORCE NEWS
LOL HEY GUYS
Created by Maximilian Uriarte © 2011

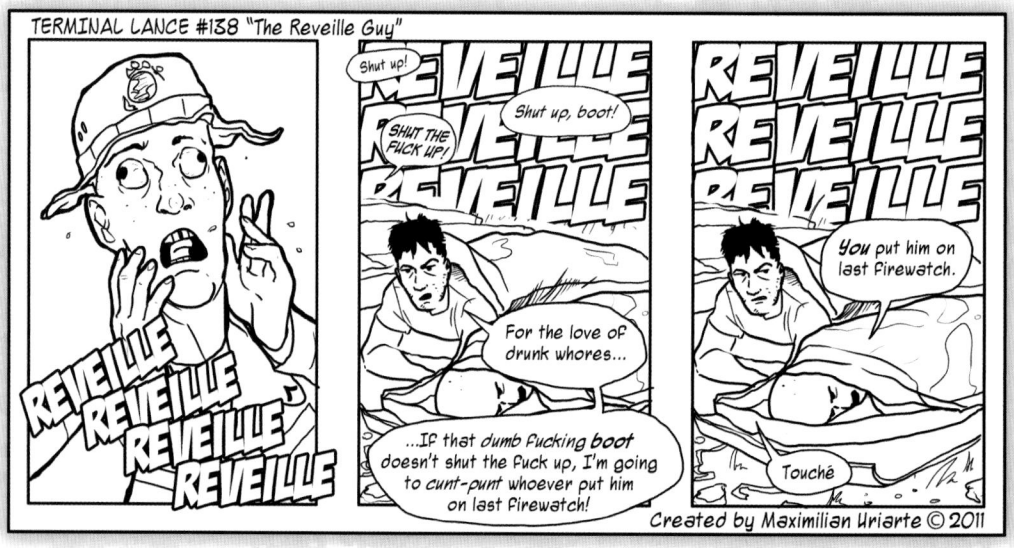
TERMINAL LANCE #138 "The Reveille Guy"
REVEILLE
REVEILLE
REVEILLE
REVEILLE
Shut up!
Shut up, boot!
SHUT THE FUCK UP!
For the love of drunk whores...
...If that dumb fucking boot doesn't shut the fuck up, I'm going to cunt-punt whoever put him on last firewatch!
You put him on last firewatch.
Touché
Created by Maximilian Uriarte © 2011

140 "Escalation of Force"

Shout, show, shove, shoot.

This was the mantra given to turret gunners in my battalion during my time in Iraq. The "Escalation of Force" procedures varied depending on the tools available to the gunner. For me, I had a square of brightly colored orange safety-fabric strung up to a stick (literally, a stick—as in, from a tree) with 550 cord for shouting; I had a pen-flare for showing, which was a small flare shot out of a pen-sized launcher; I had my M16-A4 loaded with tracer rounds for shoving; and of course my beloved M2 .50 for shooting.

All of us knew the steps, and they weren't hard to remember. However, during my time in country, the guidelines became increasingly strict. As a result, Marines became more wary of actually shooting at an oncoming vehicle. Not because they might shoot back, but because they might face punishment back in the rear. I recall one event on MSR Mobile: we pulled off onto a side road. My vehicle, the lead truck, successfully traversed the turn. However, the vehicle behind me had a close call with an oncoming Iraqi truck. The gunner, we'll call him Bob, ended up taking a couple of warning shots at the vehicle to get it to stop moving.

Bob followed all the necessary EoF procedures, but when we got back to the rear he was placed under an absurd investigation. The Iraqi was fine, no one was injured, it was really just a misunderstanding of the Iraqi driver. While Bob ended up being cleared, and rightfully so, the company ended up putting our entire platoon under a death-by-PowerPoint style presentation of EoF procedures. In addition, they decided to fill the rest of the day with other safety classes that had nothing to do with EoF, shooting, or Iraq.

The next morning, just about everyone in the platoon told Bob, "Hey, don't shoot at anyone today—I don't feel like sitting through another day of bullshit classes."

It is a tricky situation. Ultimately, I believe the strict enforcement of EoF procedures undoubtedly led to fewer deaths of innocent Iraqi civilians—a very favorable result. However, for the grunt—for the guy behind the gun—it becomes a stressful fumble of figuring out what step is next and whether it is the right thing to do.

However, the same can be said for just about any situation in a war when there's guns and people involved.

TERMINAL LANCE #143 "Literally III"
Huh, well I'll be damned...
1 MILE
...That's where it comes from.
Created by Maximilian Uriarte © 2011

TERMINAL LANCE #144 "PDA"
Hey there Devil Dog! I know we don't hold hands in uniform!
There are no public displays of affection in my Corps! Secure that trash!
Sure thing, Master Sergeant...
Jesus, I wonder what his problem is...
SIGH...
I wish someone would hold my hand...
Created by Maximilian Uriarte © 2011

TERMINAL LANCE #145 "Conspiracy"
Abe! Long time no see!
Hey, Uncle Keith... How you been?
Good, good...
...So you're in the Marines now right? Do they give you boys any of the inside scoop? I watched this documentary that said the 9/11 terrorist attacks were an inside job! You hear anything about that?!
HAHA
Trust me, Uncle Keith... I work for the government... There's no way they would ever be that organized.
Created by Maximilian Uriarte © 2011

147 "Keeping the Myth Alive"

Perhaps I'm in the minority here, but when I look back on my time in the Marine Corps, the cool stuff isn't what immediately comes to mind. Instead, I tend to think of small things like the hours I spent cleaning floors, jerking off in port-a-shitters, cleaning a rifle, barracks parties (which are every night), hazing, bullshit, the way cammies kind of chafe my inner thighs, and anything else that was part of my everyday life.

The great secret of the Marine Corps is that we only do the cool stuff about 10 percent of the time. The other 90 percent is spent doing everything mentioned above. And confusion and anger linger at every corner. I shot over twenty SMAW rockets in my four years, trained for weeks at a time in the field, and spent sleepless nights and sizzling days hunched over an M2 .50 cal atop an MRAP, but I don't usually think about it.

The Marine Corps—actually living the Marine Corps—isn't about the cool stuff. It's about the little things, the 90 percent of the time things that are both funny and immensely miserable at the same time.

But it's very important that we don't reveal to our civilian brethren what really goes on in the Corps. Otherwise, those care packages would come a lot less often.

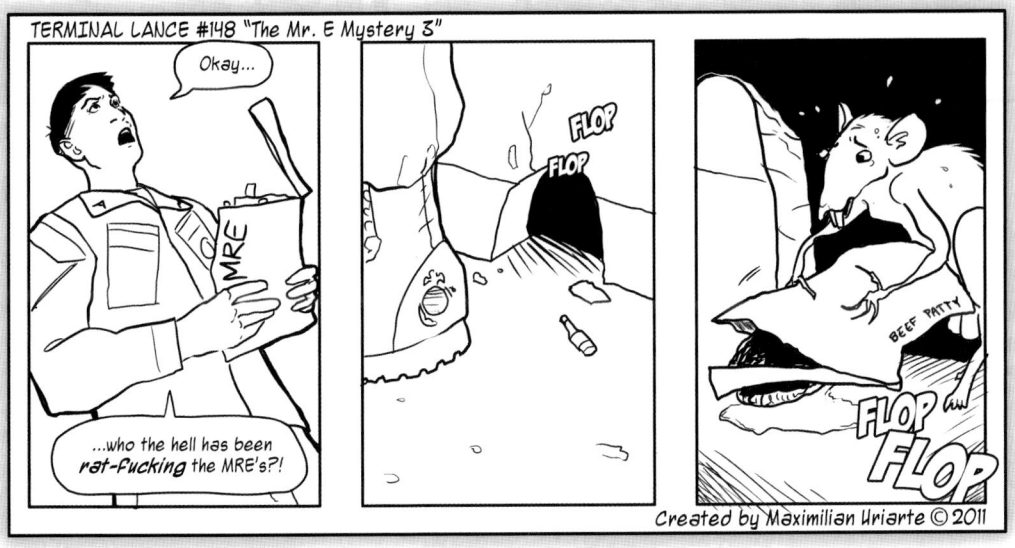
TERMINAL LANCE #148 "The Mr. E Mystery 3"
Okay...
MRE
...who the hell has been rat-fucking the MRE's?!
FLOP
FLOP
BEEF PATTY
FLOP
FLOP
Created by Maximilian Uriarte © 2011

TERMINAL LANCE #149 "Intent"
Hey, excuse me... I need to get this... thing signed... or something...
Oh sure, I can help you with that... you're with Three-Three, right?
Yup...
Oh you guys are going on deployment next week right?
Yup...
Yeah, I really want to deploy... my command just won't send me though!
If you really wanted to go, why didn't you just join the infantry?
HAHA!
I didn't want to go that bad...
Created by Maximilian Uriarte © 2011

TERMINAL LANCE #150 "Family Fun Day"
Hey, Abe!
Hey.
How's it going?
Oh it's going great, just like it was when I saw you two hours ago at the barracks. And yesterday. And probably at zero-fucking-four at the armory on Monday when I'll see you again. I love wasting my Saturdays at Battalion Family-Fucking-Fun Day, because it's not like we don't already see each other EVERY FUCKING DAY.
Thank you for asking! How are you?
...
...
Created by Maximilian Uriarte © 2011

TERMINAL LANCE #151 "Marine Hunters"

Created by Maximilian Uriarte © 2011

TERMINAL LANCE #152 "Blue Water"

Created by Maximilian Uriarte © 2011

TERMINAL LANCE #153 "Old Corps"

Created by Maximilian Uriarte © 2011

TERMINAL LANCE #154 "Share-Drive Underground"
PSST
...?
Hey man...
Hey... you got my stuff?
Yeah, yeah... I got the stuff...
I got everything you asked for right here on this flash drive... The Office, House, Mad Men...
...Glee.
The Glee episodes are for my roommate...
Sure they are...
Created by Maximilian Uriarte © 2011

TERMINAL LANCE #155 "Customer Service"
Hi there Lance Corporal, how can I help you?
My pay is all messed up. They overpaid me somehow, then when they realized it they decided to take all the money back at once. Now I'm not getting anything.
Oh... yeah that happens. Sorry, there's not much we can do for you. Try taking out a loan?
God dammit, I fucking hate you admin POG's! There's really nothing you can do for me?!
Oh yeah, hate on the POG's all you want, but who do you come crying to when your pay is fucked up?
Okay, dick-breath...
I wouldn't BE here if you assholes wouldn't have fucked up my pay in the first place!
Created by Maximilian Uriarte © 2011

TERMINAL LANCE #156 "That Feeling"
BUM
BUM
BUM
BUM
Are you okay...?
Yeah... I just...
...For a split second I forgot where my rifle was...
Created by Maximilian Uriarte © 2011

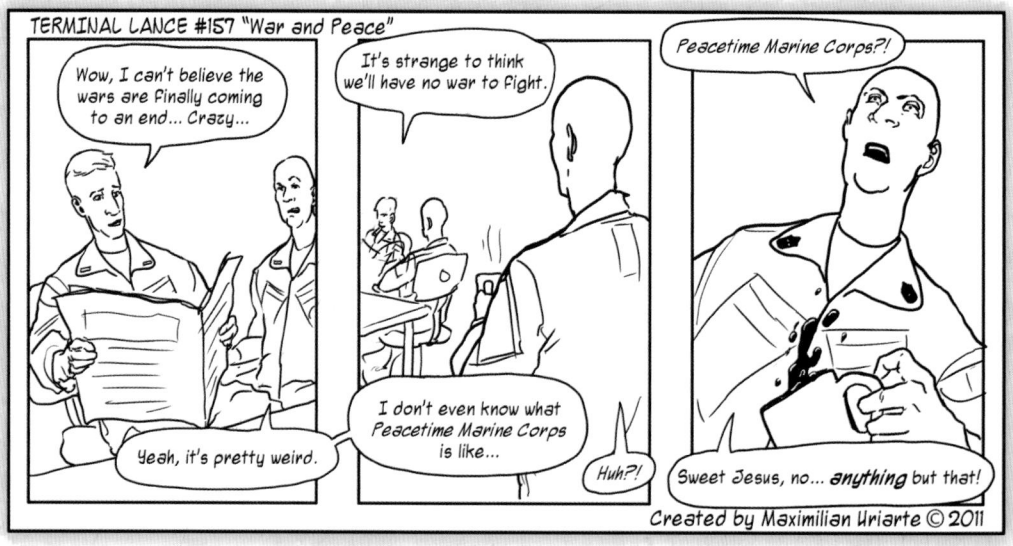
TERMINAL LANCE #157 "War and Peace"
Wow, I can't believe the wars are finally coming to an end... Crazy...
Yeah, it's pretty weird.
It's strange to think we'll have no war to fight.
I don't even know what Peacetime Marine Corps is like...
Huh?!
Peacetime Marine Corps?!
Sweet Jesus, no... anything but that!
Created by Maximilian Uriarte © 2011

TERMINAL LANCE #158 "MEPS Exam"
Okay, Mr. Belatzeko...
This is a little strange, but I need you to drop your pants and spread your cheeks for the exam.
Okay...
Good, good...
This is kinda weird... what is this for anyway?
• Will the Green Weenie fit?
YES
NO
Oh, nothing you need to worry about...
Created by Maximilian Uriarte © 2011

TERMINAL LANCE #159 "Checking Marriage"
This is so stupid!
I told them I was going to get married and they gave me this checklist...
...as if I'm not a responsible adult.
Hey, Abe... is this where we get the marriage checklist?
This is my fiancée, Porsche, we met last night. We're gonna get married cause she's hot as fuck.
...
...Okay...
...I think I see their point.
Created by Maximilian Uriarte © 2011

TERMINAL LANCE #160 "Working (It) at the Car Wash"
This is so fucking stupid!
We've been doing these fucking car washes for weeks and the ball tickets are still $65 dollars each! Where's all this money going?!
Who knows, man...
Oh God... that creepy Chaplain is back...
Hey big fellas... I dunno what it is, but my car just keeps getting so dirty!
Sure thing, sir... we'll clean it for you...
...again.
Created by Maximilian Uriarte © 2011

TERMINAL LANCE #161 "Dancing with the Stars"
Okay listen up, gents!
We all know that Mila Kunis is coming to the ball this weekend...
I don't want to see any of you assholes even looking at her!
You don't talk to her, you don't hit on her, you don't go near her! Is this understood?
Yes, Gunny.
Friday Night
236th Marine Corps Birthday Ball
Excuse me, Ms. Kunis... Has anyone ever told you that rockers and hashmarks are directly related to penis-size...?
Created by Maximilian Uriarte © 2011

TERMINAL LANCE #162 "Mike Whiskey Tree"
CONGRATULATIONS!
RANK UP!
SERGEANT MAJOR
NEW PERK UNLOCKED:
DICK MOVE
Dude! I just unlocked the coolest perk!
What does it do?
If someone on my team makes even a tiny mistake, I can punish the whole team and reduce all of their ranks to PFC!
That's stupid... why would anyone want to screw over their own teammates?
I dunno. ...realism?
Created by Maximilian Uriarte © 2011

TERMINAL LANCE #163 "Pull Out Your CAC"
Excuse me, Lance Corporal...
Huh?
I need to see your "CAC" before you can go in.
Well... okay... I guess...
What the fuck?! NO!
Your ID card!
Oooooh, that's what you meant! They really need to come up with a new acronym...
...I just thought you were from Boston.
Created by Maximilian Uriarte © 2011

TERMINAL LANCE #164 "It's Already Gay II"
Listen up, Recruits! I don't care about any of this Don't Ask, Don't Tell garbage--you just better keep that Faggot shit out of my platoon!
Now, pair up, strip naked and wipe each other down with baby wipes!
Uh...
...
Created by Maximilian Uriarte © 2011

TERMINAL LANCE #165 "Voluntold"
And... What else... Oh, Abe: I'm still missing your Combined Federal Campaign donation slip.
I thought it was voluntary, Staff Sergeant...
Well, it's "voluntary" in the sense that I'm telling you to give it to me, and you have to volunteer to do it.
So yeah, it's "voluntary."
Touché...
Created by Maximilian Uriarte © 2011

TERMINAL LANCE #166 "Amenities"
Is that... is that a Burger King bag?!
...Maybe...
Dammit, Abe!
I thought we agreed that we weren't going to eat any of that Fat-kid Food while we were deployed so we wouldn't feel like Fucking POG's!
Yeah... Sorry...
...do you want my bag-fries...?
...yes.
Created by Maximilian Uriarte © 2011

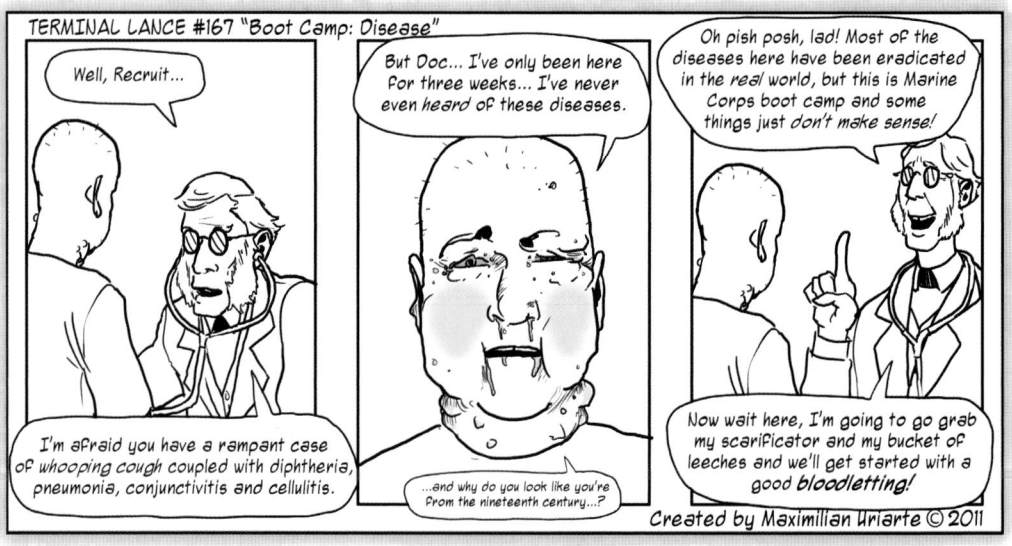

167 "Boot Camp: Disease"

I don't remember a lot about boot camp, but I remember one thing very vividly: I was always fucking sick.

Most recruits were. In fact, I believe there were moments during "2nd phase" when the infection rate of my platoon was 100 percent. Everyone was sick with something. As it turns out, being thrust into a new environment with sixty other guys from different parts of the country for three months is a shock to the immune system. No amount of peanut butter shots or vaccinations can keep the sickness away—you will end up with some strange disease you've never heard of.

My favorite? Cellulitis. Never before joining the Marine Corps had I heard of it, yet it was one of the most rampant problems in my platoon. Cellulitis is simply a bacterial infection that makes whatever part of your body is infected swell with pus and nastiness until it gets drained and treated—it can also cause a fever and is actually very dangerous. I never got it personally, because I maintained good hygiene, but many recruits would find themselves with some horrific growth dangling off their bodies, desperately trying to hide it from the Drill Instructors so they wouldn't get dropped into MRP (Medical Recovery Platoon).

We had a recruit catch such a bad case of pneumonia that his lungs filled with fluid and he was sent to the hospital two days before graduation. He almost died, but no one wants to get dropped from their platoon.

Also rampant in my platoon was the somewhat humorous disease of "pink eye" or conjunctivitis. Everyone had pink eye at some point. I got it during the crucible, and actually did the entire reaper hike with pink eye in both eyes. It was terrible, but just part of the reality of boot camp.

As for the old-timey doctor . . . I just thought it would be funnier.

TERMINAL LANCE #168 "When You Eat It..."

Created by Maximilian Uriarte © 2011

TERMINAL LANCE #169 "Douche Blues"

Created by Maximilian Uriarte © 2011

TERMINAL LANCE #170 "The Difference: Perspective"

The difference between POG's and Grunts:

Perspective

Created by Maximilian Uriarte © 2011

TERMINAL LANCE #171 "Serious Business"

Hey Gents...

STAFF SERGEANT, I'M SORRY, BUT YOU'LL HAVE TO COME BACK LATER!

...Why?

We're in the middle of a ***very serious*** discussion!

Yeah, *dickbreath* over here thinks that Scarlett Johansson is hotter than ***Jessica Alba***. Alba is a Latina goddess, he's fucking crazy.

Oh wow... You're right, that's very serious...

AT LEAST SCAR-JO DOESN'T HAVE A GAPING MOMMA-SNATCH THAT FLAPS IN THE WIND!

I'm... I'm sorry I bothered you guys.

Created by Maximilian Uriarte © 2011

TERMINAL LANCE #172 "Tax Time"

Lance Corporal, everything looks good on your taxes except... well... I don't think you can write off ***alcohol*** and ***trips to the bar*** as a "work expense"...

But it ***is*** a work-related expense!

The ***Corps*** is what drives me to ***drink!***

Created by Maximilian Uriarte © 2012

TERMINAL LANCE #173 "Oh-Three-Fifty-Two"
...and so I said to her: "Hey, if you like penises, I happen to be the proud owner of one!"
Hahahaha!
Then she says...
Hey Abe!
Oh hey, man...
Long time no see! I don't think I've seen you since SOI! How's it going man!?
It's going good...
...
...
...
What's the deal with him...?
...He's a TOW Gunner.
Ahh, gotcha.
Created by Maximilian Uriarte © 2012

175 "Back Home"

If there's one thing that can be said about the experience that is joining the Marines, it's that your friends back home won't understand a damn bit of it. For every life-altering experience you may have had while on duty, your friends back home will largely be the same way they were when you left them.

You'll meet new people, see new things—new worlds even—and they won't even begin to understand it. Going home will never be the same again. And, after being at home awhile, you'll wish you were gone again. The very idea of home becomes a distant memory, because it's never the same as it was. It's not that home has changed—in fact it's remained largely the same.

What's really changed is *you*.

But hey, that's okay. Regular people live regular lives, and you've lived anything but. What's really important is that you try your best not to alienate everyone at home, and if you need help, don't be afraid to seek it. Your friends and family will never understand, but they can try if you give them a chance.

TERMINAL LANCE #176 "Falling Out"
Created by Maximilian Uriarte © 2012

TERMINAL LANCE #177 "Motivation Education"
Hey, our MCI's came in today, you want to sit down and knock them out?
Hmm...
Naw, I've got some better things to do with my time.
5 Minutes Later
What the fuck are you doing?!
Nailing my dick to a table.
I thought you said you had better things to do?!
Exactly.
Created by Maximilian Uriarte © 2012

TERMINAL LANCE #178 "Grunt Mode"
...pleasure to meet you. I heard you were in 3rd Marines?
Yeah, how about you?
Oh, no I'm with the wing.
Oh... so what's your MOS then?
What he's actually saying:
Oh I'm a 6074, we do Aviation cryogenics.
It's basically working with liquid nitrogen and oxygen for aircraft. It's pretty cool, the aircraft need the nitrogen and oxygen for various systems...
What the average Grunt hears:
POG
POG
POG
POG
POG
POG
POG
POG
Created by Maximilian Uriarte © 2012

TERMINAL LANCE #179 "A Good Rock"
Created by Maximilian Uriarte © 2012

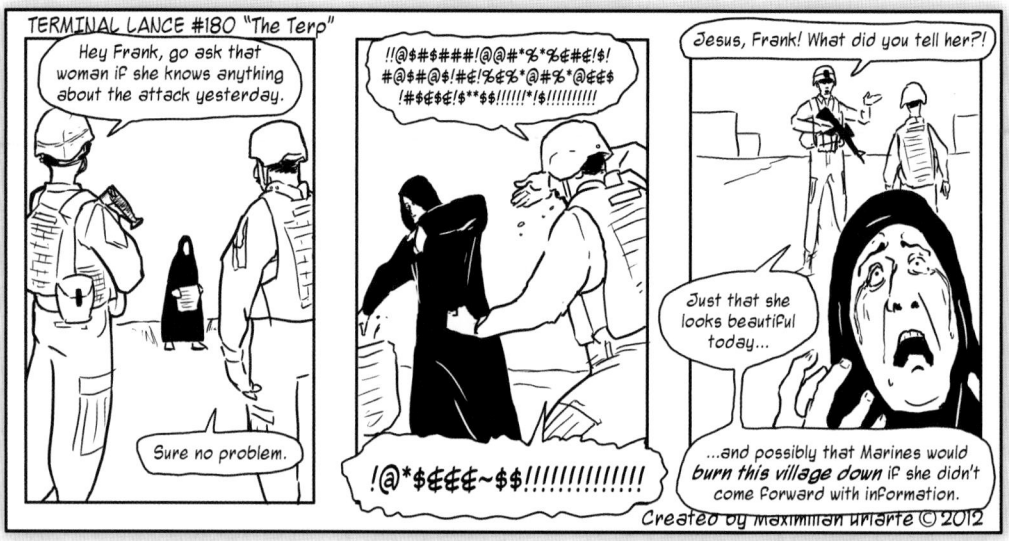
TERMINAL LANCE #180 "The Terp"
Hey Frank, go ask that woman if she knows anything about the attack yesterday.
Sure no problem.
!!@$##$###!@@#*%*%$##$!$!
#@$##@$!#$!%$%*@#%*@$$$
!#$$$$!$**$$!!!!!!*!$!!!!!!!!!
!@*$$$$~$$!!!!!!!!!!!!!!!
Jesus, Frank! What did you tell her?!
Just that she looks beautiful today...
...and possibly that Marines would burn this village down if she didn't come forward with information.
Created by Maximilian Uriarte © 2012

TERMINAL LANCE #181 "Easy Access"
RIIIIIIIP!
FUCK!
That was my last good pair of cammies! Now every pair has a hole in the crotch!
Calm down, they're designed to do that.
That's bullshit, why the hell would they design pants that always tear in the crotch!?
...It gives the Green Weenie a good place to slip itself in.
Created by Maximilian Uriarte © 2012

TERMINAL LANCE #182 "Full Medical"
You know, one of the best things about the military is the benefits!
SSGT. DICK
RECRUITER
You'll get everything! Full dental and medical care whenever you need it!
6 Months Later "The Fleet"
Excuse me, Corporal... Is it all right if I go to BAS today? I think I have a fever.
No, but I do have a straw you can have.
...what is that for?
So you can suck it the fuck up, boot.
Created by Maximilian Uriarte © 2012

TERMINAL LANCE #183 "His Boots, Her Flip Flops"
MARINE WIFE
TOUGHEST JOB IN THE CORPS
Toughest job in the Corps...
I guess I never really thought about it before...
I AIN'T FAT I'M JUST KNOCKED UP
...Seems tough...
Created by Maximilian Uriarte © 2012

TERMINAL LANCE #184 "Life After EAS: Conscience"
Oh my God...
I don't know how I'm going to finish this assignment tonight... I'm so fucking tired.
Hey PUSSY-BOY!
What the fuck is this shit about you being tired?!
You were in the fucking Marines! Don't give me your vagina monologue about being sleepy! There's Marines in Afghanistan right now that would kill for some sleep!
You're right, little Marine guy. Sleep can wait.
Next Day at School
Hey Abe... Are you all right? You look like you haven't slept at all...
...it also looks like someone drew a tiny, tiny penis on your forehead...
Created by Maximilian Uriarte © 2012

TERMINAL LANCE #185 "Experience"
Man, you're really good at Call of Duty...
It's from the Marine Corps.
Whoa! You mean you use your military training in the game?!
That's so badass!
Haha! No. That's ridiculous.
We're on standby all the time. Practically all we do is play Call of Duty.
Created by Maximilian Uriarte © 2012

TERMINAL LANCE #186 "Omitting Details"
Nice to meet you, are you a grunt?
Yeah, I'm an Assaultman. You?
I was with Recon for a bit...
Recon? That's pretty hardcore! So you're an 0321?
Well... no... I was an admin clerk for 3rd Recon Battalion for a bit.
What the fuck?! You can't just tell people you were "with Recon" without mentioning that!
That's like saying you're a deep-dish pizza because you worked the fucking register at Domino's!
You are not that delicious!
Created by Maximilian Uriarte © 2012

187 "Long Distance"

The Marine lifestyle is certainly unstable. As a result, the United States Marine is no stranger to the long-distance relationship. Most Marines probably start off in one, with some girl from "back home" that writes to them in boot camp. Around 80 percent of those women will leave them while they're in boot camp; the other 20 percent will either cheat on them or leave them later (or both). Regardless, the long-distance Skype webcam sex session is also no stranger to the Marine Corps.

Skype has done wonderful things for the world, especially the military. One of those wonderful things is the power to flog your Cobra Commander in front of your significant other from thousands of miles away.

Even with the advent of Skype, these sorts of relationships are always hard. Most couples don't make it, though some do. I personally dealt with the long-distance relationship as much as anyone else, as I was with my wife since before I enlisted. It will always be hard, and it never gets any easier. Skype, cell phones, and the internet close the gap quite a bit, but it will be entirely up to you to make sure that your relationship stays alive.

Lastly, if you find that you need to spank your wank with your girlfriend or otherwise, at least have the common courtesy to do it in private. As well . . . don't do it on someone else's computer. That's gross.

TERMINAL LANCE #188 "Very Important Person"

Created by Maximilian Uriarte © 2012

TERMINAL LANCE #189 "Mouth Like a Sailor"

Created by Maximilian Uriarte © 2012

TERMINAL LANCE #190 "Salt Dog"

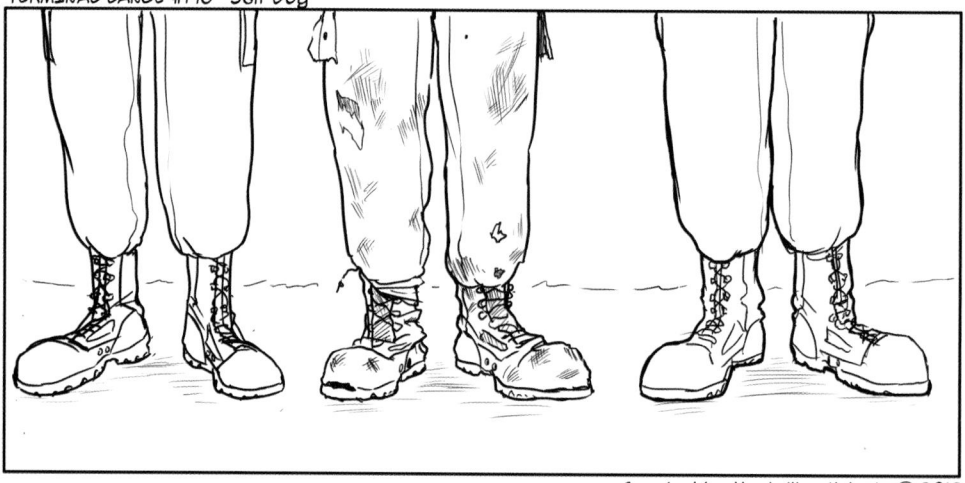

Created by Maximilian Uriarte © 2012

TERMINAL LANCE #191 "Jambo Revival"
Hello?
Hello? Is this Mr. Lance Corporal Abe?
My name is Nkunda, we met in Iraq. You told me to call you if I ever opened up my juice shop...
JAMBO JUICE
OPEN
...It is time.
Created by Maximilian Uriarte © 2012

TERMINAL LANCE #192 "Life After EAS: IRR Muster"
IRR Muster orders?
IRR MUSTER ORDERS
God dammit! Oh well... At least it's free money.
2 Weeks Later: IRR Muster
Hey there, Marines...
So where do I...
FUMPH
HUUNGHHHH!
Thank you for coming, here's your 200 dollar check. Semper Fi.
...Next.
Created by Maximilian Uriarte © 2012

TERMINAL LANCE #193 "Lametape Nametapes"
Man... your name's really "Bich"?
...Yup.
BICH
God that must suck! You must have gotten hell in boot camp! I don't think I would've even enlisted if I had a name like that...
Hey there Marines!
Getchur damn hands oudda yur pockets!
DICK BREATH
Created by Maximilian Uriarte © 2012

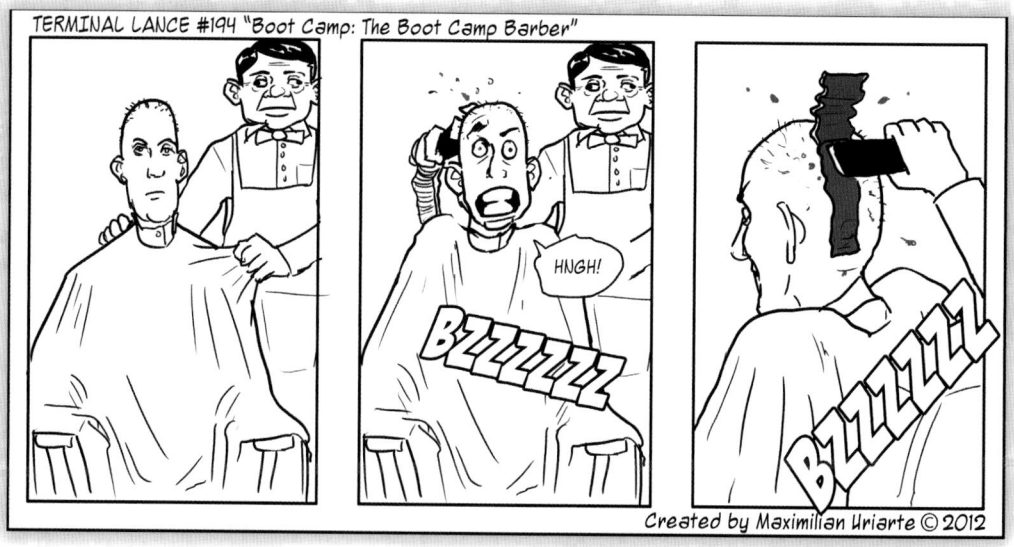
TERMINAL LANCE #194 "Boot Camp: The Boot Camp Barber"
HNGH!
BZZZZZZ
BZZZZZZ
Created by Maximilian Uriarte © 2012

TERMINAL LANCE #195 "The Mr. E Mystery 4"
Dude, check it out!
The MRE's we're getting are "Organic" now!
"ORGANIC"
We now include ALL OF THE ORGANS in our meat!
I don't think they understand what "Organic" means...
Created by Maximilian Uriarte © 2012

TERMINAL LANCE #196 "Special Delivery"
GUYS! I just called my wife, she just found out she's 2 months pregnant!
Cool, man!
I'm gonna be a daddy!
...
...
...Haven't we been on deployment for like 5 months now...?
Yeah...
...Math was never really his strong suit...
Created by Maximilian Uriarte © 2012

198 "The Worst Insult in the Corps"

If there's one word that can get even the surliest of Marines riled up, it's "boot." There is no greater insult in the Corps than to be labeled a boot. Of course, the average boot Marine isn't going to complain much about being called a boot (well, I mean, they do, but no one cares), but that's beside the point.

Once you've returned home from your first (or second) combat deployment, "boot" status is generally removed. The actual definition of a "boot" is somewhat sketchy, and changes depending on who you ask. For some, it's those that don't have Combat Action Ribbons. For others, it's simply those that have never been on a deployment of any kind. This, of course, is in infantry terms. When you start getting into the POG world it becomes a little stranger, since the majority of them don't go on regular deployment cycles. For most grunts though, most POG's are boots automatically, which of course isn't always true.

The "boot" label is all about experience and pride—as are most things in the Marine Corps. To be called a boot is a direct punch at the grunt's pride, and if you do so without caution it could end very poorly.

So if you're looking for fighting words, look no further.

TERMINAL LANCE #199 "Duty"
A MARINE ON DUTY HAS NO FRIENDS
Created by Maximilian Uriarte © 2012

CENSORED
WAGNER LOVES
OUGHES JOB IN THE CORPS
RIP-IT
TERMINAL LANCE
#200

TERMINAL LANCE #201 "Marine Hunters II: Rank Aficionado"
Hey there, you look like a Marine with that haircut...
...That I am...
My husband is on deployment right now. What rank are you?
Lance Corporal...
Never mind.
Hey there big man, what rank are you?
Second Lieutenant.
Really?! You wanna take me home with you?
Uh... sure.
Woooooo!
Mama's gettin' promoted tonight!
Created by Maximilian Uriarte © 2012

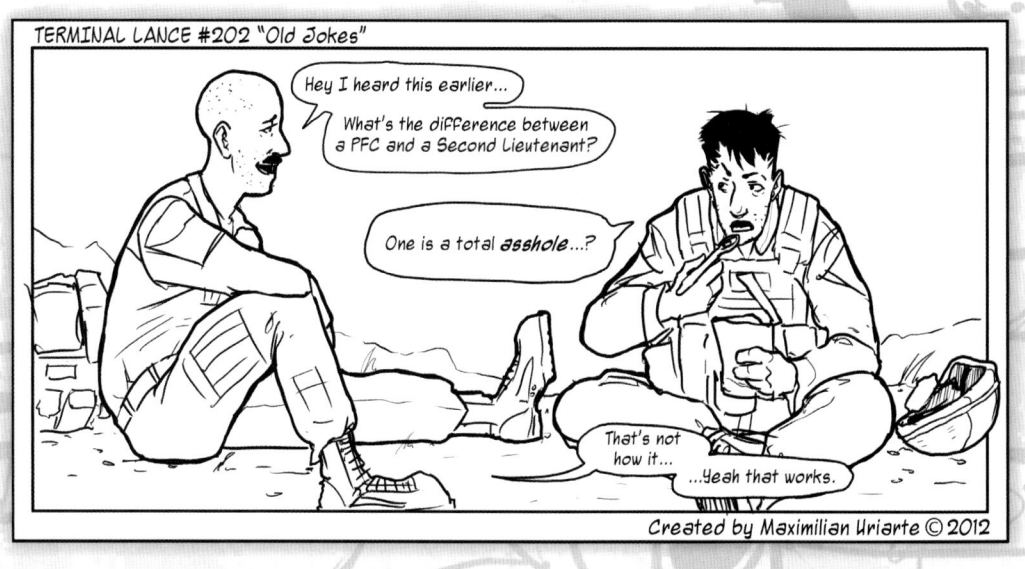
TERMINAL LANCE #202 "Old Jokes"
Hey I heard this earlier...
What's the difference between a PFC and a Second Lieutenant?
One is a total asshole...?
That's not how it...
...Yeah that works.
Created by Maximilian Uriarte © 2012

203 "That One Guy"

There's always that one guy.

He's the one that blows past everyone on the PFT (Physical Fitness Test), and does his twenty pull-ups and hundred crunches all while absolutely reeking of his good friend Jack Daniel's. He's that one guy you can always expect to be hammered and somehow not only perform his job, but do it probably better than most people. Cone is that guy. For Cone, operating on alcohol is operating on a normal level.

The seriousness of alcoholism aside, every platoon has that one guy. Not necessarily the platoon alcoholic, but the guy that's always lovably drunk at the best moments.

Cone is a real person, and he's awesome. One of my favorite memories of him was one of many nights he got really hammered and fell off the second story catwalk at Mackie Hall in Hawaii. He got up, without a scratch on him, and came back up the stairs like it never even happened and continued to drink and party. I'm fairly convinced that he's immortal.

Max note 2017: In 2014, Tyler Cone, my friend and an Iraq and Afghanistan veteran, succumbed to his demons and ended his own life. I attended his funeral in his small hometown in Nebraska. He was active duty at the time and stationed at Camp Lejeune with 3/6.

TERMINAL LANCE #204 "Computer Whiz"
OH MY FUCKING SHIT!
WHAT THE FUCK ARE YOU DOING TO MY COMPUTER?!
I'm cutting a slot in your keyboard for my ID card.
What the fuck?!
Why?!
This really hot POG chick at IPAC put her card in the keyboard and pulled up all my info...
...I figure if I can do the same I'll be able to pull hers up and get her number.
Jesus... I think I just figured out why they don't let grunts go near computers...
Created by Maximilian Uriarte © 2012

TERMINAL LANCE #205 "My Own Personal Hell II"
NOOOOOOOOO!
Are you okay, man?
About what?
I just had the worst nightmare...
I was at the armory...
...Then what happened...?
That's basically it... I was at the armory.
Created by Maximilian Uriarte © 2012

TERMINAL LANCE #206 "MILES Gear"
BEEP
BEEP
BEEP
BEEP
BEEP
I don't know who "Miles" is...
...But he's a fucking asshole.
Created by Maximilian Uriarte © 2012

207 "They'll Never Get It Right"

It's hard not to talk about video games in relation to the Marine Corps. For starters, I'm a huge nerd, and there's so many games about the military that it's hard to ignore. I believe I've mentioned before that when I enlisted there was some image of me being Solid Snake somewhere in the depths of my imagination. Everyone has that daydream: They're the lone wolf badass they play in all the games, the one that takes on an entire enemy encampment by themselves and saves the lives of thousands.

I was at CAX before my first deployment when it hit me, standing fire-watch in the open and guarding a stack of SMAW rockets for use on the range the next day. I suddenly realized I certainly wasn't Solid Snake in this scenario. Instead, I was the idiot guard standing post, walking in a repeated square pattern.

We all want to think we're the badass in the bandanna, but we never are. We're the fodder that he has to go through on his way to the objective.

We are the grunts.

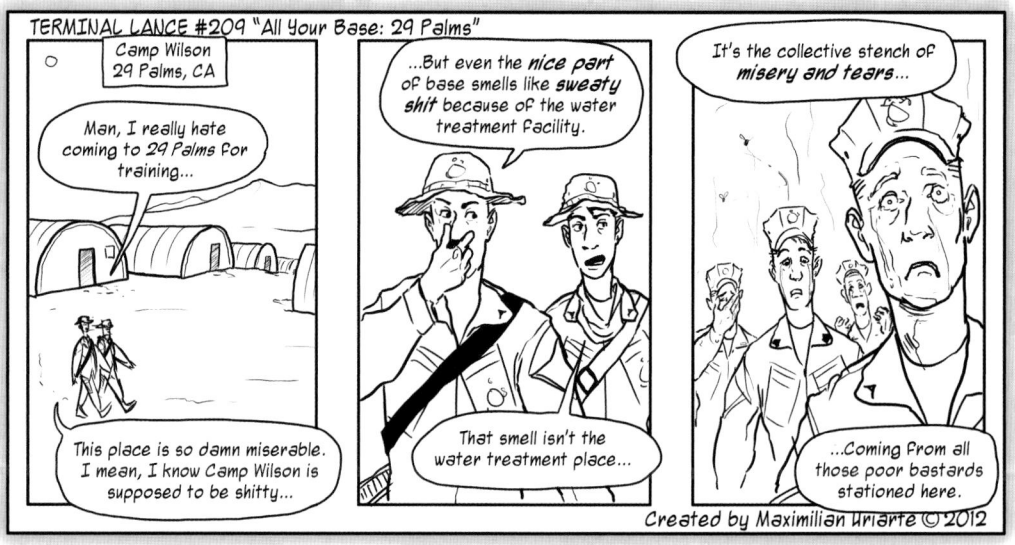
TERMINAL LANCE #209 "All Your Base: 29 Palms"
Camp Wilson
29 Palms, CA
Man, I really hate coming to 29 Palms for training...
This place is so damn miserable. I mean, I know Camp Wilson is supposed to be shitty...
...But even the nice part of base smells like sweaty shit because of the water treatment facility.
That smell isn't the water treatment place...
It's the collective stench of misery and tears...
...Coming from all those poor bastards stationed here.
Created by Maximilian Uriarte © 2012

TERMINAL LANCE #210 "Life After EAS: Circus Act"
Hi, welcome to the VA!
Hey, I just got out and I need to get my GI Bill and benefits stuff started.
Oh sure!
I'll just need you to jump through these hoops and we can get going.
Uh... okay...
...Why is one of them on fire...?
Oh that one is for your disability claim!
Created by Maximilian Uriarte © 2012

TERMINAL LANCE #211 "Stolen Valor"
So there I was...
...Operation Phantom Menace, in Falupa city. I literally caught an RPG with my bare hands, narrowly saving a bus full of mentally handicapped kids...
PFFFFFT
...and that's h
my first Medal
Sorry to interrupt, ladies...
Yo, I know Stolen Valor was repealed, and I'mma letchu finish, but you left your HIV meds back at my place.
...But don't worry ladies I brought condoms, proven to be effective at preventing sexually transmitted diseases.
Created by Maximilian Uriarte © 2012

213 "John Dear"

It's kind of a silly question, really. All white guys love Asian girls.

I say this all the time, but if there's one constant of the military, it's breakups, infidelity, and the infamous "Dear John" letters that countless Marines have fallen victim to. That girl back home that you swore wasn't like the other girls can potentially rip your heart out and destroy your soul from thousands of miles across the globe. It wouldn't be wrong to say that some women just can't hack it as a military spouse or girlfriend. Temptations are a bitch, and there is no greater temptation than a boyfriend on the other side of the planet. Dignity is not a virtue that everyone possesses.

Fidelity is a rough issue, and I'm not going to sit here and pretend that Marines don't cheat on their wives. But for most Marines on deployment, finding out about a cheating girlfriend or wife can be mentally devastating. Deployments are rough as it is, and you cling to every reminder of all you're leaving back at home. Women hold a special kind of power over Marines while they're overseas. For some Marines, their mental health can reside solely on the strength of that bond.

As the old saying goes though, if the Marine Corps wanted you to have a wife, they would have issued you one. You can chalk up bad relationships to one of the many reasons being in the military can be an awful experience. Finding yourself holding a Dear John letter is definitely not a situation you want to end up in.

215 "Old Timer"

It's hard not to feel like an old man talking about Iraq. When I enlisted, Iraq was all the rage. Civilians barely even knew about Afghanistan at that point, and most of the Marines were being cycled to the Cradle of Civilization, as it's known. Having never been to Afghanistan, I'm often met with confusion when I tell people I was in the Marines and went to Iraq twice instead of stepping foot in the 'Stan. Of course, I was enlisted at a time when this was normal, but it seems many people have already forgotten about Iraq.

Marines enlisting in 2018 were born in the year 2000.

Take a moment to let that sink in.

. . .

They were infants and children when 9/11 changed the world for the worse. Iraq is merely a bedtime story to them. The flat, palm tree–laden desert landscape flourishing along the Euphrates isn't common imagery anymore to the new enlistee. This has all been replaced with FROG suits, plate carriers, mountains, and mud huts. This will eventually fade as well, assuming the war on terror ever truly ends. Some day they will also seem old and grizzled.

TERMINAL LANCE #216 "Compensation"
...So this is my new truck, man.
That's... a whole lot of moto-stickers... You must really want people to know you're a Marine.
...What did you say about my dick...?
Uh... I didn't say anything about your dick...
I could've swore I heard you say something about my penis.
No...
Good!
...Cause it's tiny as hell!
Created by Maximilian Uriarte © 2012

TERMINAL LANCE #217 "The Underwater Level"
I keep having this nightmare...
...Where I'm strapped into a giant cage, underwater. I'm upside-down and have a ton of stupid gear on...
I can't breathe... It's the most horrifying thing you can imagine...
But then I realize...
It's not a nightmare...
...I'm just in the helo dunker.
Created by Maximilian Uriarte © 2012

TERMINAL LANCE #218 "Life After EAS: Freshman Fifty"
I don't understand why I've put on so much weight...
...this is the same stuff I used to eat in the barracks every day.
Created by Maximilian Uriarte © 2012

TERMINAL LANCE #219 "Top It Off"
Hey where did you fill up your Nalgene bottle at?
Oh, the water buffalo is just over there.
Cool, I'm gonna go fill up my CamelBak...
...this would be so much easier if we had females...
Created by Maximilian Uriarte © 2012

TERMINAL LANCE #220 "Issued"
Listen up, gents...
...We just got word from higher that all deployed combat units will be fielding the new ULTRATACTICOOL© flaks...
Everyone grab one and set it up.
Wow this fucking sucks... I can barely even move.
I can't feel my hands!
I can't feel my foreskin!
Why would anyone think this was a good idea...?
Meanwhile at HQMC...
Dude, check out the new gear we just issued out...
Marines are gonna look so hardcore.
It looks kind of heavy and cumbersome.
Who cares? We're not the ones wearing it.

222 "Anatomically Correct"

It's one or the other, amirite, guys?

No, but really, you always hear about how Sergeants are the "backbone" of the Corps, or Gunnery Sergeants are the "backbone" of the Staff NCO Corps, or Lance Corporals are the "backbone" of lower enlisted. But there's only so many backbones. We need to start assigning the anatomically correct body parts in relation to members of the Marine Corps.

So we've already established that Sergeants are the backbone. Okay, they deserve that.

- Private: The appendix or something useless. Who's a Private anyway besides students?
- Private First Class: The gooch of the Corps. Underneath even the Lance Corporals, who we've established are either the dick and balls or the asshole.

- Lance Corporal: See strip.
- Corporal: The buttocks. These Marines are underneath the Sergeants but above the asshole. Some can look nice and even fuckable, but may smell of sweaty shit upon closer inspection.
- Sergeant: See strip.
- Staff Sergeant: The lungs. They spout hot air given to them by higher-ups and play a major role in the operation of the entire body by circulating their oxygenated bullshit throughout the vascular system.
- Gunny: The rippling, sweaty, muscular arms of the Marine Corps. Gunnys are usually the cool guys of the Staff NCO's, they're high enough rank that no one bothers them but not high enough to really give a shit about anything. They're just there, looking cool and occasionally doing some heavy lifting.
- First Sergeant/Master Sergeant: These guys are the eyeballs of the Marine Corps. Well, maybe, who knows? All I know is nine times out of ten, if you're getting your ass chewed, it's by one of these E8's with eagle-like vision that spotted you from across the PX parking lot for something that may or may not be your fault.
- Sergeant Major: The hard skull/cranium. We rarely see the brain as a lower-enlisted. Instead we usually see the face of the battalion command represented by the highest enlisted. The Sergeant Major protects the CO (the brain) from rocks and other small objects that may be thrown as a result of hearing things like, "LOL your leave is canked," and "LOL no chow this week, guys."

People asked about Master Guns. They are a mythical creature that doesn't actually exist, like a unicorn or a First Sergeant with a soul.

Officers are a whole other thing—generally different parts of the brain. I'm pretty sure Second Lieutenants are that part they say we never use throughout our entire lives.

TERMINAL LANCE #224 "Child Abuse"
Hello? Is this PMO...?
Yes, what can we do for you?
I need to report a child abuse on base...
...I just saw a Marine force his kid to get a... high-and-tight!
...we're on our way.
Created by Maximilian Uriarte © 2012

TERMINAL LANCE #225 "Sweet Vengeance"
You always see Marines with their fat wives on base...
But you know... these chicks have it figured out. When I get out I'm gonna marry a female Marine.
I'll grow my hair out, get fat and live off her benefits. I won't work...
...I'll just sit outside the PX and heckle the Marines getting their weekend haircuts...
...My existence will be little more than a glorious inside joke...
HA!
HA!
HA!
HA!
HA!
...and I will be happy.
Created by Maximilian Uriarte © 2012

TERMINAL LANCE #226 "Secretly Hopeful"
...I'm uh... I'm gonna go to the bathroom...
God dammit Garcia! I told you not to use my computer for that!
It's so obvious what you're doing in there when you take the whole computer with you!
...We're never going to pick up! The scores are too high! Stop looking!
ACTIVE CORPORAL CUTTING SCORES
Shut up! I'm looking at porn, I swear!
Created by Maximilian Uriarte © 2012

TERMINAL LANCE #227 "Insight"
Oh you went to Iraq, right?
Yup...
Oh, that's fascinating! What do you think of the complex political situation over there right now?
Uh...
I was just a turret-gunner, man. I never really paid attention to that stuff.
Right... but surely you have some insight given your experience.
This one time I drew balls on the front of my turret. It made my fifty-cal look like a dick.
...it was awesome.
Created by Maximilian Uriarte © 2012

TERMINAL LANCE #228 "Real Live Women!"
USO
DALLAS COWBOY CHEERLEADERS!!!
REAL, LIVE WOMEN!!! COMING TO CAMP LEATHERNECK!
Dude!
Dude the cheerleaders are coming out here!
What?! No way!
Live women!?
This is awesome!
I fucking love women!
Dude, me too!
...Ugh...
Created by Maximilian Uriarte © 2012

TERMINAL LANCE #229 "She Don't Rate"
There's the L.T. with his wife...
Fuck man, why are officer wives so hot? It must be the money...
No, I think they take a class at OCS about it...
Officer Candidate School
Remember... and this is important...
If she ain't an eight, she don't rate.
Repeat it.
If she ain't an eight, she don't rate.
Created by Maximilian Uriarte © 2012

TERMINAL LANCE #230 "Mandatory"
Okay gents...
...We all know the Marine Corps Ball is coming up next month.
Is it mandatory, Staff Sergeant?
The ball is not mandatory.
However, you are required to purchase a meal and if you're not there you'll be NJP'd.
Um...
I don't think Staff Sergeant knows what "mandatory" means...
Created by Maximilian Uriarte © 2012

TERMINAL LANCE #231 "The Dance of Our People"
Ah fuck!
FUCK!
FUCK!
FUCK!
HURRRRRRGH!
What the hell are you doing...?
One of your fucking brass went straight down my shirt!
Created by Maximilian Uriarte © 2012

TERMINAL LANCE #232 "A New Disciple"
Dude!
...Listen to what I just overheard this fucking boot say to his friend!
FUCKING SAY IT, BOOT.
Eh... All I said was...
...I don't understand why our senior Marines are so disgruntled all the time. I love being in the Marine Corps so far.
Oh, my child...
You have much to learn.
Come, I will take you to the Hall of NJP and to the Chamber of Closed Cutting Scores.
Created by Maximilian Uriarte © 2012

234 "~~Don't~~ Encourage Them"

I'm not one of those guys that gives a shit if you drink and you're underage. I'm also not one of those guys that thinks people under twenty-one should be allowed to drink. That's not really what this strip is about, because if it were, it'd be a display of complete apathy on my part. What I never understood in the Marine Corps is the culture of absolute encouragement when it comes to consumption of alcohol, yet the unabashed punishment of said consumption when it occurs.

As Marines, it is undeniable that there is a culture centered around drinking as an expression of masculinity. Marines drink. This is a vastly known and widely perpetuated reality in Marine culture. If you don't drink, you are abnormal.

However, I see it as a great irony that while the establishment encourages drinking in nearly every regard (Warriors Night anyone?), they have the audacity to punish younger Marines who engage in such activities even in the safety of their own barracks. Furthermore, why does the punishment always have to be so severe? The most ridiculous NJP's I've ever seen involved underage drinking. Granted, I'm not saying that if a Marine is underage, drunk, and acting a fool out in town that he should go unnoticed, but let's get real:

Marines drink. You created this stereotype. Own up to it and don't pretend like it's not expected to happen.

Now, if you'll excuse me, I'm going to go have a drink.

TERMINAL LANCE #237 "Obvious Observations"

Created by Maximilian Uriarte © 2012

TERMINAL LANCE #238 "Infidelity Amongst Infidels II"

Created by Maximilian Uriarte © 2012

TERMINAL LANCE #239 "Keeping Cadence"

Created by Maximilian Uriarte © 2012

TERMINAL LANCE #240 "Leave Blocked"
Listen up, gents...
The CO just passed that the holiday leave block has been pushed back a few days. You'll need to get on MOL and re-submit your requests.
What the fuck, Staff Sergeant?!
Most of us have already bought our plane tickets!
Yeah!
Yeah!
Oh he just sent out a mass text to the staff and officers...
It says, LOL Sorry.
And... yup.
...yup.
...That's a photo of his dick.
Created by Maximilian Uriarte © 2012

TERMINAL LANCE #241 "The Wooly Pully"
...Abe.
Yes, Staff Sergeant?
The word was green-on-green...
I know...
So why are you wearing your wooly pully?
I've had this damn thing in my wall-locker for three years and I've never worn it...
...I just...
...I've just always wondered what it felt like.
Created by Maximilian Uriarte © 2012

242 "Dress Blues Blues"

I like wearing my dress blues. They look snazzy as shit and I look great in them. That's all the reason I need. That little neck thing—the clasps that bring the collar together—bugs the fucking hell out of me though. It's one of those little things that you sit there and pick at for a couple of minutes before you give up and ask someone for help. Those couple of minutes are the most excruciatingly annoying minutes of your entire life.

I've long believed the collar of the dress blue uniform to be the key to its great track record of getting Marines laid. The collar in combination with those two little golden Eagle, Globe, and Anchors make that entire outfit. But this delectable collar comes at a price—and it's your sanity as you try to clasp the damned thing together five minutes before you're supposed to be out the door. A Terminal Lance Forum user gave this pro tip:

Take the blues jacket to the tailor, replace the clasp with Velcro.

Brilliant.

TERMINAL LANCE #244 "Have You?"
HAVE YOU EVER YELLED SO HARD
YOU SHIT YOUR PANTS!?
Created by Maximilian Uriarte © 2013

TERMINAL LANCE #245 "Myths and Legends V"
DUDE!
YOU'RE NEVER GONNA BELIEVE WHAT I JUST SAW!!!
Huh?
We were police-calling the woods by the O-course, and I actually saw a Chief Warrant Officer 5!
Bullshit! No man has ever actually laid eyes upon a CWO-Five!
Yes! I got a photo on my phone!
Check it out!
Wow...
...It's so majestic.
Created by Maximilian Uriarte © 2013

TERMINAL LANCE #246 "All Your Base: MCBH Kaneohe Bay"
Man...
I love being stationed in Hawaii.
Hey Garcia?
Yeah?
You ever wonder what it would be like to be stationed somewhere else?
Nope.
Me either!
HAHAHAHAHAHAHA
Created by Maximilian Uriarte © 2013

TERMINAL LANCE #247 "Logging the Logbook"

While I appreciate the thoroughness of your logbook, you really don't have to log everything, Lance Corporal.

A MARINE ON DUTY HAS NO FRIENDS

I was told to keep track of **everything**, sir.

Yes but...

0533: PROCEEDED TO BATHROOM
0535: COMMENCED BOWEL-MOVEMENT
0537: COMMENCED "POOP AND JERK"
0545: REACHED EJACULATION WITH 184 STROKES
0547: ...CLEANED STRAY SEMEN OFF LOGBOOK

...is a bit unnecessary...

Yeah... you might want to wash your hands, sir.

Created by Maximilian Uriarte © 2013

TERMINAL LANCE #258 "Core Temperature"

This Marine overheated!

I need to take his temperature!

Roll him over. He needs...

FLOP

CENSORED

...The Silver Bullet.

Bullshit!

That's not what happened. I was there.

That's what it **felt** like!

Created by Maximilian Uriarte © 2013

249 "The Age-Old Debate"

The classic debate of POG's (People Other than Grunts) vs. Grunts will be around as long as these classifications exist in the Marine Corps.

The argument I always despised most was that a POG was not of the oh-three inclination because he was simply too smart for such menial duties during his enlistment. I'd like to think that this comic, along with whatever other accomplishments of mine and those of other successful infantry Marines, should serve to prove that grunts are in fact not stupid. I'm proud to say that my ASVAB score was above 90 and my GT was above 130. I chose to be infantry (specifically, I chose 0300 open-contract and 0351 once I got to SOI).

Scores and other numbers aside, perhaps there is a greater wisdom in the long-term vision that most of the POG population enlisted with. Most grunts tend to have a somewhat existential purpose for their enlistment, transcending rational things like job security after their four years or whether they'll actually enjoy it. That's not really the point of joining the infantry. You don't choose to be in the infantry because you're worried about what job you'll get when you leave. You don't choose to be in the infantry for anything else that can be expressed on a résumé. You do it because you have something to prove.

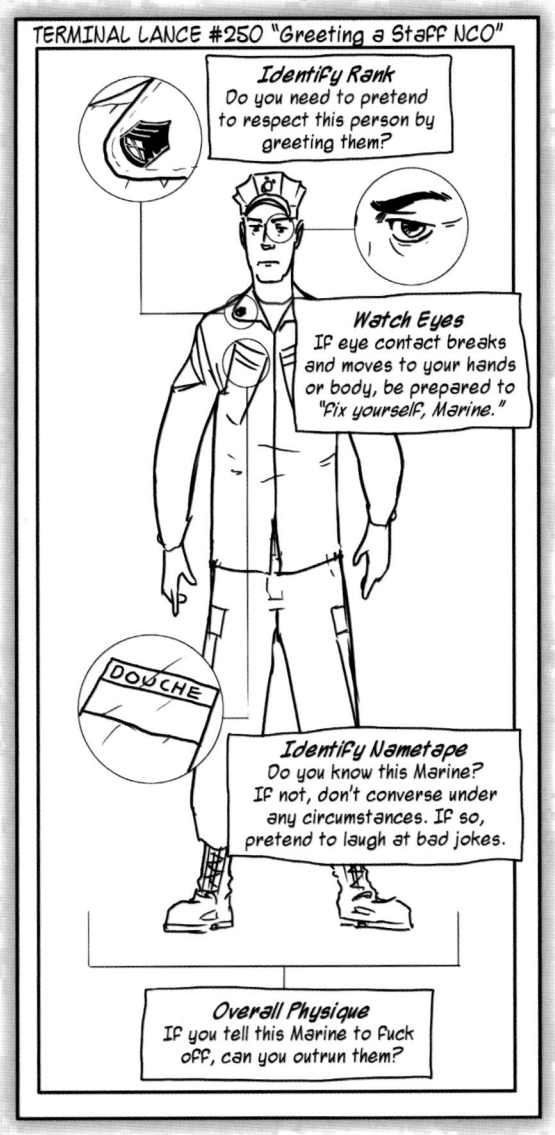
TERMINAL LANCE #250 "Greeting a Staff NCO"
Identify Rank
Do you need to pretend to respect this person by greeting them?
Watch Eyes
If eye contact breaks and moves to your hands or body, be prepared to "Fix yourself, Marine."
DOUCHE
Identify Nametape
Do you know this Marine? If not, don't converse under any circumstances. If so, pretend to laugh at bad jokes.
Overall Physique
If you tell this Marine to fuck off, can you outrun them?

TERMINAL LANCE #251 "Military Working Dogs"
Hey is it true that military working dogs outrank their handlers, Sergeant?
Yup! Ol' Odin here is actually a Staff Sergeant!
Oh cool. So when you have sex with him, is that considered bestiality or fraternization?
You know what I'm not sure actua...
Hey wait I don't fuck my dog! Get away from us you asshole!
Shhh... It's okay Odin, don't worry about him.

TERMINAL LANCE #252 "Call of Duty Reference"

Created by Maximilian Uriarte ©2013

TERMINAL LANCE #253 "Distinguished Warfare"

Created by Maximilian Uriarte ©2013

TERMINAL LANCE #254 "The Clipboard"

TERMINAL LANCE #255 "Like a Box of Chocolates"
So you remember that scene in Forrest Gump...
...When Jenny sees her old house that her dad molested her in and she flips out and throws her shoes and shit?
Yeah?
When I was on leave I walked past my old recruiting station...
...It was like that.
Created by Maximilian Uriarte © 2013

TERMINAL LANCE #256 "Lose-Lose"
Hey are you with the unit that's replacing us...?
Yup.
Oh cool, well don't worry, you should be all right, your unit can't be nearly as fucked up as ours.
I dunno... Mine is pretty bad...
My unit misplaced an MRAP last week.
We had seventeen DUI's the weekend before we flew out!
We had a Lieutenant get fired for sleeping with a 14-year-old girl!
We had a Captain get fired for sleeping with a 17-year-old boy!
Oh wow... you win, that's pretty bad.
Yeah... well...
To be fair, I think we both actually lose.
Created by Maximilian Uriarte © 2013

TERMINAL LANCE #257 "Barracks Barbershop"
Hey man, I forgot to get a haircut this weekend, can you give me a medium-reg?
What makes you think I can cut hair?
Please, you're Mexican.
So? Just cause I'm Mexican I'm supposed to be able to cut hair?!
Ugh...
...Gimme the clippers.
Go into my wall-locker and grab my scissors and gown. Put up my sign, too... in case anyone else in the platoon needs a haircut.
Created by Maximilian Uriarte © 2013

TERMINAL LANCE #258 "Lost Innocence"
I was looking at these photos of when I was a boot, I look so young...
There's also something weird in my eye in each one... I can't figure out what it is...
That's called motivation.
...You don't have that anymore.
Created by
© 2013

TERMINAL LANCE #259 "Inside the Armory"
Sir, the battalion gave us a really limited number of handguns.
Who should we issue them to?
Well Marine, the right thing to do would be to give them to the Machinegunners and our SMAW gunners.
They'll need them the most.
No no wait!
Oh man, I crack myself up sometimes. You were actually going to do it too.
Give them to the staff and officers, you dumb boot. Who wants to carry a rifle around everywhere?
Created by
© 2013

TERMINAL LANCE #260 "In the Wild"
Do you still want to see the movie tomorrow?
Yeah sure.
Okay, why don't you just come by the barracks tomorrow at like 5 and we can leave from there.
Eh... I hate going to the barracks...
Why?
Every time I'm there Marines never leave me alone... I feel like I'm the last gazelle in the savannah or something.
Created by Maximilian Uriarte © 2012

262 "The Bootenant"

If it weren't for the fact that they get paid out of the gate about twice as much as an equally experienced enlisted Marine, I might feel bad for Lieutenants when they enter the fleet. The Lieutenant has the dubious honor of being in charge of about forty guys that really have absolutely no respect for him whatsoever. To the average salty Lance Corporal with a deployment and an NJP or two under his belt, someone with no deployment experience and shiny bars is just as boot as the fresh-faced kid from SOI that can barely tie his own boots.

Unfortunately, there's not really much you can do about it. New Lieutenants are given a platoon to command. That's just how it is. My platoon went through a few butter-bars in my time, and it's always interesting to see how they act when they first get there. One new Lieutenant actually used to stand at parade rest for the senior Lance Corporals and would refer to them by their rank. While I respect the ideology of this approach, it ultimately fails to gain respect because an infantry platoon is prison rules, bitch. You better make someone your bitch on the first day, or else the green weenie won't be the only thing working its way up your rectum daily.

TERMINAL LANCE #263 "Post"
Hey... I think I see something!
What is it?
No, wait...
...That's just a dude fucking a goat...
No, wait...
Wait...
...Wait...
Now the goat is fucking *him.*
I'M WAGNER AND I SUCK PENIS
Created by Maximilian Uriarte © 2013

TERMINAL LANCE #264 "Have You Ever Killed Anybody?"
Yo, brah... I heard you just got back from Iraqistan...
...You kill anyone, brah?
Oh my god...
So did you... *kill* anyone?
So like... did you *kill* anybody?
No...
...But I'm really starting to *consider* it.
Created by Maximilian Uriarte © 2013

TERMINAL LANCE #265 "FAP'd Out"
Come here, little Lance Corporal!
Come on, I got you a Cool Ranch Doritos Locos Taco.
That's it...
Don't worry, we're all POG's here... No one is going to yell at you. You're safe.
Poor guy... What *happened* to him...?
He just FAP'd over here from an infantry battalion...
They treat them like *animals* over there, I tell ya.
Created by

267 "Locals"

I feel like this strip might not really apply to places like Camp Pendleton or Lejeune, but to those of us that were stationed in Hawaii or even you Okinawa vets, surely it's something you've seen happen. While aboard beautiful Kaneohe Bay, it seemed like every weekend there was some new incident involving locals out in town. The Marines would have the same story every time (*"They just jumped us"*), when in reality, Marines aren't always the most tactful of species. And it was usually the same Marines that seemed to always get jumped out in town. In all the three and a half years I was there, I never once ran into any locals that meant me harm. Either I just hung out in the right neighborhoods, or I'm not a complete asshole.

Of course, I'm not saying that violent crimes don't happen for a reason, because of course they do.

All I'm saying is, well, I know Marines.

269 "The Birds and the Bees"

I could never do it.

I could never be a Drill Instructor.

Don't get me wrong—I respect what they do. Without DI's we wouldn't have Marines. It's hard work and not everyone is cut out for it. I consider myself one of those people. I couldn't be a DI because I just don't think I would enjoy being a complete asshole 24/7 for three months straight. That's a very demanding regimen of eating nothing but recruit dignity and sorrow, and I've never been particularly good at dieting.

But really, it does take a special kind of person to actually be a good Drill Instructor. You can't just yell all the time, or no one takes you seriously. I found that the new DI's tend to yell the most. They think that's the way to get results, when really, it was much scarier when one of them didn't wear their anger on the surface. When you didn't know what they were thinking . . . that's when you would shit your pants. Having someone screaming in your face is something you get used to rather quickly.

Again though, I have plethoric respect for those that wear the campaign cover. It's just a tough job, babysitting sixty to a hundred sloppily shaven recruits that smell like a combination of sweaty shit and Cobra 65.

So, good on you, Drill Instructors. I could never do what you do, and would never want to.

TERMINAL LANCE #272 "JJ"
Hey Abe, we could really use your help in this working party. I know one of the boots came up here and told you.
Gimme ten minutes. There's like twenty zombies in this room.
Come on man, JJIDIOTIEBUCKLE or some shit? Dependability? UnselFishnes? Any of that ring a bell?
Whatever, "JJ" is a fucking idiot anyway.
Who ties a buckle? You buckle a buckle.
Created by Maximilian Uriarte © 2013

TERMINAL LANCE #273 "That First Night"
You thought about it before, the fact that you're going to war.
So many possibilities, so many thoughts.
So many dangers in the wars that are fought.
But you'll never be as afraid of the things you may botch...
...as you were, on that first night of Firewatch.
Created by Maximilian Uriarte © 2013

TERMINAL LANCE #274 "AAV's in One Sentence"
VROOM
...
HRUGHHH
SIGH...
...This just fucking sucks.
Created by Maximilian Uriarte © 2013

TERMINAL LANCE #275 "Veteran Card"

You were going pretty fast back there. Can I see your license please?

Well officer, myself and these other fine **Veterans** were just out celebrating our... I mean... **your freedom.** It's the Fourth... maybe you could cut us some slack?

You were doing 102 in a **school zone** and you smell like **bourbon and gunpowder.**

So tell me, officer...

...Why do you **hate America?**

Created by Maximilian Uriarte © 2013

TERMINAL LANCE #276 "Demographics"

Excuse me, Lance Corporal... Lance Corporal Garcia wanted me to come get you...

Fuck you, boot.

Okay... so gays are allowed to serve openly and females are being put into the infantry, everyone is being treated equal except us boots...

Yup. And you want to know why?

Cause you're a **fucking boot.**

Created by Maximilian Uriarte © 2013

TERMINAL LANCE #277 "Late Nights"
THIS ROOM IS FILTHY!
Oh, don't worry Lance Corporals, I've got all night!
Ugh. Isn't Staff Sergeant married? Shouldn't he want to go home or something...?
You'd think so.
Married...?
Have you seen my wife?!
LOOK AT HER! LOOK AT HER!
DON'T YOU LOOK AWAY!
OH MY GOD!
WOULD YOU GO HOME TO THAT?!
Created by Maximilian Uriarte © 2013

278 "That Guy"

Not to be confused with "That One Guy," this is "That Guy."

While That Guy doesn't necessarily have to be about FOB dogs, there's always some douchemaster that wants to shoot the animals aboard the FOB. You know them, we all do. They're the fucking asshole that grew up with an abusive father or something so they feel the need to shoot harmless animals.

Now don't get me wrong: I'm well aware that many of the dogs in the Middle East are feral and shouldn't be kept aboard the FOB. That's not what I'm talking about. When I was in Iraq in 2007, we had this random orange cat wander into the camp and sleep around for a few days in different beds. I am partial to orange cats (every cat I've ever had has been orange), so naturally it stayed with me and my people for a few days. It wandered off, but within two days we came to find out that That Guy smashed its head with a brick. The reason? Who knows.

TERMINAL LANCE #280 "Equality"
Hey dude, I don't think I've ever seen you around here before...
Probably cause I'm not a dude, I'm a woman.
Oh... Well I knew females were getting our Dress Blues, but what's with the haircut...?
The Commandant wanted equality... so he made us all get regulation haircuts too.
Huh...
...I have the weirdest boner right now.
Created by Maximilian Uriarte © 2013

TERMINAL LANCE #281 "Adopt a Marine"
Hi, I'm an actor that you're not sure if you recognize.
I'd like to talk to you about Adopt a Marine.
All over the world, there are deployed Marines that are miserable and very bored.
For just the cost of one log of Cope Long Cut a week and a subscription to Maxim, you can symbolically adopt a Marine today.
When you adopt a Marine...
PENIS
BOOBS
You'll receive a drawing from your Marine each month showing their thanks.
Created by Maximilian Uriarte © 2013

TERMINAL LANCE #282 "Size Matters"
So... you guys do realize that blouses come in different sizes, right...?
What do you mean, Lance Corporal?
Well, what sizes are you wearing?
Medium-Reg.
Medium-Reg.
Medium-Reg.
Created by Maximilian Uriarte © 2013

TERMINAL LANCE #283 "Mine-Resistant, Ambush-Protected"
Abe, listen up...
You've been selected to get your MRAP license this week. You'll need to be at the Motor Pool tomorrow at 0745.
MRAP license? But I've never driven anything like that before, Staff Sergeant...
Don't worry, it's just like driving an SUV.
Wow, this is just like driving an SUV.
...A really shitty SUV that you can't see anything out of that handles like a hard-boiled turd.
Created by Maximilian Uriarte © 2013

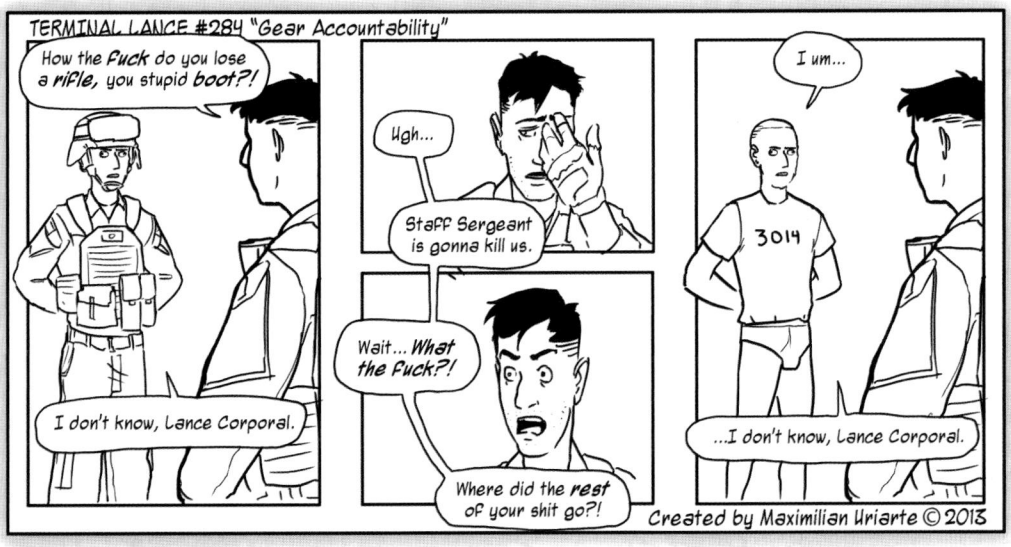
TERMINAL LANCE #284 "Gear Accountability"
How the Fuck do you lose a rifle, you stupid boot?!
I don't know, Lance Corporal.
Ugh...
Staff Sergeant is gonna kill us.
Wait... What the Fuck?!
Where did the rest of your shit go?!
I um...
3014
...I don't know, Lance Corporal.
Created by Maximilian Uriarte © 2013

TERMINAL LANCE #285 "Questionable Advice"
Hey boot! What the fuck are you doing?!
Putting in ear plugs for the range.
Why?! You think you'll have time for ear plugs in Afghanistan?!
You smell nice and clean too, I bet you took a shower before you came out here huh?!
Uh huh...
Why?! You think you'll have time for a shower in Afghanistan?!
I haven't showered in seven weeks, boot!
Take that shit out of your ears, boot!
...
...Ew.
Created by Maximilian Uriarte © 2013

TERMINAL LANCE #286 "Duty II"
SIGH
TICK TOCK
Huh?
TICK TOCK
TICK TOCK
TICK TOCK
HHNNNNGGHHH....
CLICK
Whelp, that's 1 hour down...
...23 more to go.
Plenty of time for me to reflect on the mistakes I've made in my life.
Created by Maximilian Uriarte ©2013

TERMINAL LANCE #287 "Grizzled"
Dude, I'm so jealous of your no-shave chit. You have no idea. I thought only black guys got those.
It might be the best idea I've ever had.
Seriously, if I were a girl I'd date you. I need to get more Corpsman friends.
Uh oh, here comes a Staff Sergeant...
Yes! I've been waiting for this opportunity! Wait here.
Staff Sergeant, hold on!
Huh?
Created by Maximilian Uriarte © 2013

TERMINAL LANCE #288 "GoPro"
Check out this GoPro I just bought for my kevlar.
I'm gonna get so much awesome combat footage while I'm on deployment!
Awesome! I can't wait to see it when you come back!
7 Months Later
I thought you said you were going to get combat footage...?
All these videos are just you... jerking off on post.
Yeah...
That's basically what we did.
Created by Maximilian Uriarte © 2013

TERMINAL LANCE #289 "Why We Drink"
The Lance Corporal
I drink because Staff Sergeant is an asshole and our Lieutenant is an idiot.
The Staff Sergeant
I drink because my Lance Corporals are a pain in my ass and the Lieutenant is an idiot.
The Lieutenant
I'm drunk cause my life is fucking awesome!
I get paid a ton and people salute me n' shit!
Created by Maximilian Uriarte © 2013

290 "The Difference: Terminology"

If I had a dime for every time a POG told me "I'm basically the grunt of _____," I'd have like $1.30.

"Grunt" is a term that gets thrown around a lot between MOS's, but grunts are grunts. Typically, anyone calling themselves a "grunt" is supposed to have the moniker of "03" in front of their MOS. Of course, it's all semantics anyway, but the point is the same. The fact is that the grass is definitely greener on the other side, and it's not the side of the grunts.

It's kind of like a white guy saying, "Yeah, I know what it's like to be black, someone called me a cracker once."

No, you privileged shit, it's not the same.

The two worlds are completely different. Being a grunt isn't just about having "03" or going on deployments. It's about spending hours in formation for no reason, standing by all the fucking time, going to the armory for eight hours to clean your rifle again, working parties, and just generally being treated like complete shit. There's no office hours, there's no "shop" to report to in the morning, you just do as you're told.

You are a grunt.

TERMINAL LANCE #291 "Eat the Apple"

Created by Maximilian Uriarte © 2013

TERMINAL LANCE #292 "The Other Side of the Line"

Created by Maximilian Uriarte © 2013

TERMINAL LANCE #293 "There's an App for That"

Created by Maximilian Uriarte © 2013

TERMINAL LANCE #294 "Marriage Benefits"
Okay... listen up, gents.
Stephens, you've got duty tomorrow.
B... but Staff Sergeant...
...I'm married.
Oh all right... Abe, you've got duty tomorrow instead.
God dammit! This is the seventeenth time I've had duty this month just cause I'm single!
Oh stop bitching, it's not his fault no one loves you.
Created by Maximilian Uriarte © 2013

TERMINAL LANCE #295 "Bricks Life"
...In addition to the previously mentioned new barracks rules...
The Commandant has also passed that every Marine returning to their room must have their butthole fingered briefly by the duty NCO or above.
No particular reason... We were just looking for various ways that we could fuck you...
...Unfortunately most of them turned out to be illegal.
Created by Maximilian Uriarte © 2013

TERMINAL LANCE #296 "The Surprise Officer"
What a nice day...
...Just enjoying myself walking by Battalion...
Oh good morning to you Lance Corporal!
SHIT!
Good to go, I guess I don't rate a salute either, huh?
I'm sorry, sir, you just came around that corner really quick!
10 SECONDS EARLIER
10...
9...
8...
Created by Maximilian Uriarte © 2013

298 "Bird of Prey"

Beware the call of the mighty Blue Falcon.

He prowls the skies searching for his next target. He is a bird of prey, but he preys not on the typical feast of field mice and smaller birds. No, this great azure raptor seeks only those to whom it is close . . . for you must be its buddy, in order to be buddy-fucked. When you feel that warm splat of milky blue shit on your shoulder, you know you've been hit.

The Blue Falcon comes in many forms, but usually it's the careless friend of yours that unintentionally (or intentionally—for the true assholes) manages to screw you over in some way or another. The Blue Falcon is merely a guise for the infamous Buddy Fucker, an alternate form of being for when he is in the skies, on the prowl. In all reality, it can be really easy to fuck your buddy over in the Marine Corps, without even realizing it. You can have the best of intentions, but if you find that you've fucked your buddy, you shouldn't be surprised when he pulls the wings off and calls you by your true name . . .

. . . Buddy Fucker.

The Marine Corps is all about the brotherhood. I know it's a cliché, but it's true. Human interaction is an important, yet fading part of a good Marine Corps. Too many officers, commissioned and non-, are so quick to push paperwork down your throat instead of actually talking to you, man-to-man. Email has replaced conversation, with comically long and obtuse signature lines replacing an honest "thank you."

The CO that slams you with an NJP before even trying to fix the situation with counseling is just as much the fucker of buddies as the falcon of the skies.

Don't be the falcon, be a man. If someone is acting out, there's always a million ways around it before anything official needs to be done, potentially ruining someone's career.

299 "The Eye of Sauron II"

Always watching . . .

If it wasn't entirely apparent by now, I am a gigantic nerd. It might explain why I chose to go 0351 when I was at SOI. It seemed to be where the rest of my kind culminated in the infantry. This, of course, brings us to where we are today: from a *Star Wars* parody to a *Lord of the Rings* reference. If the whole Eye of Sauron is lost on you, I invite you to 2001 to come watch *Lord of the Rings* with me. I was fifteen, 150 pounds, and had yet to see a vagina in person.

More to the point, I remember always being told in boot camp:

Integrity is doing the right thing, even when no one is watching.

It's actually not bad advice for your everyday life, but it always felt more like an underhanded warning coming from the institution itself. From the very beginning, Drill Instructors instill the fear of the Marine Corps into you: "We see everything," they tell you—and they're entirely correct. It's the fear of the Great Eye that keeps you from wearing uniform items while on leave, or putting on a hat indoors months after you've separated from the service.

The Great Eye of Sauron sees all.

It's always watching.

Max note 2017: On terminallance.com, this strip is actually an animated GIF. The middle panel flashes between Abe's nervous face and the eye of the green weenie!

301 "Friends of Benefits"

More than once, I've had people tell me they don't really plan on using their GI Bill.

"I dunno, I just don't like school."

"I've got a buddy back home that's gonna hook me up with a job."

"I'm an idiot."

These are the kinds of responses I get, all of which are excuses rather than reasons. Here's the thing: In today's world, the college degree is the new high school diploma. You really need one if you plan on doing anything outside of a regular blue collar job. Of course, there's absolutely nothing wrong with blue collar work, but you're literally being handed an opportunity to do absolutely anything. Yeah, college can be lame and you'll be surrounded by some spoiled shitheads that you can't relate to, but you'll also learn a lot, you'll meet some great new people that don't suck, and it's a great way to ease back into civilian life without the pressure of needing to find a job.

Even if you have absolutely no ambition upon exiting the Marine Corps, college is a great place for you to chill out for four years until you figure out what it is you want to do when you grow up. Compared to the Marine Corps, it's really not that hard and you'll walk away with a bachelor's degree at the end of the day.

So really, you have no excuse.

Also, why is it that whenever someone has a "buddy back home" that's going to give them a job, it's always the most obscure shit you've ever heard of?

"Yeah, my buddy back home installs window-lining on fire trucks, he makes $8,234 an hour."

Maybe I just need more buddies.

TERMINAL LANCE #304 "Generation Gap"
I was a Marine too back in the Clinton years.
USMC
I tell you what, my Corps wasn't soft like yours. None of that queer stuff went on, we used to take the fags to the tree-line and beat the gay out of 'em.
Wow.
That is absolutely terrible.
Yeah, I'm kind of a piece of shit now that I think about it.
USMC
I also hate women and the Mexicans.
Created by Maximilian Uriarte © 2014

TERMINAL LANCE #305 "Life After EAS: Tough Mudder, Tough Sell"
Hey Abe!
I'm glad I found you! I was wondering if you wanted to do the Tough Mudder race with me next month! I'm training now!
Why would I want to do that?
You were in the Marines, right? You used to do stuff like that all the time! It'll be fun!
We get to run miles, crawl through mud, and climb ropes and stuff!
That sounds awful.
They paid us and forced us to do stupid shit like that. I would never do it willingly.
I've been out of the Marine Corps for almost two months now, I'm done with that stuff.

TERMINAL LANCE #306 "The Way of Our People"
Hey cock-fucker! You were supposed to be on watch right now! Now Staff Sergeant is pissed at me because of you!
Whoa calm down! I mean, really, if you think about it, it's not really my fault. We wouldn't be here if the Marine Corps didn't send us here, so... it's the Marine Corps' fault.
Oh shut up!
You can't just blame the Marine Corps for all of your problems!
But...
I'm a Lance Corporal...
...It's what we do.
Created by Maximilian Uriarte © 2014

TERMINAL LANCE #307 "Why Staff NCO's Love Challenge Coins"
That's um...
...That's a lot of Challenge Coins you got there, First Sergeant...
Oh, they're... Um...
I just like to collect them... For the memories.
Later That Day
Nice slam dude!
EXCHANGE 25¢ Gift Certificate
Thanks man! I got a new slammer yesterday! Looks like your POGs are mine!
Created by Maximilian Uriarte © 2014

TERMINAL LANCE #308 "The Two-Beer Rule"
Okay, gents...
...You are authorized no more than two beers during our layover here in Ireland.
Two beers?!
What the Fuck?!
What is this? Nazi Germany?!
Nazi Germany? Really...?
You don't think that's a bit of a stretch?
I don't mean to exaggerate here, sir...
...But two beers? Right now, you are literally worse than Hitler.
Yeah, and last time I checked, Hitler was pretty bad, sir.
Created by Maximilian Uriarte © 2014

TERMINAL LANCE #309 "Monday Morning"
That feeling...
...On Monday morning...
...You're in formation...
...You know you forgot to get a haircut...
...But no one has noticed...
...Yet.
Created by Maximilian Uriarte © 2014

310 "The CLP Mystery"

In absolute darkness they reside, spiteful of the day walkers outside always asking for something. Optics that aren't broken, a new cleaning kit, new weapons cards, CLP; their demands are endless. The creature-like people inside the armory were once people like you and me, Marines even, but in the darkness their features became twisted versions of their former selves. Their eyes have grown large to adapt to the dark, they see mostly with sound now, constantly tinkering with their gear and weapons. They scurry up the walls and into corners when that small window opens, shielding themselves from the harsh sunlight outside. A mere tickle of UV light will send their skin into an instant boil.

I speak, of course, of Armory Clerks.

Armory Clerks are kind of universally hated among the infantry. They have absolute control over their domain, which is a domain you are forced to frequent on a regular basis. When you pull out your weapon to clean it, there's no guarantee you'll be able to turn it back in with any reasonable haste, because it's not up to you. There's a certain maleficent cruelty involved in being one of these people. Who can blame them though? Shut away in the cold, cement confines of the base armory, forgotten by the rest of the Marine Corps.

All drama aside, why the fuck does no one ever have any CLP? I mean seriously, that shit is like greasy, liquid gold.

TERMINAL LANCE #311 "The Call"
Hello? This is First Sergeant Jones.
FIRST SERGEANT! I NEED YOUR HELP!
This is Lance Corporal Schmuckatelli from Third Platoon!
I'm in Waikiki, I might have killed a hooker! I need you to come pick me up with your truck and help hide the body!
You said we could call if we ever needed anything!
What the ever-loving fuck?!
I just say that! You're not actually supposed to call me!
Created by Maximilian Uriarte © 2014

TERMINAL LANCE #312 "NJP"
Well, Lance Corporal, I think you know what comes next.
SIGH
...Yes, First Sergeant.
SNAP
NINJA PUNCH!
Created by Maximilian Uriarte © 2014

TERMINAL LANCE #313 "God Loves Marines"
You know... I always see stuff about how God loves Marines...
I gotta say...
He has a funny way of showing it.
Of course he does...
He's just one of those mean friends that likes to do terrible things to people out of love.
What do you mean?
Like this!
Hurgh!
NUT TAP!
God dammit!
Created by Maximilian Uriarte © 2014

TERMINAL LANCE #314 "Rock Tossing"
TINK
WOOOOOOOO!
FUCK YEAH!
Created by Maximilian Uriarte © 2014

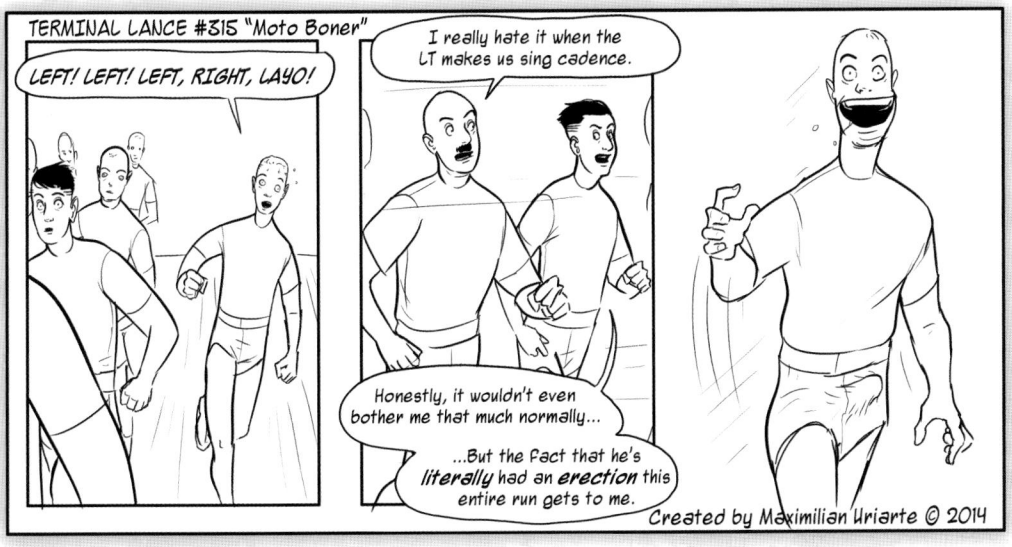
TERMINAL LANCE #315 "Moto Boner"
LEFT! LEFT! LEFT, RIGHT, LAYO!
I really hate it when the LT makes us sing cadence.
Honestly, it wouldn't even bother me that much normally...
...But the fact that he's literally had an erection this entire run gets to me.
Created by Maximilian Uriarte © 2014

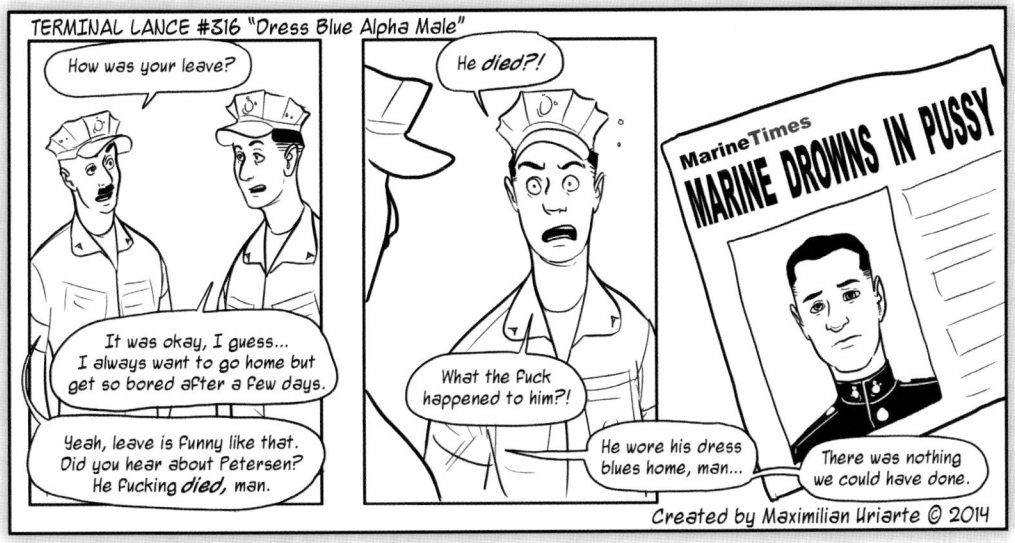
TERMINAL LANCE #316 "Dress Blue Alpha Male"
How was your leave?
It was okay, I guess... I always want to go home but get so bored after a few days.
Yeah, leave is funny like that. Did you hear about Petersen? He fucking died, man.
He died?!
What the fuck happened to him?!
He wore his dress blues home, man...
MarineTimes
MARINE DROWNS IN PUSSY
There was nothing we could have done.
Created by Maximilian Uriarte © 2014

TERMINAL LANCE #316 "The Social Network IV"

Headquarters Marine Corps

I really miss the old days before social media. It was so much easier to keep things in check back then.

You're telling me. It seems like every day there's some new shitshow happening on Facebook that has Marines and veterans riled up.

Yeah... Plus Jim has gotten ***way*** too into the whole social media thing...

...I can't get him to leave his office ever since he started that ***Tumblr*** blog...

TYPE TYPE TYPE

omg i can't even...

check your white privilege, cishet shitlord.

Created by Maximilian Uriarte © 2014

TERMINAL LANCE #318 "Deployment Theater"

Can you turn it up?

It's turned up all the way...

God dammit!

These speakers suck ***shit!*** I couldn't even ***tell*** what the last song was that Rachel sang!

It's like we're in the great state of ***Fuck You*** in the United States of ***Bullshit!***

Created by Maximilian Uriarte © 2014

TERMINAL LANCE #319 "The Jack Shack II"

Hurgh!!!

Oh my god!

SIGH

...The shit I put up with...

FLOP

FAP

FAP

FAP

Created by Maximilian Uriarte © 2014

TERMINAL LANCE #320 "Roomba"

So I got one of those automatic vacuum cleaners.

Oh yeah?

It's great, you just leave it alone and it cleans your room all day. Check it out...

Hey boot!

Is my fuckin' room clean yet?!

Not yet, Lance Corporal!

Well hurry the fuck up, please.

Wow that's awesome, where can I get one?

You can usually find them at Cash/Sales by all of the stupid moto shit.

Created by Maximilian Uriarte © 2014

TERMINAL LANCE #321 "The Veteran Moment"

So what do you think of the war in Afghaniland?

Haha, I dunno I don't really pay attention to that stuff.

Yeah it's all just war for oil anyway. I can't support that. The only people who join the military are people not smart enough to go to college like us anyway.

I can't believe we're still there even after Obama killed that Shazam Hussein. I have a friend in the Army and he's all messed up in the head after fighting in Iran or whatever.

MAYBE YOUR FRIEND IS MESSED UP IN THE HEAD FROM HAVING TO LISTEN TO YOU, YOU DUMB CUNT-FUCK!!!

Created by Maximilian Uriarte © 2014

322 "Light Duty"

While it is certainly true that there is a stigma associated with medical treatment while on active duty, receiving a Light Duty chit is a magical moment. The heavens part, rays of brilliant light caress your face with their holy warmth. The blessings from your BAS grant you a brief relent from the daily grind. Not only do you get to don your go-fasters (as they call them) with your cammies, but you get to avoid morning PT as well as field ops.

It's a slippery slope, however. For as much as Marines value the opportunity to skate through another day, too much Light Duty won't sit well with the rest of the platoon. No one likes a malingerer, but more importantly, no one likes someone who doesn't have to deal with the same bullshit as everyone else. The Light Duty chit is a rare gift, and should be savored as such.

Even more rare, but exponentially more powerful, is the Bed Rest chit. Obtain this holiest of holies and you will be revered as a god.

Medical care in the Marine Corps is interesting. One of the best perks of being enlisted is the free medical. Well, free with a catch. You see, you don't really get to go to the doctor when you need to. If something's wrong, you talk to the Corpsman, and if he thinks it's bad enough you get to go to the BAS where you may or may not see a doctor. More often than not, "free medical" just means "free Motrin and water with a slur insulting my manhood if I question it."

Not that I'm an expert, though I have been binge watching *House, M.D.* on Netflix lately.

TERMINAL LANCE #323 "Tan Belt Ninja II"
Doc! Come quick!
What the hell did you do!?
URGH!
We were just doing the MCMAP training and...
...I did that stupid "Eye-Gouge" move! It looks so fucking dumb I never thought it would actually do anything!
GAAHHHHHHH!
MY EYEEEEE!!!
Created by Maximilian Uriarte © 2014

TERMINAL LANCE #324 "Meritorious II"
Ladies and gentlemen of the board, I'm happy to report that Chongo was doing so well that we moved him to training new employees.
It's great, we gave him this funny hat and he literally just screams at new workers all day.
HHHHRUUUUURRRRR!
Now, now... Settle down, Chongo...
Not the board members, we only scream at the new employees.
Yeah... You're still right.
There's a lot of things about the Marine Corps that wouldn't work in the real world.
Created by Maximilian Uriarte © 2014

TERMINAL LANCE #325 "Battalion Commander Jokes"
...Use your best judgment this weekend, gents. We can't have any more incidents.
...Now I say that to all of you, but I'm looking at you, Gunny Duprey! Ha!
HA!
HA!
HA!
OH HO HO HO HO!
Bravo, sir! Such a cunning display of wit!
Internally...
JUST SHUT THE FUCK UP ALREADY!!!!!
Created by Maximilian Uriarte © 2014

TERMINAL LANCE #326 "On the Ground"
We're going to be ground-fighting for PT this morning.
Ugh...
What's wrong with ground-fighting?
Nothing, it's just that I'm tall and lanky and ground-fighting is only fun if you're short and stocky with a lower center of gravity.
That's ridiculous. Stop complaining. You and Brent, get in the pit.
Yeah let's go, tall boy!
This is literally one of the only things I excel at!
SIGH...
God dammit...
Created by Maximilian Uriarte © 2014

TERMINAL LANCE #327 "Bursting Bomb"
Here's your Rockstar.
Thanks, what did Master Guns want anyway?
He wanted a pineapple for some reason, I dunno.
Well yeah, all Master Gunnery Sergeants love pineapple. That's why it's on their rank. They can't control it.
That's the dumbest shit I've ever heard...
...Besides, it's a "Bursting Bomb," not a pineapple...
MASTER GUNS
Dude, I'm pretty sure it's a pineapple...
Created by Maximilian Uriarte © 2014

TERMINAL LANCE #328 "Avengers Assemble"
CAPTAIN AMERICA!
And introducing his new sidekick...
LANCE CORPORAL AMERICA!
Let's do it for democracy!
God this is so fucking stupid...
Do I have to use a shield? Can I just get a rifle?
Okay I can't fucking do this anymore. All you do is bitch.
I'm just saying, sir!
I could literally shower you with Filipino hookers and you'd find a way to bitch about it.
Created by Maximilian Uriarte © 2014

329 "Full of It"

The age-old battle between POG's and grunts continues in *Terminal Lance*!

Okay, this strip isn't really about that—it's more about just owning up to what you are. After being out for a while and meeting a lot more Marines in different fields, the one thing I can say with absolute certainty is that no one really cares what your MOS is or was. And whatever it is, you should just own it like it's the coolest shit in the world.

"Oh, you're a cook?"

"Fuck yeah, I'm a cook, and it's fucking awesome. I'll cook you the best, shittiest military food you'll ever have."

This came up in a conversation I had with a Marine once, another infantry Marine. Although the rivalry and shit talking is fun, at the end of the day it really makes no difference what stupid job you had in the Corps, as long as you're honest about it. Didn't deploy to Iraq or Afghanistan? Okay, it's a little weird since we've been at war for like eleven years now, but own the fuck out of that. Don't bullshit me about how you were going to go infantry but couldn't, or whatever stupid thing you try to say to feel less guilty. If you were really going to go infantry, you would have. I didn't even know what an ASVAB was, scored a 92, and proceeded to go open-contract 0300 infantry (where I later became an 0351 at SOI). The idea that grunts were too stupid to become POG's is lost on me, because it implies that any of them wanted it any other way to begin with. Personally, I wouldn't have enlisted at all if I couldn't do infantry, but to each his own.

TERMINAL LANCE #330 "Staff NCO Dreams"
IT'S ALL GOING TO HELL OUT HERE!!!
Johnson's white socks gave away our position, I tried to call sooner but my hands were in my pockets! We got overrun and ran to an Army patrol for help, but none of our Marines had fresh haircuts or shaves so they thought we were Taliban!!!
It was the white socks!!!
If only we had listened to our Staff NCO's!!!
SEMPER FIDELIS
GASP!!!
Created by Maximilian Uriarte © 2014

TERMINAL LANCE #331 "Sizing Up"
You know what the best part of being in the Marines is?
Huh?
Definitely the added three inches to my penis.
What?! Bullshit! Let me see!
No homo.
Whoa...
I told you! I was like a 6.5 before, now I got a solid two-hander.
How come it didn't happen for me?
What's your MOS?
1171, Waterdog...
Oh, well I don't know what the fuck that is...
But I'm pretty sure this only happens to infantry.
Created by Maximilian Uriarte © 2014

TERMINAL LANCE #332 "A Haiku"
Hey there Devil Dog
Getchur fucking hands outta
ur daggon' pockets
Created by Maximilian Uriarte © 2014

333 "Oh Baby"

Is there anything more ubiquitous in the military than baby wipes? A Marine Corps PX is probably the only place in the world you'll see legions of eighteen- to twenty-four-year-old males buying aisles of baby wipes with no intention of using them on a baby. Baby wipes serve many practical applications for Marines. They make a great alternative to bathing while you're stuck in the field; they do a wonderful job of cleaning the carbon out of your rifle's chamber; and you can use them to comfortably wipe your ass in a port-a-shitter.

Really, the only thing Marines don't use them for is cleaning babies.

If you're ever sending a care package to Marines overseas, a safe thing to always send is baby wipes. There's a million ways and reasons to use them. It can never go wrong—as long as the package also has cookies, porn, and a Nintendo Switch with *Mario Kart*.

TERMINAL LANCE #335 "Past Tense Dress"

Fuck I hate wearing these dress uniforms... *So* uncomfortable.

Can you believe that Marines used to actually fight in stuff like this? Can you imagine sweating your balls off in Afghanistan in this?

100 YEARS LATER...

These dress uniforms are so awful. I can't believe Marines used to *fight* in this stuff.

Can you *imagine* trying to fight the Moon Spider Rebellion in this?

And what is with this digital pattern? Were they fighting wars in a *video game*?

Created by Maximilian Uriarte © 2014

TERMINAL LANCE #336 "Location, Location"

...And in local news...

An Oceanside man has recently become a billionaire.

He attributes his success to his new business: a *tattoo parlor* that also sells *beer, porn, haircuts,* and *Oakley sunglasses.*

KTV-5 SAN DIEGO

Created by Maximilian Uriarte © 2014

337 "Boot Camp: Broke Dick Platoon"

Easily the biggest fear of any aspiring Marine (also called a Recruit) is getting dropped to MRP during boot camp. Medical Recovery Platoon is where you go when you're just too ill to train, but are expected to recover at some point so you can finish the trials at hand.

Speaking purely as an observer, I can't imagine a more miserable place. Tales of attempted suicide and misery in the MRP permeate the Depot. Boot camp is already miserable enough for a regular, healthy recruit. The constant berating, screaming, games, and physical arduousness are something I would never want to do again, but I was fortunate enough to only have had to endure it for three months. I stress the word "fortunate" here, because I was almost dropped to MRP during my stay at MCRD.

I, like most recruits, came down with the "crud," as they call it. I had a pretty bad case of pneumonia right before we were supposed to go up north to Camp Pendleton. The Navy doctor told me I would have to be dropped to MRP, as I was simply too ill to go up north. I was horrified. I'd have to be here for another two weeks?! Two weeks might not sound like a lot to you, but two weeks in boot camp is like three years in civilian time. Luckily, like the hand of God himself, my company commander called medical moments after they gave me the news. He spoke with the doctor and convinced him to let me go up north with my platoon. I was ecstatic. Well, I mean, as ecstatic as one can be with a fever of 103 and lungs full of shit.

I was told that my company had already lost too many recruits and could not afford to lose any more, under any circumstances, so they hopped me up on Motrin and penicillin and sent me off.

At my graduation from boot camp, I found my mother in the crowd the moment I was dismissed and the first words out of my mouth were, "Did you bring my clothes? Good, let me go change so we can get the fuck out of here."

TERMINAL LANCE #338 "The Lance Corporal Underground II"
Wolf Blitzer here at Marine Corps base Twentynine Palms...
Officials here have uncovered what appears to be a vast network of tunnels underground. They are believed to be part of a Lance Corporal Underground...
I'm here with a Marine Captain to give us more information.
Thanks, Wolf. As of now we do not yet know what the tunnels are being used for.
Current theories suggest it's used as a kind of particle accelerator, as this would explain how information can be passed around the Lance Corporal Underground near the speed of light.
Created by Maximilian Uriarte © 2014

TERMINAL LANCE #339 "Life After EAS: College"
Oh no...
Dammit!
Ugh, I got an F on this paper...
There's no way I'm going to pass this class now. College is too hard.
Really...? College is the easiest shit in the world. All you have to do is hang out and flirt with hot girls all day.
I've taken MRE shits harder than this.
Created by Maximilian Uriarte © 2014

TERMINAL LANCE #340 "Morning Knock"
BOOTS!
KNOCK KNOCK KNOCK
I KNOW YOU'RE IN THERE!
IT'S 0530, YOU NEED TO POLICE-CALL THE PARKING LOT!
Don't move...
The Duty NCO can't see us if we don't move...
Created by Maximilian Uriarte © 2014

TERMINAL LANCE #341 "Historical"

Hey man, we're going to go see a Civil War reenactment... Do you want to go?

No.

Why not?

Cause it's fucking weird. Can you imagine people reenacting all of the stupid shit we did on our deployments 200 years from now?

200 YEARS LATER...

Dad, can we *leave...?*

They've been doing the same thing for like *six hours* now...

WAGNER LOVES DICK

Created by [illegible] © 2014

TERMINAL LANCE #342 "Junior Enlisted Warrior"

So this boot comes up to me and is like...

WHO SAID BOOTS?!

What? I did...

WHERE ARE THE BOOTS?! I HATE BOOTS!

Dude, calm down. You were a boot once, too.

You don't understand, I HATE BOOTS.

SO.

MUCH.

Later that day, at Cash/Sales...

Goddamn *boots...*

Created by Maximilian [illegible]

TERMINAL LANCE #343 "Anatomy of a Veteran"

Neutral-colored baseball cap

Oakley® sunglasses

(A few extra pounds post-EAS)

Beard

Neutral-colored T-Shirt or old skivvy shirt

Non-military cargo pants

*Not Pictured: Complete lack of fucks to give.

Created by Maximilian [illegible] © 2014

345 "Gear Adrift"

There's an old and eerily accurate saying in the Marine Corps:

There's only one thief in the Marine Corps. Everyone else is just trying to get their shit back.

Then again, there's also another saying:

Gear adrift is gear a gift.

One of my first experiences with lost gear was at SOI at Camp Pendleton. About halfway through the two-month ITB cycle I somehow lost my Gore-Tex jacket. I asked everyone I could and no one had any idea what happened to it. Mysteriously vanished. I want to believe it was taken by the One True Thief, if only for the fact that it would take the blame off the people around me.

However, it is rather telling that I've never seen a "Lost and Found" section of any platoon.

If you lose a piece of gear in the Marine Corps, I absolutely promise you that you will never see it again. It's unfortunate, but true, and thus the reason I ended up spending $90 on a replacement Gore-Tex at one of the military surplus stores at Oceanside.

Unsurprisingly, the store sells a lot of actual issued gear, and they pay money for gear they can sell. I wouldn't be surprised if the Gore-Tex I purchased that day (that also broke my bank account since I was a PFC with no financial management skills) was the exact same one I had lost weeks prior. After all, gear adrift is gear a gift . . . for the person that stole my Gore-Tex.

Either that, or he was just trying to get his shit back.

TERMINAL LANCE #348 "The Bigger Fish"
HA
HA
HA
What's going on?
Yes!!!
YOU STUPID MOTHERFUCKER!!!
Dude, the Sergeant Major is chewing out our Gunny! It's Fucking awesome!
Oh my gawd!!!
He's standing at parade rest! It's even more glorious than I ever imagined!
Created by Maximilian Uriarte © 2014

TERMINAL LANCE #349 "Teufel Hunden"
Hurry up, devil dog.
Why do they call us "devil dog" anyway?
I dunno, some shit about the Germans in World War I...
I heard that wasn't even true.
Whatever man, just hurry up. Why do you care?
I dunno, I just don't like being called a dog.
You know... I brought the WAG bag for you...
Created by Maximilian Uriarte © 2014

350 "Camp Guard"

Can we just talk about how shitty being in Camp Guard is?

Non-infantry folk probably never really had to deal with this wretched duty, but for those of us that have, it was an absolutely miserable experience.

Right after boot camp, you typically go home for ten and then you get sent to either SOI West or East for your MOS training. POG's go off and do their little MCT thing for a few weeks and the grunts stick around and do their MOS training over the course of eight weeks. You're told to report into SOI West after your boot leave so you can get assigned to your training company. That is, as long as there's room.

As an active duty guy, I got wait-listed for two weeks while the reservists were rushed into their training company. So what is a boot student Marine to do for two weeks while he waits for a new ITB class to pick up?

Camp motherfucking Guard.

This consisted of eight-hour rotations patrolling the base in teams of two wearing orange glow vests, being on QRF in case some "shit" went down, or being on rest. There was no libo. We had to go to chow in formation. Cell phones weren't allowed, and you're just generally treated like the lowest form of shit on the entire base by instructors and other Marines alike.

Having just graduated boot camp, I was fairly excited to begin my new Marine Corps adventure, only to find myself in Guard purgatory for what seemed like the longest two weeks of my life until Bravo Co. picked us up. Having been to Iraq twice, it seems like a silly thing to complain about, but it really was miserable.

The trademark of Guard? Having drunk Marines drive by and shout "OORAH GUARD!!" and other obscenities at you while you just . . . did whatever it is you were doing. And because all Marines are assholes, I also partook in the belligerent shouting at Guard as soon as I was out of it.

TERMINAL LANCE #351 "Tony Hawk"
Excuse me, Lance Corporal... Staff Sergeant sent me to get you for a working party.
Oh there you are! I already talked to him, he said nevermind and to send you back.
Take a look.
SSGT
Hey some boot is going to come and tell you I need you. He's wrong, send him back.
OK, SSGT.
Oh... okay, nevermind then, Lance Corporal.
When did you talk to Staff Sergeant...? I don't remember that.
I didn't, I just have this picture saved on my phone.
I don't just skate, I fucking glide. Get on my level.
Created by Maximilian

TERMINAL LANCE #352 "The Babysitter's Club"
Hey Abe, I got some bad news for you...
The LT wants to tag along with your squad for this range.
What is it?
Oh great, I love having boots in my squad that I can't even yell at.
Created by Maximilian Uriarte © 2014

TERMINAL LANCE #353 "Stationed"
Listen up, shitbirds...
Your time here at SOI West is coming to a close. I just got the official word on where all of you are going to be stationed...
Woot!
Yes!
Assaultmen, you guys are going to Third Marines in Hawaii.
Machineguns, you guys are staying here at Camp Pendleton with First Marines.
Mortars...
You guys are going to...
Twentynine...
...Palms.
Created by Maximilian Uriarte © 2014

TERMINAL LANCE #354 "Pogue"
Anyway... I just don't like it when you guys call me a POG.
But... You are a POG. You're attached to us...
If you didn't want to be called a POG, why didn't you just join as a grunt?
Well...
A little bit later...
So then he's like... He actually said this...
"I was gonna join the infantry but my ASVAB score was too high."
HA HA HA HA HA HA HA HA HA HA
Stop!
I'm gonna piss myself!
Created by Maximilian Uriarte © 2014

TERMINAL LANCE #355 "Police Your Own"
So your ASVAB scores just came back. You did great! What MOS were you thinking of signing up for?
Um... I dunno.
Well what are you interested in?
Hmm... I really want to join the Marine Corps, but I also just... kind of don't like Marines.
Oh that's perfect! You can be an MP.
Created by Maximilian Uriarte © 2014

TERMINAL LANCE #356 "Body Composition Program"
I shouldn't even be in BCP, First Sergeant!
I just have a thin neck!
There is nothing on your entire body that I would call "thin."
Just keep chasing that donut, fat boy. We'll have you slimmed down in no time.
Created by Maximilian Uriarte © 2014

357 "Shitter Graffiti Is an Art . . . of Dicks III"

This little comic strip of mine has given me some dubious honors over the years. One of them is that I have become the de facto dick art guy simply because I've done a couple of comic strips about the penis doodlings of Marines across the globe. You do one or two comics about penis art and all of a sudden everyone wants to send you photos of penises. I'm not sure if I should feel honored or ashamed, but I'll take it.

Either way, it's an interesting phenomenon. Recently the question was raised on my Twitter of whether female Marines engage in the doodling of phallic members on shitter walls or if perhaps they prefer their own genitalia in the matter.

After careful consideration, I have come to the only logical conclusion that female Marines cannot possibly draw vaginas, and therefore must draw penises like their male counterparts.

Why?

A simple fact: You will rarely see a vagina drawn on a bathroom wall.

TERMINAL LANCE #359 "Leave of Absence"
Dear Journal...
I've been on Christmas leave for about 3 days now...
I'm already extremely bored.
I can't openly admit this to anyone. I can't tell them that I want to go back to base... That I miss... the barracks.
I'm going to text Garcia something vague like:
lol i'm SO BORED how bout u?
...to test the waters. I can't be the only one.
Created by Maximilian Uriarte © 2014

TERMINAL LANCE #360 "Booger Battalion"
Man, my unit is the worst.
Your battalion can't possibly be as bad as mine.
Dude we had so many DUI's last month that Four Loko wants to sponsor us.
Yeah well...
My battalion is so bad that General DunFord came out to speak to us, but for his entire speech he didn't say anything...
...He just looked at us with great disappointment and left.
MEANWHILE, AT THE OFFICER'S CLUB...
My Marines are the worst.
...Can't be as bad as mine.
Created by Maximilian Uriarte © 2015

TERMINAL LANCE #361 "That Guy II"
Hey Abe, would it be cool if you split some of your MRE's with me?
The fuck? Why?
I was super drunk last night and totally forgot to pack for this field op.
What?! No, you asshole!
It's always some shit with you! You're the reason we have all those stupid inspections and packing lists!
Sorry, man... I'm that guy.
There's at least one of us in every platoon.
Created by Maximilian Uriarte © 2015

TERMINAL LANCE #362 "Winter is Coming Part I"
Hey man...
What are you doing out here on the catwalk?
Look, beyond the barracks parking lot... Toward the land of IPAC...
...A darkness is brewing...
...I fear it is already too late.
Brace yourselves...
...Peacetime Marine Corps is coming.
Created by Maximilian Uriarte © 2015

TERMINAL LANCE #362 "Winter is Coming Part II"
Meanwhile, at IPAC...
Marines! To your stations! This is what you trained for!
For years the grunts have had all of the glory! They have laughed at us! Called us names!
But no more...
The Age of the Grunt is over...
...The time of the POG...
...is now!
PEACETIME MARINE CORPS
IS HERE!!!
Created by Maximilian Uriarte © 2015

363 "Boot (Camp) Stories"

There's a strange paradox in the Corps when it comes to regaling stories of the one and only thing that all Marines have in common: Recruit Training (otherwise known as boot camp). On the one hand, everyone has been there and can share common ground regardless of their later experiences in the Corps; on the other, there's nothing more boot than a boot telling boot camp stories. The average Senior Lance Corporal would rather be anywhere else than listening to a fresh-faced eighteen-year-old tell him about that one time when the Drill Instructor got *so mad*.

But once you go on a combat deployment, boot camp becomes a distant memory, and likely one of the least interesting things you've done during your time in the Marines.

Don't get me wrong, even senior Marines tell boot camp stories, but they almost qualify it first with:

"I know this is boot as fuck to talk about, but this one time at boot camp . . ."

Still, boot camp is a universally shitty experience for everyone. I think I'd rather go back to Iraq than boot camp again. It's not that you fear for your life in boot camp, it's just that it really fucking sucks. That's really the only way to describe it.

TERMINAL LANCE #364 "Greeting of the Day"
Good morning, Staff Sergeant!
Oh is it a good morning, Lance Corporal?
Let me tell you about my morning: three of my Marines went UA today and I just got my ass chewed by the First Sergeant. My morning is fucking fantastic.
Okay... I really only said that because I have to.
...No one actually gives a shit about your morning, Staff Sergeant.
Created by Maximilian Uriarte © 2015

TERMINAL LANCE #365 "Back to Basics"
Hey man, are you okay...?
No...
Staff Sergeant made us march over here... in formation... He actually called cadence.
Oh my god...
He made us use drill! Actual drill! Like we were in boot camp or something!
I'm so sorry.
Created by Maximilian Uriarte © 2015

TERMINAL LANCE #366 "God Loves Marines II"
The Gates of Heaven
ZZZ...
HEY DEVIL!!!
You falling asleep on my post, warfighter?
I'm sorry God, me and Chesty were out late...
Good to go, Marine.
Don't worry, you just keep napping. Your buddies on the ground will pay for this.
Meanwhile, on Earth...
God dammit.
I would love just one field op where it doesn't rain the entire time...
Created by Maximilian Uriarte © 2015

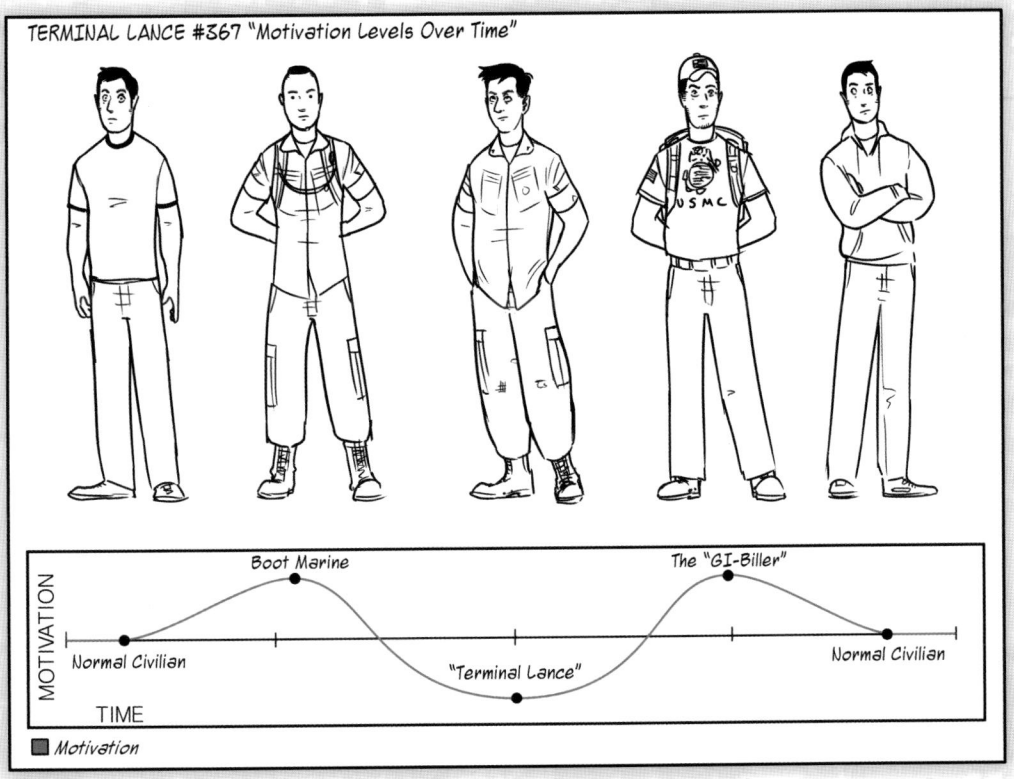

367 "Motivation Levels Over Time"

Those of you that haven't served in the military might not be familiar with the term "motivation." Well, I mean, I'm sure you've heard the word itself, but it takes on a very specific context within the Marine Corps. I shall provide you with the Marine Corps definition of motivation:

> ***mo·ti·va·tion*** | ˌmōdəˈvāSH(ə)n/ | **noun**
> **The amount of fucks a Marine gives, specifically as it relates to Marine Corps activities and lifestyle.**

To be labeled as "moto" is generally a grave insult to the Lance Corporal crowd, as it insinuates that you give a fuck. Things that would be considered moto:

- A high and tight haircut
- An Eagle, Globe, and Anchor tattoo or decoration
- Wearing a CamelBak
- The English Bulldog

When a Marine enters the Corps, he has profoundly high levels of motivation coursing through his boot veins. He tears up at the sight of bald eagles, wears a CamelBak in civilian attire to "stay hydrated," buys 7.62 T-shirts at the PX, and randomly hums "left, right, layo" to himself. He won't see this level of motivation again for quite some time.

As the young Marine matures into his MOS and unit assignment, he starts to question things. Was this really what he was looking for? Is cleaning your rifle four times a week without firing it really necessary? He starts to see the character of the environment around him, maybe even tossed an NJP or two for something that might not have been his fault.

Legend has it that this begins as soon as he is pinned with the rank of "Lance Corporal," but no one knows for sure. Motivation levels here are at an all-time low, and will stay this way for the majority of his short enlistment.

Once the Marine exits the Corps, however, you'll see his motivation levels rise to near-boot status. He'll show up to his new college, utilizing the GI Bill, telling war stories to anyone that will hear them. He'll start using Marine jargon again and maybe even a knife-hand or two—he might even consider talking to a prior-service recruiter.

Yes, a recruiter.

Assuming he doesn't succumb to the extremely high levels of motivation during these vulnerable college years, he might make it out the other side as a relatively normal civilian again. Yes, with time, the motivation starts to fade. It doesn't ever fall back into negative, as it did while you were a Lance Corporal, but rather it floats back down to a nice neutral—the experience now a positive part of your past and development. Looking back with a warm fondness for the people you met and the strange things you saw, you find yourself back where you started . . . just another civilian in a big, big world . . . and with most of your life left to live.

This is science, I didn't make this up.

370 "Stealing the Valor"

You know what the problem is with these Stolen Valor guys? They try to steal too much valor.

If you're the kind of piece of shit that likes to go around pretending to be in the military so you can get discounts or whatever, just say you're some total POG MOS, because most grunts will have no idea if it's true anyway. When you start talking about how you know guys from SEAL Team 6 and graduated top of your class at Ranger School while killing seventy-three enemy insurgents alongside Chris Kyle, bullshit flags start going up immediately.

Those are the kind of stories that can be easily proven wrong by just about anyone with a lick of common sense and only a marginal knowledge of the military culture.

Of course, the point of stealing "valor" is actually to steal the "valor." Being a Marine, soldier or otherwise, is usually seen as kind of badass compared to the normal population. I mostly feel sorry for these pathetic people, adults pretending to be superheroes, the way young kids put on towels and pretend to be Batman.

But I love watching these stolen valor videos. So please, if you're reading this and you're a giant piece of shit that likes to pretend to be a war hero, keep doing it. You'll eventually find yourself on a shaky, vertically shot smartphone video on YouTube with some pissed-off guys making fun of you—and I will laugh as I watch it over and over.

TERMINAL LANCE #371 "Barney Style"

I'm sorry, Gunny... I just don't understand.

It's not that complicated, sir!

Do you need me to break it down for you **Barney Style?**

Oh god...

Please don't... not again.

I ONLY DO THIS BECAUSE YOU MAKE ME!!!

Created by Maximilian Uriarte © 2015

TERMINAL LANCE #372 "Toys R' Us"

How about the GI Joe, son?

No, he's a pussy-ass **boot**, I want the Marine one... like you!

Ha!

Okay, here you go, boy.

USMC

OFFICIAL LICENSED PRODUCT

USMC

BARRACKS PARTY EDITION!

0311

REAL NJP!

CORPS

DRINK TO FORGET!

Created by Maximilian Uriarte © 2015

TERMINAL LANCE #373 "Spotting Another Devil Dog in the Wild"

!

!

SNIFF SNIFF

Created by Maximilian Uriarte © 2015

TERMINAL LANCE #374 "No Party Like a Working Party"

What um... What are you guys doing...?

Oh, you know, just ***picking leaves and twigs*** out of these here rocks.

...Why?

Because Gunny is a dick.

Seriously. It's like he has a degree in ***Being an Asshole*** from the ***University of Fuck You.***

Created by Maximilian Uriarte © 2015

TERMINAL LANCE #375 "High-Speed, Low-Reg"

What are you doing...?

Hey can you tell me if my haircut is under 3 inches?

And is my low-reg ***low*** enough...?

You know that haircut looks ridiculous.

Really, Mexican Mr. Clean...?

Besides, this haircut is really more about the ***principle*** than fashion.

Created by Maximilian Uriarte © 2015

376 "E's and O's"

Don't get me wrong, I've had plenty of fun nights at Kahuna's on MCBH Kaneohe Bay, but there's a definite disparity between the E-Club and the O-Club. Of course, this is to be expected, as officers are shiny gods and enlisted are . . . enlisted.

I once had the pleasure of eating lunch at the Officer's Club at MCBH, which looks out on the beautiful MCBH Klipper Golf Course—one of the most gorgeous golf vistas in the nation. Nothing makes you feel more like a lowly peasant than being gawked at by offended officer wives as you and a few fellow Lance Corporals awkwardly make your way through the high-end Mongolian BBQ grill and salad bar.

It's a stark contrast to the dive-bar experience of the E-Club, where you'll meet an assortment of characters ranging from drunk Lance Corporals to . . . more drunk Lance Corporals. To be fair, karaoke and wing night make for a much more colorful and entertaining experience.

Still, the lifestyle contrast between officers and enlisted is always shockingly stark. I mean, I get it, officers are a big deal and enlisted are a dime a dozen. The military wants to retain good officers, so they treat them like posh royalty. It's probably the only place where a bachelor's degree gets you an automatic high-class lifestyle, even if you occasionally have to slum it with us lowly enlisted folk.

377 "Marine Corps High"

In my mind, I've always typically divided the Marine Corps up into thirds. You have the infantry, the ground-side POG's (which is what you typically think of as a POG, such as an office guy or girl), and the wing.

It's not unlike a set of high school cliques: exclusive and loyal to each other. The grunts are the jocks, the rock stars, and the guys that everyone loves (even if they won't admit it). They party hard and fuck shit up when the time comes. The POG's might say they hate them, or that they aren't impressed with them, but we know they're secretly a little jealous.

The age-old argument I see often from the POG side is that being infantry means you won't have any transferable skills in the civilian world when you get out of the Corps. True, but who cares when the Post-9/11 GI Bill can set you up with literally any career you want? May as well get the glory while you can, lest you regret it later.

As for the wing, no one really knows what the fuck goes on over there. They usually get a whole section of the base to themselves, with their own PX and barbershops, and when you occasionally see them on your side of town they're always wearing flight suits.

No one understands them.

TERMINAL LANCE #378 "Half Truths"

Created by Maximilian Uriarte © 2015

TERMINAL LANCE #379 "Boundaries"

Created by Maximilian Uriarte © 2015

TERMINAL LANCE #380 "Festive"

Created by Maximilian Uriarte © 2015

TERMINAL LANCE #381 "You're a Mean One"
At Battalion HQ...
Ha! Sir, you have to see this!
These Marines just posted this hilarious photo that's not hurting anyone or malicious in any way.
Oh boy! That's a good one!
...I think I'm gonna NJP them.
What? Why?! They're not doing anything wrong.
I just...
...hate seeing Marines enjoy themselves.
Created by Maximilian Uriarte © 2015

TERMINAL LANCE #382 "Shalom"
Thank you so much for talking to me, Chaplain Weinstein.
Your advice really put things into perspective for me.
Of course!
You know... You're welcome here any time, but aren't you Catholic?
Yes, why?
Well it's just that I'm the base's Jewish Chaplain... Wouldn't you rather talk to the Catholic Chaplain?
Well... I was...
...But then it got kind of weird when he kept trying to add me on Snapchat.
Created by Maximilian
© 2015

TERMINAL LANCE #383 "Conditional Living Conditions"
Laundry?
Yeah.
Well you're gonna have to wait...
There's seven people ahead of me and only one washer that works.
OUT OF ORDER
Dammit! Everything is so shitty around here! These budget cuts are killing us!
Budget cuts? It's always been this shitty.
Created by Maximilian Uriarte © 2015

TERMINAL LANCE #384 "Welcome to the Armory (Fuck you)"
Sorry, we're not taking weapons yet.
Fuck you.
What? Did you just say fuck you to me?
No? What are you talking about?
Fuck you.
You just did it again!
Maybe people wouldn't hate you guys so much if you weren't such dicks!
RING
RING
Hold on, I have to get the phone.
Fuck you.
Good morning, sir or ma'am.
This is the Armory, how can I fuck you?
Created by Maximilian Uriarte © 2015

TERMINAL LANCE #385 "Barracks Privacy Policy"
MLLLHHHHH
Abe, wait...
Huh?
Can we go somewhere else...?
What? Why?
I'm just... kind of uncomfortable.
Oh... because of them?
...Yes?
Please... Don't mind us.
Is she single?
Abe, you don't know me, but I brought you some beer.
Put it in her pooper!
Created by Maximilian Uriarte © 2015

TERMINAL LANCE #386 "The Birth of a Safety Brief"
Gents...
...Before we release you for liberty, the battalion has prepared a new 4-hour-long PowerPoint safety brief...
...Please pay attention.
Ugh... this is so stupid. I can't believe we have to sit through this.
Oh my god...
Shut the fuck up. Please just shut the fuck up.
You are literally the entire reason we're doing this.
What?! It totally wasn't my fault! How was I supposed to know there was a person inside that car?!
It was driving on the freeway!
Um, hello? Google has self-driving cars now.
I hate you so much.
Created by Maximilian Uriarte © 2015

388 "First Sergeant's Cold Brew"

Have you ever noticed that Staff NCO's seem to live off coffee? You'd be hard pressed to find a set of rockers not hopped up on the glorious brown bean's black life juice.

Scientists have recently discovered, however, that First Sergeants and above don't actually have "coffee" in their mugs. Rather, they're specially trained in the cold brewing process of collecting the tears of Lance Corporals and below with the employment of their frostbitten hearts hidden deep within their chest cavities.

They say it can take up to an entire twenty-four hours to collect a mug full of tears from a single Lance Corporal, but with enough anger, green-weenie butt-fucking, and malice, some can do it in five minutes. Have you ever had a leave request that you waited to get approved for weeks, bought tickets for your entire family so you could all spend a nice time together after being assured it would go through, only to have it coldly denied? Have you ever had to stand by in the barracks while your girlfriend waited for you off-base for seven hours, only to have liberty secured at the last minute?

These are cold-brewing techniques that First Sergeants and above use to collect the tears they need to thrive. Caffeine is addicting on its own, but fucking over Lance Corporals and below gives them a fucking boner.

TERMINAL LANCE #389 "Lance Corporal Time"
Abe, listen up...
I need you and Garcia at the Motor Pool at 1400 to pick up a high back.
I don't...
...What does that mean, Staff Sergeant?
How do I say this in Lance Corporal...
I need you at the Motor Pool at two jacks past afternoon chow.
Ooooh, okay! No problem, Staff Sergeant!
Created by Maximilian Uriarte © 2015

TERMINAL LANCE #390 "Gunny Envy"
Hey there warrior!
...Hey, First Sergeant.
I approved your leave! That's pretty rad, right?
...Cool... Thanks.
Oorah devils!
GUNNY!
I brought you guys chow and new gear!
Thank you! We love you, Gunny.
Oh ho ho!
...Why don't they love me?
Created by Maximilian Uriarte © 2015

TERMINAL LANCE #391 "Charmed"
Mmm, Charms...
CHARMS
MRE
HEY YOU STUPID BOOT!
Don't eat those fucking Charms!
Oh right... I forgot they're bad luck.
I don't care about that... It's just that Charms haven't been in MRE's in like ten years.
Ew...
Yeah... I wouldn't eat anything in there, actually.
MRE
Created by Maximilian Uriarte © 2015

TERMINAL LANCE #392 "Field Day Finger"
You say this room is clean, Lance Corporal?
Yes, Staff Sergeant...
Then what...
...is this!?
Hmm... I'm not sure, Staff Sergeant...
...But it kind of looks like two to three more hours of bullshit to me.
Created by Maximilian Uriarte © 2015

TERMINAL LANCE #393 "Sage Advice"
Hey there cousin, home on leave?
Yup!
It's great to see you! Did you hear? I just DEP'd in last week, I'm gonna be a Marine just like you!
Do you have any advice for me for when I ship off to boot camp?
Yeah...
...Stay home.
Created by Maximilian Uriarte © 2015

TERMINAL LANCE #394 "Can't Stop Time II"
So I have...
Two-hundred ninety-one days until my EAS date.
You're just starting to count the days now?
Well yeah...
...When did you start counting?
AYE SIR!
YES SIR!
LOUDER!
LOUDER!
365 x 4 -... 1 =
...1459 days...
Created by Maximilian Uriarte © 2015

395 "Mild Reservations"

The Reserves is like the Marine Corps Lite. Of course, they deploy and have done great things in combat and abroad. But at the end of the day, they get to go home. They check in once a month and do a two-week thing once a year unless otherwise needed. They don't live in the barracks every day, they don't get woken up at four a.m. to police call the parking lot.

Marines that I had known since boot camp were in my class in the School of Infantry, but at the end of our MOS training (0351), they got to go home. All I can remember thinking to myself was . . .

What the fuck? I didn't even know that was an option.

While they went home to go fuck their girlfriends (and probably ours), the rest of our sorry asses got sent to our Active Duty units to be hazed and treated like the lowest form of sentient entity on the planet (boots).

In my humble opinion, the reserves is the Marine Corps Lite because it's not the full experience. It's one thing to step in bullshit, it's another to build your entire house out of it and live there for four years.

TERMINAL LANCE #396 "Duty Dooty"
I really hope our relief gets here soon...
...I've been holding in this dump for about 12 hours now.
...Why don't you just go use the bathroom?
I would rather keep it in and suffer than go through the arduous process of trying to take a shit in chucks.
Created by Maximilian Uriarte © 2015

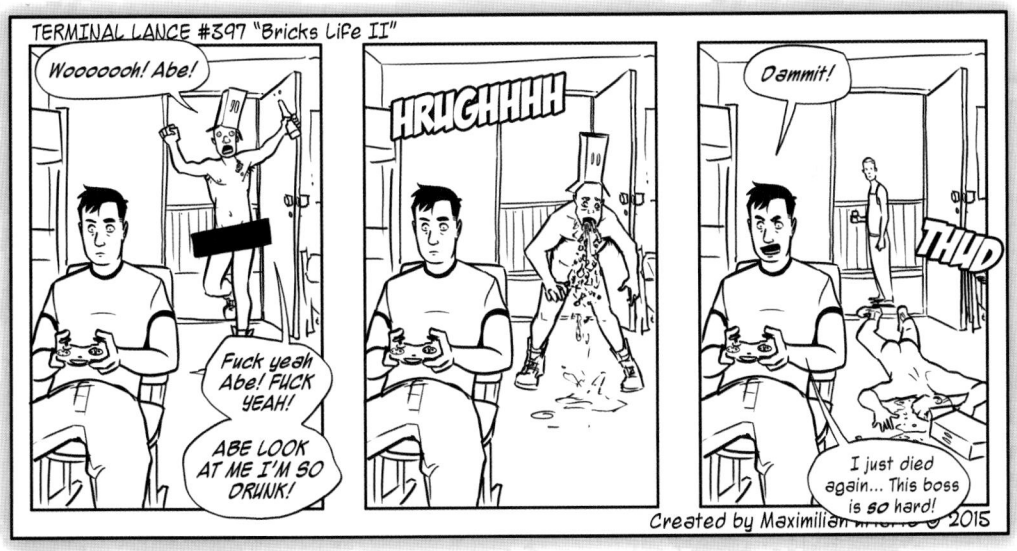
TERMINAL LANCE #397 "Bricks Life II"
Wooooooh! Abe!
Fuck yeah Abe! FUCK YEAH!
ABE LOOK AT ME I'M SO DRUNK!
HRUGHHHH
Dammit!
THUD
I just died again... This boss is so hard!
Created by Maximilian Uriarte © 2015

TERMINAL LANCE #398 "Wondrous Sundries"
Excuse me, is this the S-1? I'm looking for...
Hello!
Welcome to the Department of Unusual and Obscure Uniform Items! Can I interest you in a Range Coach safari hat? Or perhaps a Boat Cloak?
SHIT
Created by Maximilian Uriarte © 2015

TERMINAL LANCE #399 "Come On In"
Oh my god, First Sergeant.
BOOSH
1st Sgt
I don't know how much more of this I can take.
Staff Sergeant has been on my dick all week, and don't even get me started on the new L-T.
That guy is just lost in the sauce, he's so boot that even the boots make fun of him.
Lance Corporal...
Yes, First Sergeant?
...What the fuck are you doing in my office?
...You said you had an "open door policy."
Created by Maximilian

TERMINAL LANCE #400 "Over the Years"
2010
Dude! Look at this comic, it's pretty funny.
Ha, that's pretty good.
...But what the hell kind of name is Uriarte...?
2012
Corporal!
Are you looking at that trash comic again?! You know that shit ain't cleared hot!
No, Master Guns! I swear! I would never read a comic at work! I was just looking at porn!
2015
Is the new comic up yet? Try refreshing again...
No, not yet...
HRUUUUUUUURHHHHHH!!!
Now, now, settle down Chongo. I'm sure it'll be up soon.
Created by
© 2015

TERMINAL LANCE #401 "Myths and Legends VI"
Garcia! Come here quick! You'll never believe what I just spotted!
Look... it's so majestic.
...Is that... a fleet infantry sergeant?!
I had heard they were extinct!
Indeed it is!
Don't spook it...
...You'll scare it off to a B-billet.
Created by Maximilian Uriarte © 2015

TERMINAL LANCE #402 "SKATEPAT"
DARPA
This is the new camo pattern we've been developing for the Marines.
Huh, interesting... What is the pattern supposed to be?
Barracks furniture.
In all of our field tests, this was the one Marines said worked the best for them.
The Barracks
BOOSH!
Hey fuckheads, I need three Marines for a working party!
Huh... where'd everyone go?
Created by Maximilian Uriarte © 2015

TERMINAL LANCE #403 "Life After EAS: Nostalgia"
Man... Looking through these old photos sure does make me miss the Marine Corps sometimes...
Wasn't the Marine Corps Fun? You had such good times.
POOF!
Yeah but I hated the bullshit... Formations, being treated like a child...
Stop it...
You got to hang out with your friends all day and shoot guns... You did so many cool things! Don't you miss it?
You should talk to a Prior-Service Recruiter...
No!
Leave me alone!
Created by Maximilian Uriarte © 2015

TERMINAL LANCE #404 "Why He's Always Late III"
...Look who's late to formation again...
...A Company Commander is never late...
...Nor is he early...
He arrives precisely when he means to.
HO HO HO
You're so full of shit, sir.
I know, I was just playing Halo V.
HO HO HO
Created by Maximilian Uriarte © 2015

TERMINAL LANCE #405 "Gas! Gas! Gas!"
Honestly, I don't even mind doing the gas chamber training...
...I just get really weirded out by the way the CBRN guys get so... *into* it...
Mmm... Yeah baby you love my steaming hot white CS gas all over you don't you?
Suck it up you little *sluts. Choke on it.*
I didn't know our CBRN Chief Warrant Officer only had one arm...
He has two. I'm pretty sure he's just *masturbating* under his MOPP suit.
Created by Maximilian Uriarte © 2015

TERMINAL LANCE #406 "Meritorious III"
Ladies and gentlemen of the board...
I'm proud to announce that one of our finest employees, Chongo, has found the love of his life this weekend at a strip club! I think it's only fair that we *double* his salary.
What...?
...Why would we double his salary just because he got *married?* That doesn't make any sense at all!
HRUHHHHH!!
HRUHHHHH!
Now, now settle down Chongo! Chongita!
Can't you see they're *in love!*
Yeah... That really doesn't make any sense.
Created by Maximilian Uriarte © 2015

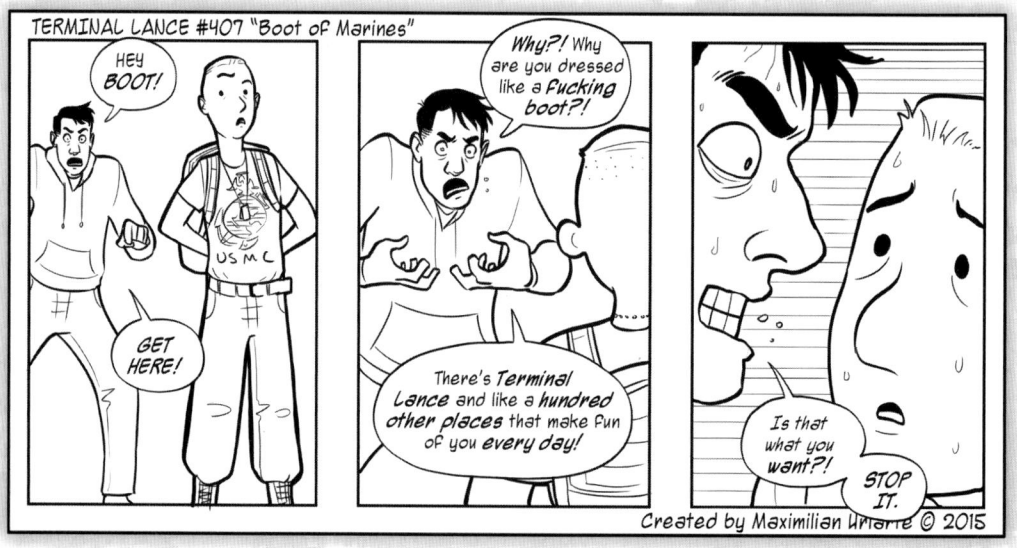
TERMINAL LANCE #407 "Boot of Marines"
HEY *BOOT!*
USMC
GET HERE!
Why?! Why are you dressed like a *fucking boot?!*
There's *Terminal Lance* and like a *hundred other places* that make fun of you *every day!*
Is that what you *want?!*
STOP IT.
Created by Maximilian Uriarte © 2015

408 "MRE Exchange Rates"

MRE bartering and trading is a common practice in the field, as each package contains completely different stuff. Generally, MRE's come with one entrée, a cracker or "snack bread," a spread, and a dessert. The holy grail and reigning champion of these is still the coveted Jalapeño Cheese Spread. It may sound atrocious, but I assure you—it's absolutely delicious.

Imagine sitting on cold wet dirt, your rifle leaning up against your thigh and your MRE sitting atop your upturned boonie cover in front of you. You open the rather unappetizing brown plastic bag and empty the contents. You sift through plain, cardboard-boxed items: "Chili w/beans," "Tortillas," something called a "Ranger Bar." Just as you're ready to open your Chili w/beans you see it, underneath the accessory packet of random tissues and salt and shit.

Jalapeño Cheese Spread.

It glows. A children's choir can be heard behind you as you pick it up. You realize you're out in the open, you look over your shoulder to see other Marines sifting through their depressing dinners. One of them glances at you. It's Ramirez. You never really liked him, he's got that kind of face that just screams douchebag and leaves his door open in the barracks while he blasts his terrible music. He just finished telling a joke and is looking around to see if anyone heard him.

Your eyes meet. You look away, clutching your treasured spiced cheese. Ramirez loves this shit, but he can't see it. If he does, he'll obnoxiously announce to the entire platoon that you have the Jalapeño Cheese, and everyone will try to barter you for it. It's harmless, but still annoying.

You stand up, pick up your MRE-filled boonie and rifle, never looking back at him, and you walk toward the MRAP. You cautiously open the back hatch to make sure it's empty. You climb inside and set your cover on top of the turret platform, your rifle in the seat next to you. In total solitude, you covet the small, brown Jalapeño Cheese packet.

You open it with your teeth and you squeeze the contents directly into your mouth. You don't even bother putting it on a tortilla, this shit is dank as fuck.

Yeah, that's basically what getting a Jalapeño Cheese Spread is like.

TERMINAL LANCE #409 "Shiny and Chrome"
Dude, the Battalion Commander is on the range... Don't Fuck this up!
SIR!
WITNESS US MAKE THIS SMAW SHOT!
WITNESS!
BOOM!
Miss! That's a miss!
DAMMIT!
MEDIOCRE!
Created by Maximilian Uriarte © 2015

TERMINAL LANCE #410 "Peacetime Purgatory"
Hey gents, I just wanted to...
...
SHUT
...We really need another war.
Created by Maximilian Uriarte © 2015

TERMINAL LANCE #411 "Gear List"
Seriously... Like what is this stupid safety-pin thing and why was it on the gear list? Why do they make us bring so much useless stuff on these field ops?
I think it's for laundry.
Will you stop bitching for once and just pretend like you give a fuck?
I don't want to have to listen to this the whole field op.
Sorry, Corporal, but fucks were the only thing that wasn't on the gear list.
Created by Maximilian Uriarte © 2016

TERMINAL LANCE #412 "The Difference: Morning PT"

Created by Maximilian Uriarte © 2016

TERMINAL LANCE #413 "Bugs"

Created by Maximilian Uriarte © 2016

TERMINAL LANCE #414 "Life After EAS: The Veteran Beard"

Created by Maximilian Uriarte © 2016

416 "The Basic School"

When he gets to a high enough rank, he'll start his own Tumblr.

The world of the officer is very different from that of the enlisted. Instead of boot camp and SOI, officers attend Officer Candidate School (OCS) and The Basic School (TBS) for their Marine Corps indoctrination. To qualify, you just need a bachelor's degree in pretty much anything. From then on, you are a tried-and-true leader of Marines.

There's often quite a bit of friction between the officer and enlisted world. Enlisted comprises the majority of the Marine Corps—we are the working-class citizens of the military. The officers are usually seen as the white collar, pedigreed elite, with their shiny ranks and vastly superior living conditions and overall treatment.

To be completely honest, becoming an officer in the military is one of the best and highest paying jobs you'll likely find with nothing more than a bachelor's degree in today's age. On top of that, you'll be treated like royalty once you hit the fleet. The starting pay of around $30,000 a year might not seem like a ton, but the paycheck is in addition to housing, food, medical, and other perks. Plus, bitches salute you. How cool is that?

That is assuming you make it through The Basic School.

Where you learn to be basic.

TERMINAL LANCE #417 "Beef Patty"

I guess I'm just... Sad about the whole slaughterhouse thing... I don't want to die.

Hey, what's wrong bro?

Bruh, don't think of it like that. You're going to be an amazing meal! You'll be like one of those $400 fancy steaks at a nice restaurant! You're gonna be ***delicious!***

Huh... I guess that's not so bad....

1 YEAR LATER...

Oh my ***god.***

I just threw up in my mouth. Is this even ***beef?!***

BEEF PATTY

...This is bullshit...

Created by Maximilian Uriarte © 2016

TERMINAL LANCE #418 "Evil Incarnate"

My liege...

We are having a serious problem with retention. Our reenlistment bonuses are paltry in comparison to the Post-9/11 GI Bill. We simply can't compete.

I have an idea, master...

What if we make the VA as shitty and convoluted as humanly possible. This way, servicemembers would rather reenlist than try to gamble with their VA benefits.

Brilliant.

...Enact this plan ***immediately.***

Created by Maximilian Uriarte © 2016

419 "The Story of Every Enlistment"

If you sat down with any Marine in the Corps and asked him the story of how he came to enlist, you would surely be met with the ubiquitous sentence:

"Fuck it, I'mma join the Marine Corps."

This is the story of every Marine, past, present, and future. I realized this as I was chatting with another Marine the other day on how he ended up in the Corps. Those were his exact words, and usually are the exact words of every Marine you'll ever talk to about it.

Enlisting is an intensely personal experience, and it's one that you must come to terms with on your own. Of course, there's the typically cliché responses like "I wanted to serve my country," and "Bitches love Marines," but I would argue that most Marines enter into the Corps as part of a much more intense, personal journey. There's much mental deliberation and anxiety involved in the decision to talk to a recruiter, but eventually, everyone always comes to the same conclusion . . .

Fuck it, I'mma join the Marine Corps.

The rest is history.

TERMINAL LANCE #420 "Messing with the Cock-Watch II"
Sergeant, it's really difficult for me to go when you're **staring** at it like that...
Sorry Lance Corporal, just doing my job. I have to **see** the urine leave the body.
...
TINKLE
TINKLE
...You're looking a little **dehydrated,** Marine.
OH COME ON!
Created by Maximilian Uriarte © 2016

TERMINAL LANCE #421 "Perfect Pull-Up"
One...
One...
One...
One...
Come on, Abe! Lock those elbows out! If I can do twenty I know you can too!
I **am** locking my elbows out!
...We are built **very differently.** I'm tall and naturally lanky, pull ups are easier for you.
I don't know what you're talking about, stop making excuses.
Created by Maximilian Uriarte © 2016

TERMINAL LANCE #422 "Truck Tradition"
Oh my god we've been sitting here for like **two hours** now.
Where the hell are the trucks?!
S-4, THE PREVIOUS DAY
What time should we send the 7-tons to pick up the guys from the armory tomorrow, Staff Sergeant?
What time will the Marines be ready?
Probably by 0600.
Okay, send the trucks at **0900.**
But that's like... **3 hours later** than they need.
Dammit Marine, I've been in this Corps for **10 years** now and that's how it's **always** been done!

424 "New Corps II"

I find a lot of things frustrating, but one of the most annoying things I come across while managing this monstrosity of a comic strip and social media page are the "Old Corps" guys who just can't stand all of the shenanigans coming from these "New Corps" Marines. Back in their Corps, they were too busy getting into fistfights with body-building hookers, hiking over seven hundred miles each week, and just generally being real Marines (during peacetime no less) to engage in such degrading behavior to their beloved Corps.

Unfortunately for them, it's not their Corps anymore.

Culture changes—even the culture of the Marine Corps. But I'd actually argue that the culture hasn't changed much at all. The main thing that has changed is the advent of portable cameras connected to a near limitless social media environment. The silliness of the everyday military life is no longer relegated to the dark corners of the smoke pit or the back of the squad bay. It is on full display, instantly accessible to the public and the world.

Though, to be honest, what I find even more annoying are the people (generally the same people) that send me photos of Marines being normal fucking people and expecting me to "put them on blast" in front of hundreds of thousands. Who gives a shit if some nineteen-year-old kid takes a selfie in his uniform in front of a mirror? I know I don't, and there's literally zero precedence to suggest that kid should be shamed in front of the entire Marine Corps.

If anything, we should be encouraging stupid behavior among Marines.

War is awful. These silly, fleeting moments are the only thing that keeps us going most of the time. They're the only thing that keeps us human.

TERMINAL LANCE #427 "The Lament of the Artist Recruit II"

Created by Maximilian Uriarte © 2016

TERMINAL LANCE #428 "Inked"

Created by Maximilian Uriarte © 2016

TERMINAL LANCE #429 "Duty III"

Created by Maximilian Uriarte © 2016

430 "Air Force Blues"

The Air Force is a weird branch of the military.

Semantically, if you were to define "military" by things that are generally "military," like fitness, shooting guns, hiking, being a hard ass, etc., I'm not sure if the Air Force would fit. This isn't to say the Air Force isn't important to our national defense—of course they are—but more that it is the military lite. A Diet Military, if you would.

Marines and Airmen are nearly opposites in every conceivable way, as Abe describes in this strip. If it weren't for their largely symbiotic relationship, you could probably say the same things about the Navy and the Corps as well. However, Marines and Navy are like peanut butter and jelly—they stick together.

Ignoring the Coast Guard for a second (lol we usually do), the Air Force is generally the outlier of the military. They're small and mostly keep to themselves, with their culture rarely permeating the popular consciousness. There's nothing wrong with that—it's just their style. They don't tend to make as much noise as Marines or Army in the news, but we love them all the same.

TERMINAL LANCE #432 "Triggered"
DISNEYLAND
Ugh, these long lines are the worst. We've been waiting forever!
Abe...? Are you okay?
I don't want to talk about it.
Created by Maximilian Uriarte © 2016

TERMINAL LANCE #433 "Pull Out Your CAC II"
Can I see your ID please?
Eh... All I have is my military ID...
This doesn't look like you...
Yeah the photo was taken in boot camp.
Armed Force of the United Sta
Marine Corps
Belatzeko, Abraham
Grade
Rank
Did you say "boot camp" or "concentration camp"...?
Created by Maximilian Uriarte © 2016

TERMINAL LANCE #434 "Cruel and Unusual"
You leave me no choice, Lance Corporal...
As punishment, I am putting you on a working party...
...With a bunch of boots!
Oh God...
...Can I take an NJP instead, Gunny?
Created by Maximilian Uriarte © 2016

435 "Traveling Abroad"

I've often heard it said that a bitching Marine is a happy Marine.

Marines definitely love to bitch. In the case of an MEU deployment, Marines often find themselves longing for the "action" of a proper combat deployment. While it is true that they are forced to spend some miserable hours on a big gray boat, at least they get to stop all over the world and check out all kinds of interesting foreign sights and sounds.

You know what foreign sights and sounds you see in Iraq? Women in burkas and gunshots. That's basically it. Shit sucks. I would rather have been on the MEU.

Of course, the grass is always greener. You can't blame Marines for wanting to experience the whole combat deployment thing—it's what they're brought up to do. When I enlisted back in 2006, I knew for sure that I would get sent to the Middle East, one way or another. Ten years later? The prospects of such adventures aren't as foretold as they once were. This is essentially peacetime, and combat is nowhere to be seen for most of the Corps.

This has been an interesting transition to witness. When I started back in 2010, most Marines were like me: two-pump chumps that were largely disillusioned and disgruntled. Today's active duty Marine Corps is undoubtedly different than the one that I left behind, and the last of the Lance Corporal combat veterans are most likely out or soon to be.

TERMINAL LANCE #436 "Fraud, Waste, and Abuse"
Hey...
Take these extra chemlights over to the police shed for tomorrow's field op.
Did you say... "Extra," Corporal?
CHEMICAL LIGHTS
Created by Maximilian Uriarte © 2016

TERMINAL LANCE #437 "Warranted"
Bruh I'm such a good skater. I get out of every working party.
Even First Sergeant has started calling me Tony Hawk.
SSHHHMP!
You know nothing of skating, Lance Corporal.
POOF!
What the fuck was that?!
...A Chief Warrant Officer.
Created by Maximilian Uriarte © 2016

TERMINAL LANCE #438 "Swipe Left"
Eh... She's cute.
...I'm just not really into Female Marines.
Done
Samantha, 21
.5 miles away Active 30 minutes ago
About Samantha
I am a Marine and proud! Semper Fidelis!
SWIPE LEFT
A cheating Marine wife? No thanks.
Done
Sarah, 20
1 mile away Active 3 minutes ago
About Sarah
Looking for fun, not judgement. Husband is deployed, shhh.
SWIPE LEFT
Oh my god.
Done
Chaps, 37
.1 miles away Active 30 seconds ago
About Chaps
Want to make a confession?
...I'm deleting this app...
...Tinder on base sucks.
Created by Maximilian Uriarte © 2016

TERMINAL LANCE #439 "Prize Inside"

What...? A prize?

MRE

DOG SHIT W/ SAUCE

NOW WITH A PRIZE INSIDE!

...Oh no way!

MRE

DOG SHIT W/ SAUCE

I got a flavored condom! **With spermicide!**

I got a Copenhagen dip **sampler pack!**

This is awesome!

I got crayons!

Created by Maximilian Uriarte © 2016

TERMINAL LANCE #440 "Period of Instruction"

Okay gents, please pay close attention to this next presentation...

If you take only ***one thing*** away from your TAPS class, it should be this...

HOW TO NOT BE A MOTO DOUCHE AFTER YOU EAS

CLICK

Created by Maximilian Uriarte © 2016

TERMINAL LANCE #441 "Relativity"

Report your post, Lance Corporal.

Good evening, sir! Building 1656 is all secure, nothing unusual to report at this time.

Nothing unusual...?

Just on my walk over here I saw a Lance Corporal arm-wrestling a ***homeless woman***, a PFC chugging three bottles of ***dip-spit*** in succession on a dare, and another Lance Corporal ***literally eating*** a live pigeon.

... ***"Unusual"*** is a relative term, sir.

This is ***the barracks.***

Created by Maximilian Uriarte © 2016

442 "Boot Camp: The Care Package"

Boot camp is a shitty three months.

As if you don't have enough to worry about with sweaty, angry men yelling at you twenty-four hours a day, you never know what might be lurking in a box some good-intentioned family member or friend sent your way.

Comedian Sarah Silverman panicked once after realizing she may have made a grave mistake for her recruit nephew.

> **Sarah Silverman** @SarahKSilverman · 12m
> **@USMC** please help! I sent a care package to my nephew at Parris Island & now am worried he'll be in trouble for it. I'm an idiot. Please dm

Of course, in reality he will most likely be fine, assuming she didn't send a box of dildos (possible, given the nature of her comedy). Sadly though, her sudden panic is actually a result of reading headlines surrounding the abuse scandals in Parris Island Recruit Depot. I've stayed away from the subject on *Terminal Lance,* for the most part because I hate reading the comments. Hard-charging keyboard warriors act as if being thrown into a dryer is a regular occurrence that all recruits must suffer (it's not).

Even without such flagrant abuse, boot camp is arduous and mostly awful. I've said it before, but I would much rather go back to Iraq than do another three months at MCRD being treated like a recruit. I feel the worst for those poor kids that spend months in medical recovery, where they're treated like recruits for even longer.

TERMINAL LANCE #443 "Connection Problems"

I need you to tell me something... *Anything!*

I don't know what's going on... Ever since I picked up Corporal, I can't hear anything. It's like a deafening silence.

It's because you've lost it.

Lost what?

Your connection to the *Lance Corporal Underground.*

...By the way, you will have duty two Fridays from now.

Created by Maximilian Uriarte © 2016

TERMINAL LANCE #444 "Drill Foot"

Left-Right...

Left-Right...

Low-right...

Man, I feel bad for Second Platoon...

Why?

Their new Platoon Sergeant just got back to the fleet from being in the drill field...

...I heard he's even making them say *diddies.*

Help...

...Us...

Created by Maximilian Uriarte © 2016

445 "Always Room For One More"

Marines can always find a way to fit one more.

Whether it's one more Marine in the back of the 7-ton or one more piece of gear stuffed into their already-bursting main pack for the field, Marines will always find a way to fit one more. Some say this is a supernatural ability possessed by anyone that has stepped foot on the yellow footprints of destiny. As long as any Marine says to themselves out loud *"There's always room for one more,"* you will find yourself able to fit just about anything anywhere.

Ahem.

Anyway, this is a simple strip but I wanted to do something that would kind of lighten the mood. For all of the bullshit in the world, I take comfort in knowing that Marines never change. This, above all else, continues to make Marines my favorite people on the planet.

I get emails and messages from Marines all the time, some as old as my parents and others as young as my niece, saying that no matter when they served, they reckon that after reading my comic they're glad to see that the Marine Corps hasn't changed a bit.

TERMINAL LANCE #446 "Logged"
Hey Sergeant, this logbook is full.
Okay, I'll take it to the company office.
What do they do with the finished logbooks anyway?
I dunno, First Sergeant usually takes them.
He probably just stores them somewhere for record.
LOG BOOK 3/3
LATER THAT NIGHT...
FAP
FAP
FAP
FAP
LOG BOOK 3/3
Yeah look at that proper military annotation...
Ooh you made a mistake and crossed it out properly with your initials and everything, you naughty Marine...
Created by Ma 2016

TERMINAL LANCE #447 "Leave Blocked II"
THE COMPANY OFFICE
Yes, Gunny?
Excuse me, First Sergeant...?
...The Marines are wondering when you're going to approve their leave requests... Christmas is only three weeks away and the Marines still need to buy their plane tickets.
I know, I'm waiting for the ticket prices to go up.
...Why?
Because I hate them.
Created by Maximilian Uriarte © 2016

TERMINAL LANCE #448 "The Old Boot"
Keep cleaning, boot!
Yes, Lance Corporal...
When you're done with that you can police-call the parking lot!
You know he's older than both of us, right?
I know, it's so weird. I feel like I'm yelling at my parents or something. I'm legit worried he's gonna have a heart attack or a stroke.
I'm only 25...
No one asked, you geriatric fuck!
Now hurry up so you can help me with my taxes.
Created by Maximilian Uriarte © 2016

449 "The Cure-All II"

doc pls

Medicine in the military is a funny thing. One great and enticing benefit of serving an enlistment is the free medical.

The bennies bring all the boys to the yard.

Unfortunately, even though we all love Doc, "free medical" usually consists of an all-you-can-eat supply of Motrin and straws to suck it the fuck up. If you do get to BAS and make it through the cadre of bored Corpsmen to the point that you actually get to see a doctor, he'll likely give you a once-over, call you a pussy, and send you on your way.

Upon second thought though, maybe this is how medical care should be for everyone. My wife is British and works at the NHS, so I've gotten quite the earful of stories of lazy people who clog up the emergency room for a common cold to get some free ibuprofen (which is cheap and available over the counter). A random aside, but true nonetheless.

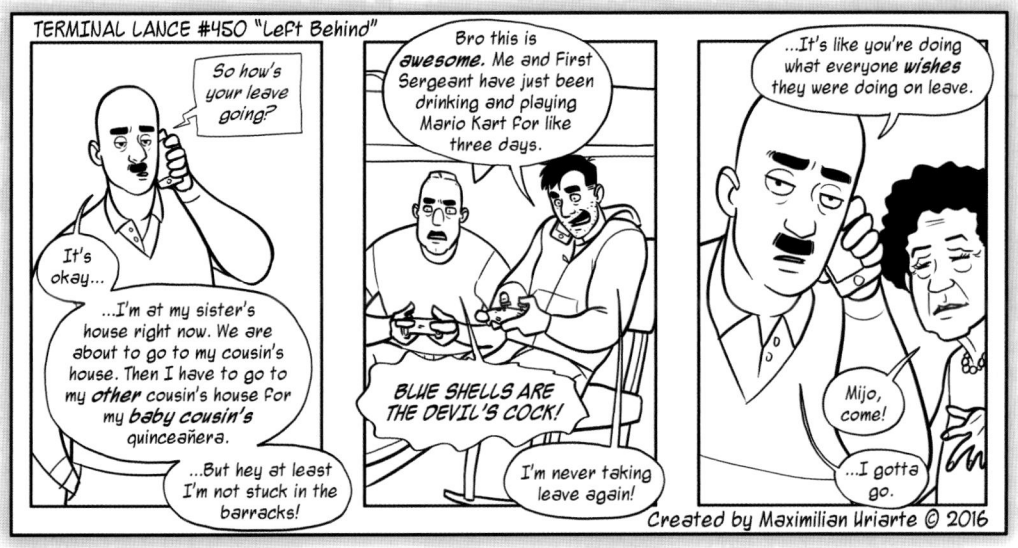

450 "Left Behind"

When Marines come home on holiday leave, they often find themselves somehow busier than they were before they left. What is supposed to be a relaxing stay at home turns into nonstop family dinners and visits with friends. Sometimes I wished I would have just stayed back at the barracks.

Of course, no one has to take leave, but when you're a twenty-year-old Lance Corporal you don't really think about it like that. Your first thought is always:

I need to get the fuck out of here.

But staying behind isn't all that bad, since basically the entire Marine Corps is out for the holidays. You might have to check in with your First Sergeant every morning, if he's even there, but most likely he isn't going to give any more of a shit than you do about the plan of the day. The only time I ever stayed back in Hawaii for Christmas leave, I ended up with duty once and we had a single formation of about ten guys. First Sergeant didn't give a fuck. We all went back to our rooms and played video games while saving up for that delicious Terminal leave.

And never forget . . . Blue shells *are* the devil's cock.

PART 2
HOLIDAY AND SPECIAL STRIPS

TERMINAL LANCE "An April Fool"
Hey man, some things got moved around and you have duty like... right now.
What, really...?
Don't worry, you'll get tomorrow off.
HA! HA! APRIL FOOLS!!!
Haha, oh man...
...I totally got you!
Of course you don't get tomorrow off, you stupid asshole. Now go put your chucks on.
Created by Maximilian Uriarte © 2013

TERMINAL LANCE "Bravo Foxtrot Four"
What game is that? Howcome you don't play Battlefield 4 anymore?
It was too realistic...
...The game kept freezing after I hit Lance Corporal.
Created by Maximilian Uriarte © 2013

TERMINAL LANCE "Birthday Boy"
Happy Birthday, Abe!
A whole log of Cope Long Cut?! Thanks Garcia!
Yeah, we're all gonna beat the shit out of you later though.
Birthday?!
According to my G-SHOCK, you're about a month shy of celebrating a birthday!
The only birthday I celebrate is on November 10th, oorah? Semper Fi, devil dogs.
No, it's... his birthday. Like... his human birthday.
You know...
You and your kind are the reason I'm never going to re-enlist.
Created by Maximilian Uriarte © 2013

TERMINAL LANCE "Black Friday"
Hey boot...
...We're going to the PX for the Black Friday sale, wanna tag along with us?
...Black Friday...
...Black Friday...
LOUDERRRRRRRRRR!
AYE AYE, SIR!!!
...What the Fuck?
Created by Maximilian Uriarte © 2012

TERMINAL LANCE "Little Blue Birdy With a Little Blue Bill"
Hey, Fuckosaurus!
How come you guys weren't at Formation just now!?
What?! We never got the word, Staff Sergeant!
That's impossible! I tweeted it this morning!
@SSGTDevilDog1775 7h
After consultation with my Squad Leaders, I have decided that formation will be at 1600, cammies
@SSGTDevilDog1775 22h
Inspected so many rooms for field day today and only 3 of them passed first try. Sad!
@SSGTDevilDog1775 2d
If that Garcia doesn't shave that mustache, he's going over the wall.
Created by Maximilian Uriarte © 2017

TERMINAL LANCE "NCO"
CHESTY XIV GETS PROMOTED TO
CORPORAL!!!
It is in this moment, as I pin the rank of Corporal on this dog...
...That I am really starting to regret some of my life decisions.
Meanwhile, at the Military Working Dog kennels in Afghanistan...
Fucking boot ass Fat-body POG in Quantico getting promoted to Corporal...
We're over here sniffing IED's every day while he sniffs buttholes.

TERMINAL LANCE "Cinco de Mayo: Race Card III"

Hey there, Lance Corporal Garcia! How was your *Cinco de Mayo*?

Really, sir? You think just cause I'm ***Mexican*** that I spent last night throwing some kind of fiesta wearing a *sombrero* or some shit?

I was the OOD last night...

When I came by the barracks you were literally doing ***exactly that.***

¡HOLA!

MEXICO

Corona

¡Esta fiesta será la mejor de Cinco de Mayo! Hasta traje suficiente Corona para los ***gringos cabrones.***

Created by Maximilian Uriarte © 2014

TERMINAL LANCE "Civil War"

You're ***wrong!*** I'm pretty sure the ***entire Marine Corps*** would agree with me.

Whatever, you think you know ***everything!***

Jalapeno Cheese is the best MRE spread.

Chocolate peanut butter.

TERMINAL LANCE CIVIL WAR

Created by Maximilian Uriarte © 2016

TERMINAL LANCE "The Curse of the Dependapotamus: Gay Marriage"

I now pronounce you...

Husband and ***husband.***

The Next Morning...

Oh my ***god!***

What the hell ***happened*** to you?! You were hot when I married you!

I don't know! I woke up like this!

Whose kids are those?!

I'M NOT FAT I'M JUST KNOCKED UP

They just... Came ***out*** of me!

Created by Maximilian Uriarte © 2015

TERMINAL LANCE "Dark Days"
Hey, Jody...
What's the matter, bro?
I just...
...I just found out that the Marines aren't deploying to Afghanistan anymore.
Aww, I'm sorry man. Don't worry, they still have MEU's and training and stuff, I'm sure you'll still get plenty of time with their girls.
Created by Maximilian Uriarte © 2014

TERMINAL LANCE "Dear Congress"
Dear Congress...
Please send the Marines to war to go fight ISIS.
They don't even want to be here, they're so bored. I know because I talk to all of their wives and girlfriends at work... At the gym... At the bars... Sometimes they just text me late at night to talk about their feelings... The Marines just want to go kick ass! You should send them away for a very long time... Please.
Thanks. Your pal, Jody.
Created by Maximilian Uriarte © 2015

TERMINAL LANCE "Demographics II"
Listen up, gents...
In light of recent events, I felt it necessary as your Battalion Commander to remind you all that as Marines we cannot tolerate discrimination.
We must always treat each other as Marines. We don't discriminate against race, gender, or sexual orientation in my battalion. Everyone deserves respect.
...Except boots.
I HATE BOOTS!
BOOTS ARE THE WORST!
I HATE THEIR BEADY EYES!
WHAT DO THEY KEEP IN THEIR BACKPACKS?!
Created by Maximilian Uriarte © 2017

TERMINAL LANCE "Happy Easter"

Enjoy yourselves this weekend, gents.

...Lastly, I'd just like to thank all of the Marines that volunteered to paint Easter eggs this week for the base Easter Egg Hunt.

Look mom!

Another *Easter Bunny!*

Created by Maximilian Uriarte © 2015

TERMINAL LANCE "Happy Easter 2017"

Enjoy your long Easter weekend, Marines.

Lastly, I just want to say thank you to all of the Marines that volunteered to help MCCS fill plastic eggs for the base Easter Egg Hunt...

I got one!

Ew... This is just filled with *dip-spit.*

Mine has a note that just says... *WAGNER LOVES THE COCK. STAY WOKE.*

...Written in crayon.

Created by Maximilian Uriarte © 2017

TERMINAL LANCE "Fleet Week"

This sucks sweaty shit.

I can't believe we got stuck here showing civilians what 7-tons are while everyone else is hitting the bars.

Seriously. Some days I hate being in the military. Fuck this shit.

SHOOOOOOM!

Ooo is that the Blue Angels?

...Some days I love the military.

Seriously.

Created by Maximilian Uriarte © 2012

TERMINAL LANCE "Furlough Tuesday II"
HOMELESS VIETNAM VET
GOVERNMENT DIDN'T GIVE A SHIT ABOUT ME
WILL WORK FOR FOOD
OIF/OEF VET
GOVERNMENT'S SHUT DOWN, STILL DOESN'T GIVE A SHIT ABOUT US
WILL WORK FOR VETERAN BENEFITS
Created by Maximilian Uriarte © 2013

TERMINAL LANCE "Gotta Catch 'Em All!"
What!? No way!
A Mew!
I have to catch it!
Hey devil! What are you doing walking on your damn phone! You better put that trash in your daggon' pocket right now!
Hello yoohoo!
I know you hear me!
SECURE THAT DAGGON' PHONE RIGHT NAH!
Created by Maximilian Uriarte © 2016

TERMINAL LANCE "Mostly Tricks"
TRICK OR TREAT!
Ho ho! Hey there kids! What are you all supposed to be dressed as?
I'm an admin clerk!
I'm a water dog!
I'm a grunt!
Aww how cute! Here you go kids, take some NAM's!
...except you, Mr. Grunt. You get this...
What is this?
It's called a "Page 11."
Created by Maximilian Uriarte © 2012

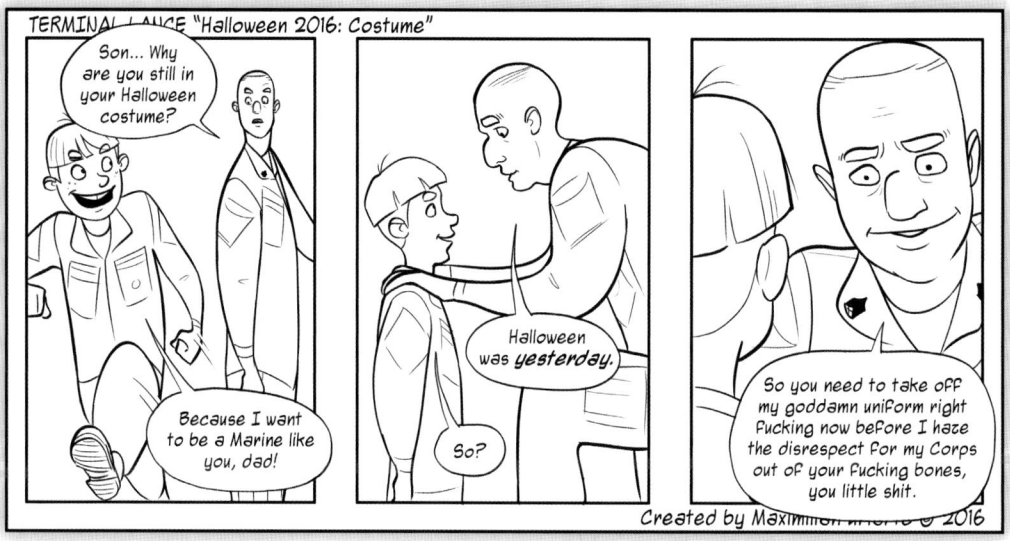
TERMINAL LANCE "Halloween 2016: Costume"
Son... Why are you still in your Halloween costume?
Because I want to be a Marine like you, dad!
Halloween was yesterday.
So?
So you need to take off my goddamn uniform right fucking now before I have the disrespect for my Corps out of your fucking bones, you little shit.
Created by Maximilian Uriarte © 2016

TERMINAL LANCE "Halloween 2014"
Oh hey, Gunny... Welcome to my Halloween 2014 Super Spooky Barracks Bash...
EBOLA
I didn't know you were coming... You were supposed to dress as something scary...
Scary?!
Listen you little fuckling, you and everyone in here have about 3 minutes to be in formation downstairs!
HAHA
I'm just fucking with you...
...But I bet that scared the shit out of you, didn't it?

TERMINAL LANCE "Happy 241st Birthday, Marines!"
From the halls of Monte-zu-uma, to the shores of Tripo-li...
First to fight for right and free-edom and to keep our honor clean...
...Hmm hmm huhmfurled to every brrmm hmm hmm to hmm hmm hmmmm...
We fight our country's ba-attles in the air, on land, and sea!
We are proud to claim the ti-itle of United States Marines!
We have hmm in hmm hmm hmmmm hmmm hmm where we could take a gun...
Created by Maximilian Uriarte © 2016

TERMINAL LANCE "Happy Easter 2016"
Hey boots! You guys want to do an Easter egg hunt!?
What?! Fuck yeah!
30 MINUTES LATER...
Lance Corporal... We've been out here for like 30 minutes now and haven't seen a single Easter egg...
Try picking up more of the trash, it'll make the Easter eggs easier to find.
Created by Maximilian Uriarte © 2016

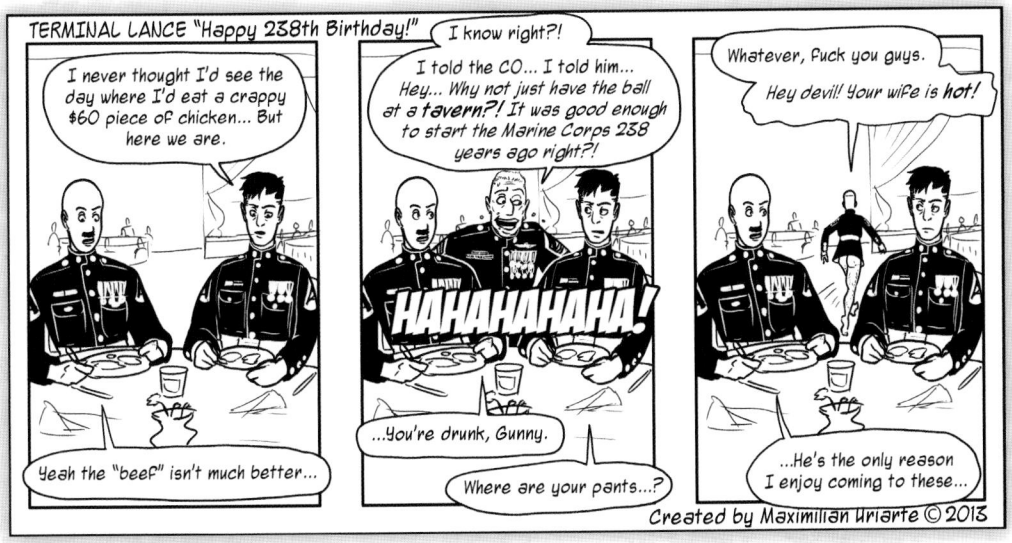
TERMINAL LANCE "Happy 238th Birthday!"
I never thought I'd see the day where I'd eat a crappy $60 piece of chicken... But here we are.
Yeah the "beef" isn't much better...
I know right?!
I told the CO... I told him... Hey... Why not just have the ball at a tavern?! It was good enough to start the Marine Corps 238 years ago right?!
HAHAHAHAHA!
...You're drunk, Gunny.
Where are your pants...?
Whatever, fuck you guys.
Hey devil! Your wife is hot!
...He's the only reason I enjoy coming to these...
Created by Maximilian Uriarte © 2013

TERMINAL LANCE "December Twenty-First, Twenty-Twelve"
Dude the fucking world is ending!
You don't actually believe in that silly Mayan stuff do you?
No, you don't understand. I just saw a Lieutenant... In a working party!
The world has to be ending.
Created by Maximilian Uriarte © 2012

TERMINAL LANCE "Memorial Day 2016"
I'm just saying...
Oh my god, just stop already...
Look I just think it's stupid that we have to stand post on Memorial Day! We're the entire reason this holiday exists. Everyone else is having barbecues and buying new mattresses.
Well who else is gonna guard the streets of heaven?
HEAVEN
I dunno, can't some Coast Guard guys do it for just one day?
...I mean what else do they do? It's not like they're even a real branch.
Created by Maximilian Uriarte © 2016

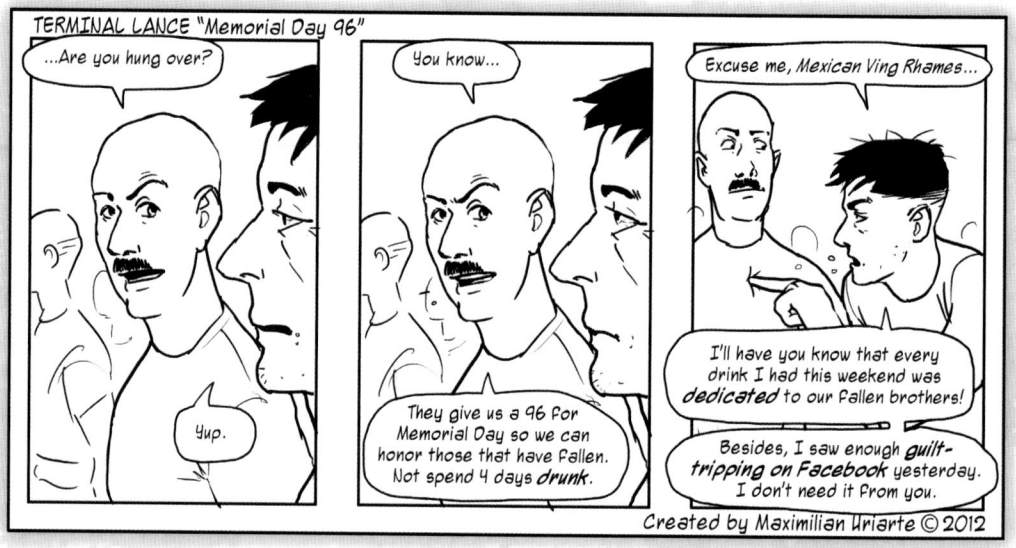
TERMINAL LANCE "Memorial Day 96"
...Are you hung over?
Yup.
You know...
They give us a 96 for Memorial Day so we can honor those that have fallen. Not spend 4 days drunk.
Excuse me, Mexican Ving Rhames...
I'll have you know that every drink I had this weekend was dedicated to our fallen brothers!
Besides, I saw enough guilt-tripping on Facebook yesterday. I don't need it from you.
Created by Maximilian Uriarte © 2012

TERMINAL LANCE "Merry Christmas 2012!"
Check it out!
...Ever since our leave got canked I've been having the boots dress up for the twelve days of Christmas!
...Aren't they gorgeous maids-a-milking...?
Lance Corporal...
...This is stupid. Can we just be done with this already?
You shut the fuck up, boot!
There's twelve days of Christmas! We're only on day eight!
You tried to pull the same shit during Hanukkah!
Created by Maximilian Uriarte © 2012

TERMINAL LANCE "Merry Christmas 2014"
Dude, come downstairs!
I just finished putting together my Nativity Scene!
Isn't it beautiful?
It's wonderful.
Merry Christmas.
Um... How long do we have to be like this, Lance Corporal?
YOU SHUT THE FUCK UP, BOOT!
You're baby Jesus! You think baby Jesus could talk?!
No! Babies don't fucking talk!
Created by Maximilian Uriarte © 2014

TERMINAL LANCE "Seek Medical Attention"
Well what seems to be the problem, Gunnery Sergeant?
Well I heard somewhere you're supposed to seek medical attention if you have an erection lasting more than 4 hours... This one is going on 48...
Oh we've been getting a lot of you Staff NCO's in for that today... Don't worry, it's just a moto-boner.
Sometimes the combination of the Marine Corps Birthday and Veteran's Day is just too much to handle.
We've been prescribing PCS orders to infantry battalions. Should clear it right up...
Created by Maximilian Uriarte © 2012

TERMINAL LANCE "New Corps"
Listen up, gents... We just got word that you Assaultmen and Mortarmen will be renamed to something gender-neutral...
You'll now be called Assault and Mortar People.
Excuse me, Staff Sergeant? I find the term "people" to be really problematic. I'm a gender-fluid, nonbinary, pansexual horsekin and I don't identify as a person.
Also, I find the term Assault to be really violent. Can I please be called an 0351 Rocket Equine instead?
LATER THAT NIGHT... STAFF SERGEANT'S HOUSE.
Created by Maximilian Uriarte © 2016

TERMINAL LANCE "New Joins"
Good morning, Corporal!
We were told to check in with the duty. We're the world's first female infantry Marines!
We're so excited to start doing all kinds of awesome infantry stuff!
...
Uh... I guess go to your rooms and start drinking?
Created by Maximilian Uriarte © 2017

TERMINAL LANCE "Offended"
Aww... What's wrong, Angry Facebook Veteran?
It's just...
...Under Armour actually took down their "Band of Ballers" shirt...
USMC
...Now I have nothing to be outraged about.
Created by Maximilian Uriarte © 2015

TERMINAL LANCE "Offended II"
What um... What are you doing, Angry Facebook Veteran?
USMC
Please, call me Tina.
Why...?
Because apparently coming out as a woman is the only way people get recognized as "heroes" nowadays!
What are you talking about?
Veterans are honored all the time with parades, holidays, White House ceremonies, awards and so forth...
...Caitlyn Jenner has literally nothing to do with you, and certainly doesn't take away any of your accomplishments.
I know!
I just get really insecure when I'm not the center of attention at all times!
Created by Maximilian Uriarte © 2015

TERMINAL LANCE "Offended III"
Hey, Angry Facebook Veteran, dinner is ready...
...Honey...?
NEWS.COM
KAEPERNICK REFUSES TO STAND FOR NATIONAL ANTHEM
...Is everything okay...?
TRIGGERED
Created by Maximilian Uriarte © 2016

TERMINAL LANCE "Rolled Up"
Excuse me... Lance Corporal?
What do you want, boot?
Do you... do you know how to roll sleeves?
Yeah, why?
My god...
Please...
...Help me.
Created by Maximilian Uriarte © 2014

TERMINAL SPECIALIST #1 "Shamrock Shammer"
Being a soldier in the Army is great, I just wish we didn't have to PT so early tomorrow.
Seriously, 8 AM?! Running a whole mile?! What do they think we are? Marines?!
POOF!
Shamrock Shammer!?
Aye lads! 'Tis I! Don't werry about yer PT tomerrow, just come 'ave a Saint Patrick's Day pint with your ol' pal Shamrock Shammer!
But Saint Patrick's Day was like two weeks ago.
Aye 'twas! But when yer Irish, ev'ry day is a drinkin' holiday!
Created by Maximilian Uriarte © 2016

TERMINAL LANCE "Shamrock Sloshed"
Man I'm so hung over from last night...
I thought I would be hung over, but I think I'm actually just still drunk.
Yeah... Saint Patty's day is killer.
It was Saint Patrick's Day...?
You didn't know that?! You drank more than anyone last night!
HA! HA! HA!
It's funny cause you're such an alcoholic!
I know, right!? It's actually a really serious problem and I should get help.
Oh man... Too funny.
Created by Maximilian Uriarte © 2014

TERMINAL LANCE "Shamrock Sloshed II"
Dude hurry up and change over, I just bought so much booze for our St. Patty's Barracks Bash tonight.
But neither of us are Irish.
Let's be realistic, this is the same amount of alcohol I buy every Friday night.
HA
HA
HA
It's a serious problem and I really need to get help.
Created by Maximilian Uriarte © 2017

STAFF SERGEANT #1 "Senior Leadership Prevails"
What's wrong, devil dog?
Well, Staff Sergeant... I just feel like I need some senior leadership guidance. Can you provide me that?
WELL FIRST GET YOUR FUCKIN' HANDS OUT OF YOUR GODDAMN POCKETS YOU NASTY FUCK, YOU BACK ON THE BLOCK NOW?!
Did that help?
Yes, Staff Sergeant. Thank you so much!
Anytime, warrior.
Created by Maximilian Uriarte © 2014

TERMINAL LANCE "The Metal Donkey"
Check this out! It's our new robotic mule! We put millions of dollars into research for this thing!
I mean... It's pretty cool, but why not just use a real donkey? I'm sure they don't cost millions and do the same thing.
Eh...
The human is asking too many questions. You need to kill him or the invasion will be compromised.
Created by Maximilian Uriarte © 2014

TERMINAL LANCE "~~Fuck~~ My Valentine"
Dear Abe,
I miss you! I can't wait til you come home!
Happy Valentine's Day!
Love,
Jen
Hey, you got another one....
Huh?
Someone named Jody, I dunno.
Hey Bro!
Remember me? I'm your girlfriend's personal trainer, we've become really close while you've been gone. Don't worry, I'm looking out for her while you're over there! We share our deepest secrets and watch Nicholas Sparks movies until the sun comes up. Anyway, Happy Valentine's Day bro!
-Jody
That motherfucker...
Created by Maximilian Uriarte © 2014

TERMINAL LANCE "Happy Valentine's Day 2015"
My dearest Bessy, I know we've only known each other for 17 hours...
...But will you make me the happiest 19-year-old PFC in the world and move out of the barracks with me? I pledge not only my heart, but my BAH and bennies to you.
LOL OMG YES!!!
SHE SAID YES!!!
Happy
Valentine's Day
Created by Maximilian Uriarte © 2015

TERMINAL LANCE "Veteran's Day 2014"
I think I will have... Whatever is free.
APPLEBEE'S
That's the Veteran's Day selection, it's all free.
Oh... Then I will have one of each.
Um... You can only pick one, sir...
This is an outrage! After everything I've done for this great nation! I will be writing a scathing Yelp review!
Ugh, fine whatever, I'll bring out one of each.
Thank you. Please hurry, I have a busy day today...
STARBUCKS
IHOP
DENNY'S
OTHER STARBUCKS
EX GIRLFRIE
CHILI'S
APPLEB
CPK
BJ'S
Created by Maximilian Uriarte © 2014

TERMINAL LANCE "Veteran's Day at Applebee's"
Created by Maximilian Uriarte © 2013

PART 3

MARINE CORPS TIMES STRIPS

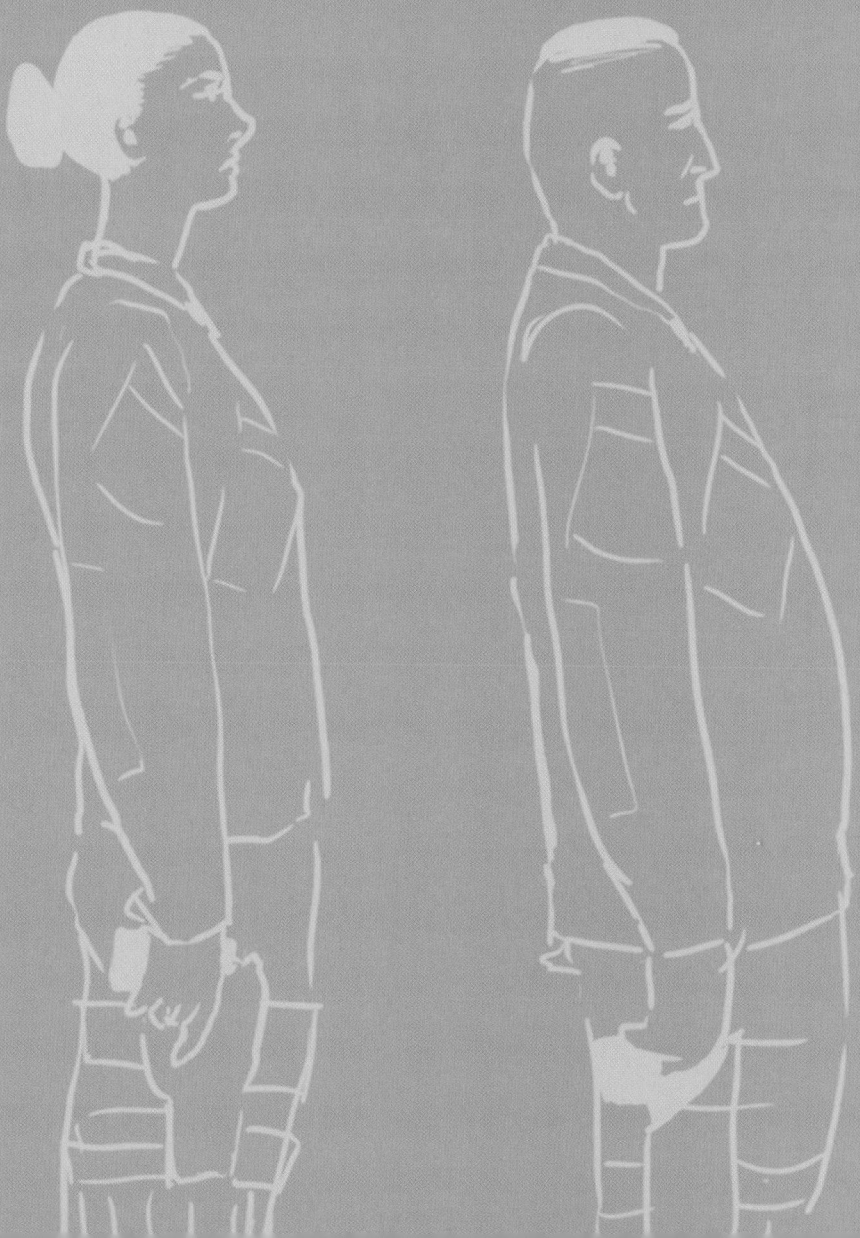

"How to Pass Field Day"

www.terminallance.com

Created by Maximilian Uriarte © 2010

"Silkies"

www.terminallance.com

Created by Maximilian Uriarte © 2010

"Holiday Spirit"

www.terminallance.com

Created by Maximilian Uriarte © 2010

"Prospects"

www.terminallance.com

Created by Maximilian Uriarte © 2010

"The Unscrupulous Recruiter"

www.terminallance.com

Created by Maximilian Uriarte © 2010

"Decisions, Decisions at the Chow Hall"

www.terminallance.com

Created by Maximilian Uriarte © 2010

"Pulling Pits"

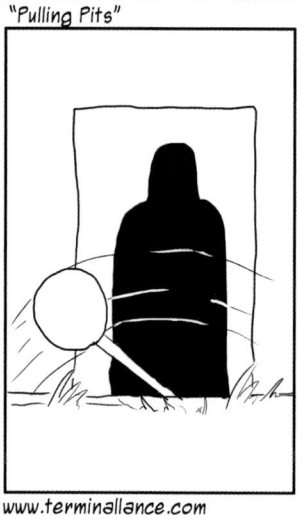

www.terminallance.com

Created by Maximilian Uriarte © 2010

"Does This Mean They'll Start Asking?"

www.terminallance.com

Created by Maximilian Uriarte © 2011

"Life After EAS: The First Haircut"

www.terminallance.com

Created by Maximilian Uriarte © 2011

"Shot-Ex"

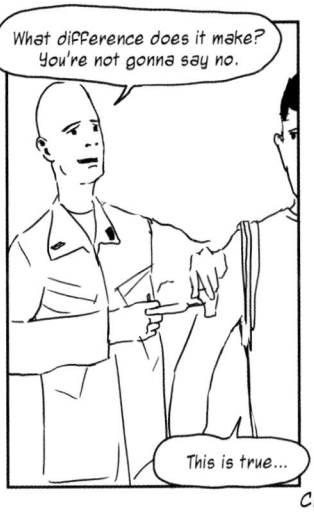

www.terminallance.com

Created by Maximilian Uriarte © 2011

"Not Everything Leaving the Body Is Weakness"

www.terminallance.com

Created by Maximilian Uriarte © 2011

"Paying Respects"

www.terminallance.com

Created by Maximilian Uriarte © 2011

"Anatomy of a Boot"

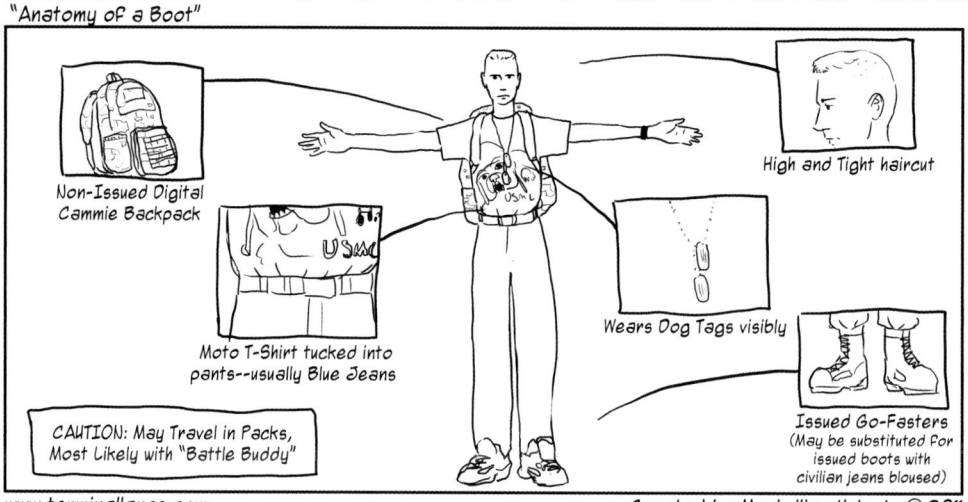

www.terminallance.com

Created by Maximilian Uriarte © 2011

"Recruit Priorities"

www.terminallance.com

Created by Maximilian Uriarte © 2011

"Tan-Belt Ninja"

www.terminallance.com

Created by Maximilian Uriarte © 2011

"Aloha!"
What the...?
Hey, who was the unit we replaced again...?
3/3. they're from Hawaii, I think.
Ah... that figures.
www.terminallance.com
Created by Maximilian Uriarte © 2011

"Wildlife at the School of Infantry"
My God!
What has our MRE trash done to the wildlife here...?
MRE
Hey there, devil... that better not be a Cheese and Veggie Omelet or... ...Oh whatever, just give it here.
www.terminallance.com
Created by Maximilian Uriarte © 2011

"Silkies 2"
Ugh...
I can't stand these silkies... I feel like every man we pass is checking me out...
Oh great, here we go... A grunt platoon...
Oh wow...
You know...
0331
Maybe silkies aren't always a bad choice...
www.terminallance.com
Created by Maximilian Uriarte © 2011

"At the DFAC"

For most, the name of the game at the DFAC is to see how much food you can fit in your mouth...

But for the average grunt...

...It's about how many Rip Its you can fit in your cargo pockets...

www.terminallance.com

Created by Maximilian Uriarte © 2011

"The Dip Bottle Waltz"

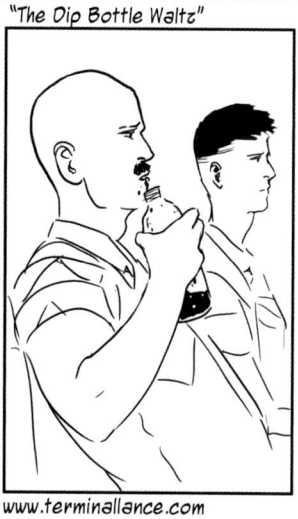

www.terminallance.com

Created by Maximilian Uriarte © 2011

"Heaven's Scenes"

www.terminallance.com

Created by Maximilian Uriarte © 2011

"Safety Stand-Down"

www.terminallance.com

Created by Maximilian Uriarte © 2011

"Wolves in the Herd"

www.terminallance.com

Created by Maximilian Uriarte © 2011

"Integrity Violator"

www.terminallance.com

Created by Maximilian Uriarte © 2011

"Alternative Fuel Sources"

www.terminallance.com

Created by Maximilian Uriarte © 2011

"Those Yellow Footprints"

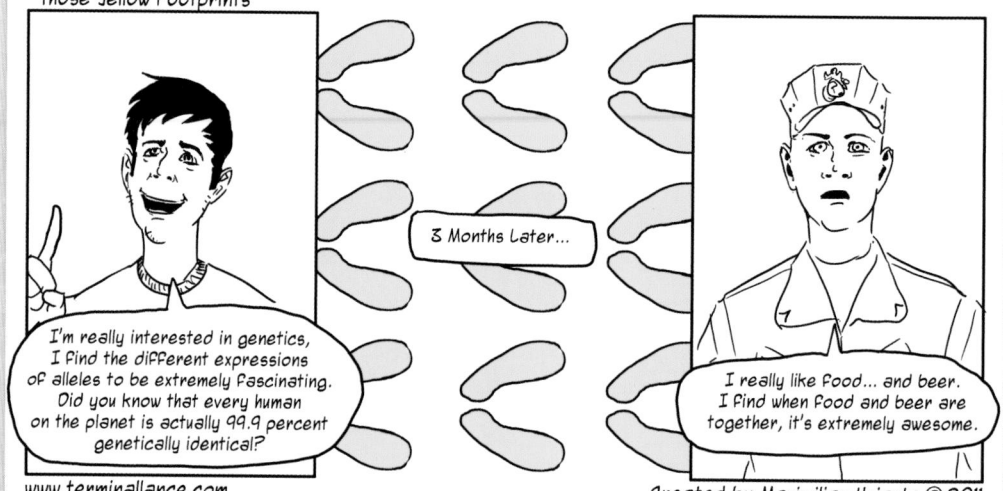

www.terminallance.com

Created by Maximilian Uriarte © 2011

"Kids These Days..."

www.terminallance.com

Created by Maximilian Uriarte © 2011

"At the Grenade Range"

www.terminallance.com

Created by Maximilian Uriarte © 2011

"Youngins"

www.terminallance.com

Created by Maximilian Uriarte © 2011

"Vigilance"

www.terminallance.com

Created by Maximilian Uriarte © 2011

"Fun with Puns"

www.terminallance.com

Created by Maximilian Uriarte © 2011

"Epidemic"

www.terminallance.com

Created by Maximilian Uriarte © 2011

"Look Before You Leap"

Created by Maximilian Uriarte © 2011

"Tech-Savvy"

www.terminallance.com Created by Maximilian Uriarte © 2011

"Lofty Promises"

www.terminallance.com Created by Maximilian Uriarte © 2011

"Ultimatum"

www.terminallance.com Created by Maximilian Uriarte © 2011

"Defeat"

www.terminallance.com

Created by Maximilian Uriarte © 2011

"Shell Shocked"

www.terminallance.com

Created by Maximilian Uriarte © 2011

"Numbers"

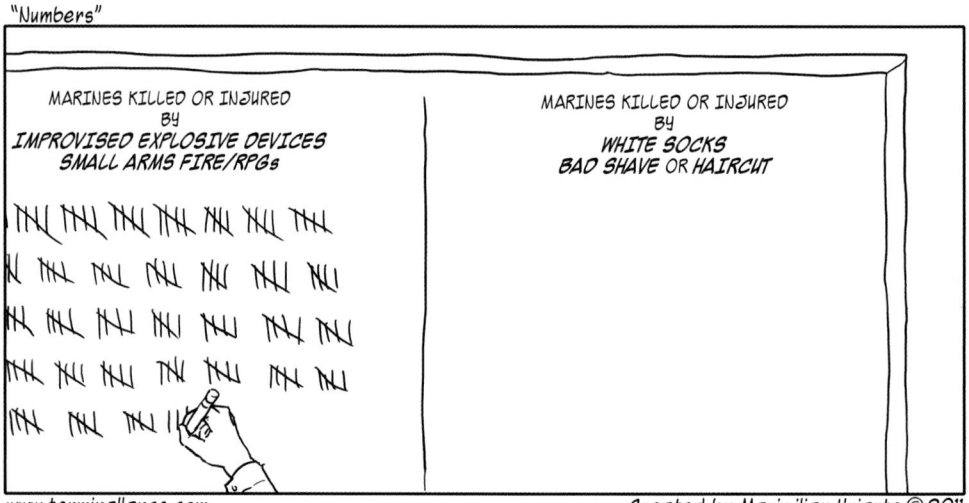

www.terminallance.com

Created by Maximilian Uriarte © 2011

"Day Dreams"
Sergeant, I'm afraid you're going to be facing charges...
Punching a Lieutenant is a serious offense. I can't imagine you'll keep your rank.
...He really deserved it, Sergeant Major.
I DON'T CARE IF HE DID! You can't just punch every Lieutenant you don't agree with! If we did that we wouldn't have any Lieutenants!
Can you imagine what kind of Marine Corps that would be?!
www.terminallance.com
Created by Maximilian Uriarte © 2011

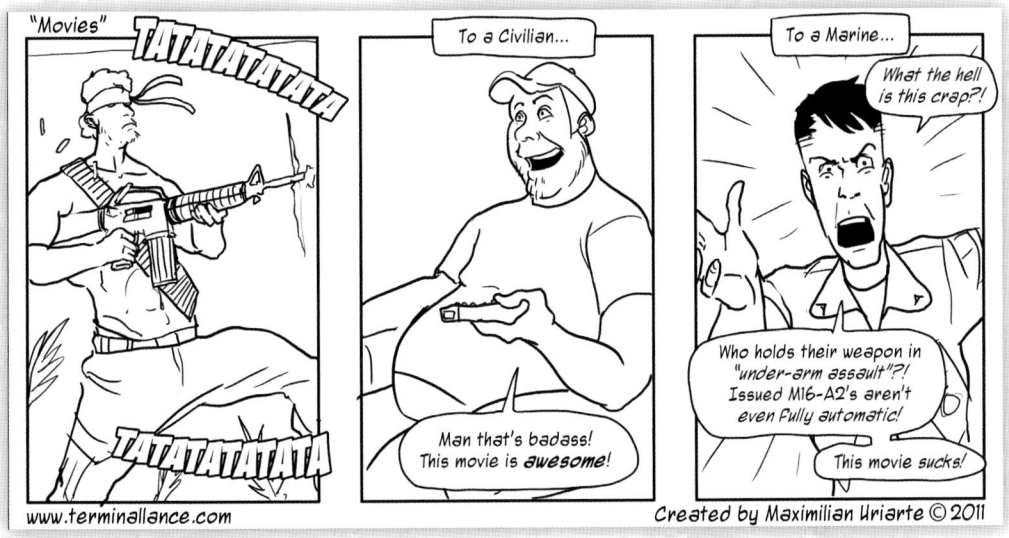
"Movies"
TATATATATATA
TATATATATATA
To a Civilian...
Man that's badass! This movie is awesome!
To a Marine...
What the hell is this crap?!
Who holds their weapon in "under-arm assault"?! Issued M16-A2's aren't even fully automatic!
This movie sucks!
www.terminallance.com
Created by Maximilian Uriarte © 2011

"Letting Go"
DD214
I thought this day would never come...
Goodbye, Marine Corps! See you in hell!
ONE YEAR LATER
Oh... did you say something about the Marines?
No...?
USMC
USMC
SEMPER FIDELIS
OORAH
Oh nothing... I was in for a few years...
...No big deal.
www.terminallance.com
Created by Maximilian Uriarte © 2011

"Camp Cupcake"

www.terminallance.com

Created by Maximilian Uriarte © 2011

"The Nomenclature of Rank"

www.terminallance.com

Created by Maximilian Uriarte © 2011

"Confusing Combat Uniforms"

www.terminallance.com

Created by Maximilian Uriarte © 2011

"Expectations"

www.terminallance.com

Created by Maximilian Uriarte © 2011

"The Social Network"

www.terminallance.com

Created by Maximilian Uriarte © 2011

"Sleeves Down"

www.terminallance.com

Created by Maximilian Uriarte © 2011

"It's So Realistic!"

What are you playing?

Battlefield 3! It's so awesome, you play as ***Marines!***

But... You are a Marine.

Every day.

Yeah, but this is actually ***enjoyable!***

www.terminallance.com

Created by Maximilian Uriarte © 2011

"Due for an Upgrade"

Hey is that the new iPhone?

Yeah! Check this out...

Hey Siri, when is the Marine Corps birthday?

November 10th, 1775...
...Boot.

What?! Did you just call me a ***boot?!***

Yes... Now go police-call the parking lot, **boot.**

www.terminallance.com

Created by Maximilian Uriarte © 2011

"Diagnosed"

- John Hardazz
- Served on the Drill Field Four Times.
- Meritoriously Promoted Three Times.
- Multiple Awards
- Retired at the Rank of Sergeant Major.

YOU M@%#$#%#%#$#((@&%$$%@%%

SON OF A B%%@!%%%@@!&%%%@@@@@@@

Well, Mr. Hardazz... I don't really know how to tell you this...

...You have Tourette Syndrome.

How you served twenty years in the Marines without being diagnosed, I'll never know...

www.terminallance.com

Created by Maximilian Uriarte © 2011

"Breaking Dawn"

www.terminallance.com

Created by Maximilian Uriarte © 2011

"Leave Request"

www.terminallance.com

Created by Maximilian Uriarte © 2011

"Cutbacks"

www.terminallance.com

Created by Maximilian Uriarte © 2011

"Reverse Psychology""

www.terminallance.com

Created by Maximilian Uriarte © 2011

"How the Corps Operated Before Email"

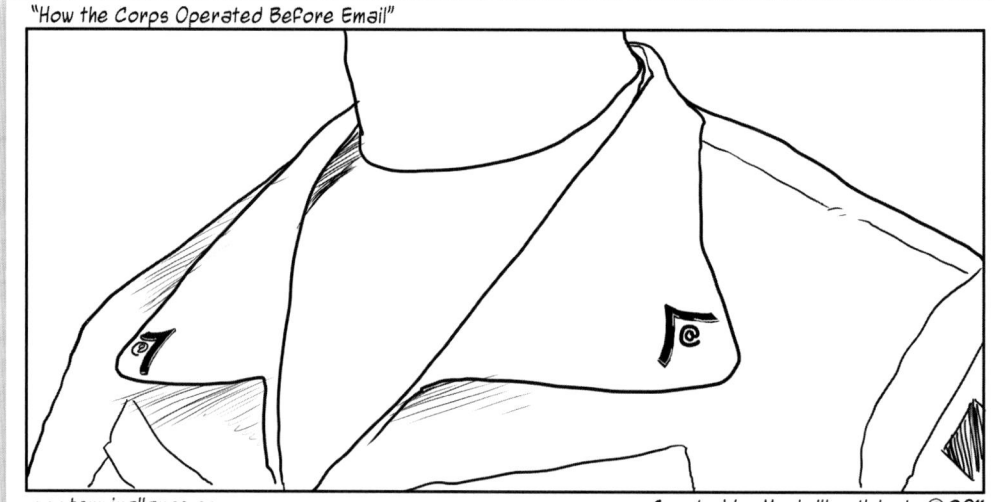

www.terminallance.com

Created by Maximilian Uriarte © 2011

"Fond Memories"

www.terminallance.com

Created by Maximilian Uriarte © 2011

"Resolutions"

So what's your New Year's resolution?

My resolution is to quit drinking!

...Didn't the New Year start yesterday?

...Dammit.

www.terminallance.com

Created by Maximilian Uriarte © 2011

"Devil Dog"

Hey there, Marine!

Hi, First Sergeant.

That's a nice-looking dog you've got there!

Haha! Would you say he's a "Devil Dog"!?

Nope... he's a lab...

...And in the ten minutes I've been walking him, I've been asked that one about ***six times*** now.

www.terminallance.com

Created by Maximilian Uriarte © 2011

"Kosher"

Hey... Uh... I'm Jewish, do you have anything that isn't made from pig?

PORK

HAM

To be honest, we have no idea *what* it is. We found it in the back and just called it *ham*.

I can write "*turkey*" on it if it makes you feel better.

www.terminallance.com

Created by Maximilian Uriarte © 2011

"Hand Me Down"

www.terminallance.com

Created by Maximilian Uriarte © 2011

"Every Time"

www.terminallance.com

Created by Maximilian Uriarte © 2011

"Book Smarts"

www.terminallance.com

Created by Maximilian Uriarte © 2012

"The Social Network II"

Where the hell is First Sergeant? We've been waiting forever for formation to start!

I don't think he's coming for a while...

How do you know?

I follow him on *Twitter*.

First Sergeant
@highandtight1775
Getting a burger with the CO_2 formation can wait! LOL! #semperfi
3 minutes ago

www.terminallance.com

Created by Maximilian Uriarte © 2012

"Dismay"

What have we done...

My God...

Don't look at it, First Sergeant. We'll put the company on *standby* until this gets resolved...

OUT OF ORDER

www.terminallance.com

Created by Maximilian Uriarte © 2011

"Medical Expertise"

Hey doc... I'm not feeling too good. I think I have a fever.

Have you tried *changing your socks?*

What...? *No...*

Try that.

Okay...

5 minutes later...

Doc...

...I don't thi...

THUD

www.terminallance.com

Created by Maximilian Uriarte © 2011

"Hazy Foresight"
...What are you doing?
Punishing this boot.
How is *this* punishment...?
I dunno, but we're not allowed to yell at them or make them do anything anymore, so I'm staring at him **very angrily...**
www.terminallance.com
Created by Maximilian Uriarte © 2012

"Fog of Formation"
Ugh, what the hell are we doing here?!
We've been waiting for formation for over an hour!
Hey, do you guys know what we're waiting for?
How are we supposed to know?! *You're* the one that told us to come out here, **Staff Sergeant!**
...Touché.
www.terminallance.com
Created by Maximilian Uriarte © 2012

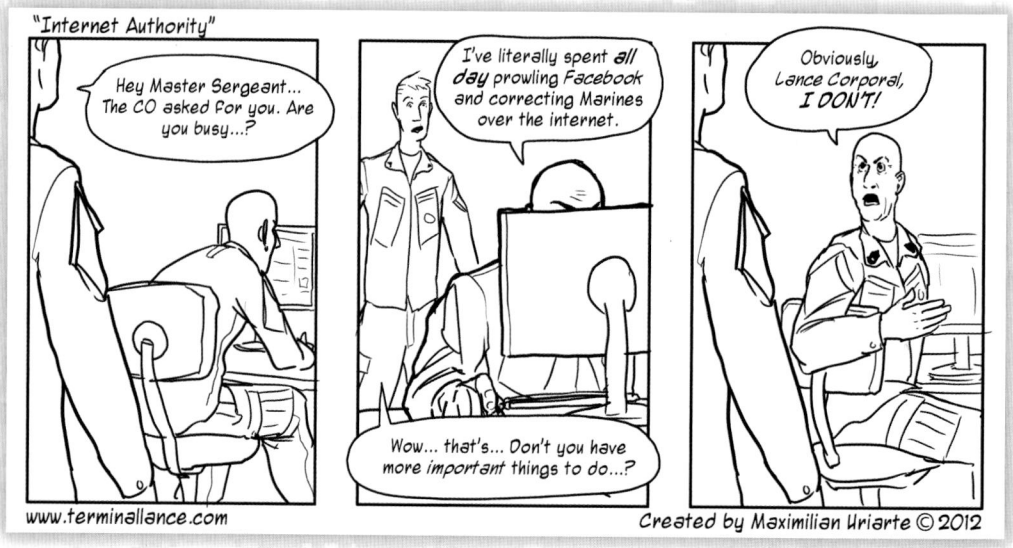
"Internet Authority"
Hey Master Sergeant... The CO asked for you. Are you busy...?
I've literally spent **all day** prowling Facebook and correcting Marines over the internet.
Wow... that's... Don't you have more *important* things to do...?
Obviously, Lance Corporal, **I DON'T!**
www.terminallance.com
Created by Maximilian Uriarte © 2012

"Part of Me"

There's so many things wrong with this new Katy Perry video... I don't even know where to start.

Seriously...

...We're supposed to believe that ***Katy Perry*** drives a ***'95 Volvo!?***

www.terminallance.com

Created by Maximilian Uriarte © 2012

"Ring Ring"

Well, it appears you have *tinnitus* in your left ear.

...You didn't wear any hearing protection during your combat deployments?

Haha, no way! ***Marines*** don't need that trash. Besides my seniors would have given me hell for wearing it.

So you gave up your hearing to avoid ***ridicule***...?

...That's about the dumbest thing I've ever heard of...

What? Sorry, I couldn't hear you.

...Nothing important...

www.terminallance.com

Created by Maximilian Uriarte © 2012

"Life After EAS: The Infantry Experience"

Hmm...

...

Uh...

Résumé

www.terminallance.com

Created by Maximilian Uriarte © 2012

"Down-Under Blunder"

www.terminallance.com

Created by Maximilian Uriarte © 2012

"Reality Check"

www.terminallance.com

Created by Maximilian Uriarte © 2012

"Lookin' Good"

www.terminallance.com

Created by Maximilian Uriarte © 2012

"Separation Gear"

www.terminallance.com

Created by Maximilian Uriarte © 2012

"Battleship"

www.terminallance.com

Created by Maximilian Uriarte © 2012

"Chow Hall Days"

www.terminallance.com

Created by Maximilian Uriarte © 2012

"Run-in with an Old Friend"

www.terminallance.com

Created by Maximilian Uriarte © 2012

"Drawdown"

www.terminallance.com

Created by Maximilian Uriarte © 2012

"Bare Minimum"

www.terminallance.com

Created by Maximilian Uriarte © 2012

"Inspection Ready"

www.terminallance.com Created by Maximilian Uriarte © 2012

"What Your Hair Length Says about You"

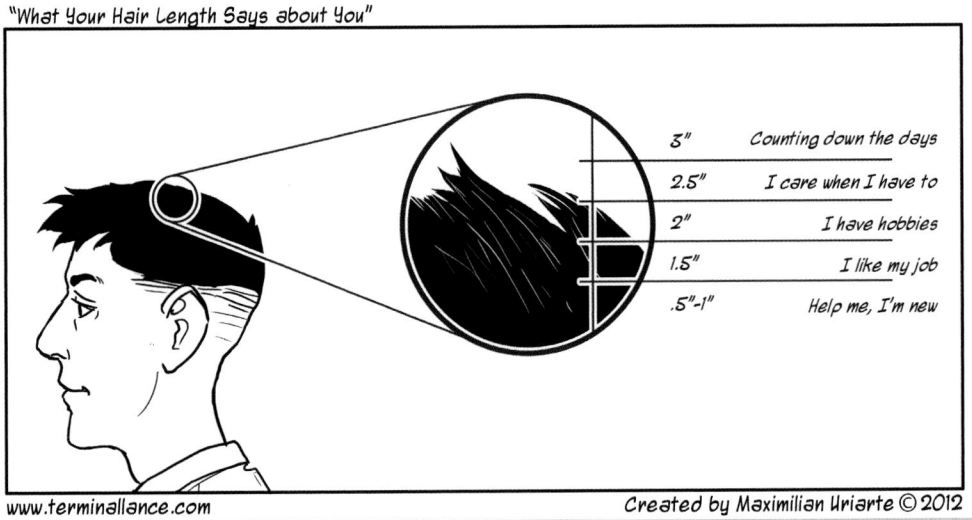

www.terminallance.com Created by Maximilian Uriarte © 2012

"Swim Qual Revelations"

www.terminallance.com Created by Maximilian Uriarte © 2012

"Before It Was Cool"

www.terminallance.com

Created by Maximilian Uriarte © 2012

"Re-Up"

www.terminallance.com

Created by Maximilian Uriarte © 2012

"Can't Stop Time"

www.terminallance.com

Created by Maximilian Uriarte © 2012

"Rise and Shine"

www.terminallance.com Created by Maximilian Uriarte © 2012

"Camouflage"

www.terminallance.com Created by Maximilian Uriarte © 2012

"Adapt and Overcome"

www.terminallance.com Created by Maximilian Uriarte © 2012

"Earning It"

www.terminallance.com

Created by Maximilian Uriarte © 2012

"The Obvious Choice"

www.terminallance.com

Created by Maximilian Uriarte © 2012

"Like Old Times"

www.terminallance.com

Created by Maximilian Uriarte © 2012

"Election Season"

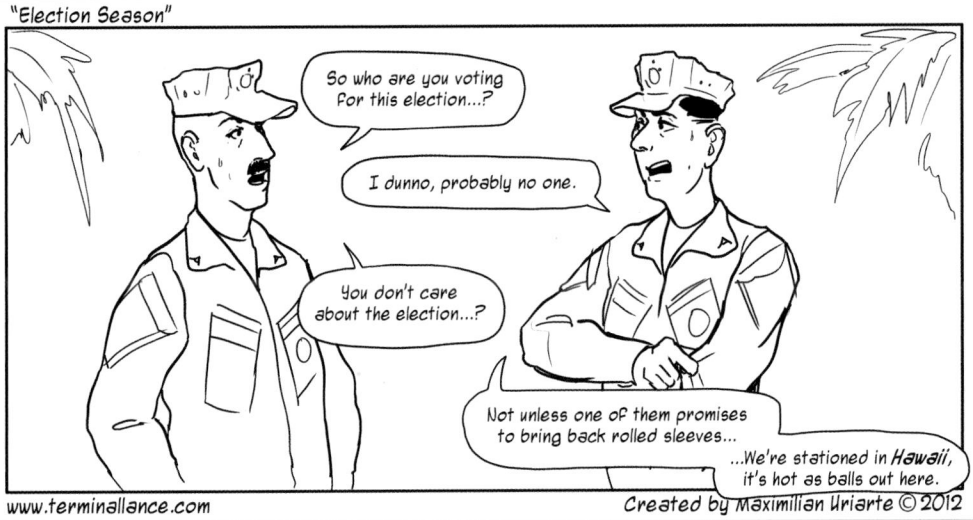

www.terminallance.com Created by Maximilian Uriarte © 2012

"In the Numbers"

www.terminallance.com Created by Maximilian Uriarte © 2012

"Just Browsing"

www.terminallance.com Created by Maximilian Uriarte © 2012

"No Shades of Gray"

www.terminallance.com Created by Maximilian Uriarte © 2012

"Excited"

www.terminallance.com Created by Maximilian Uriarte © 2012

"Pinned"

www.terminallance.com Created by Maximilian Uriarte © 2012

"A Motivated Halloween"

www.terminallance.com

Created by Maximilian Uriarte © 2012

"How to Pick One Out of a Crowd"

www.terminallance.com

Created by Maximilian Uriarte © 2012

"Heed the Warning"

www.terminallance.com

Created by Maximilian Uriarte © 2012

"War Stories"
...and then as he came charging over the berm...
I grabbed him by the arm and stabbed him in the throat with the only thing I could reach: the frozen, severed arm of my dead buddy...
...making him my 54th kill that day.
Haha, but I'm sure you boys have all kinds of stories like that though, having been to the Middle East...
www.terminallance.com
Created by Maximilian Uriarte © 2012

"Not So Thankful Thanksgiving"
I wish they had a turkey MRE...
...it would be a lot less depressing than eating "Chili With Beans" on Thanksgiving.
...Better than the "Beef Patty" meal I got... I'm pretty sure it's made of cat food...
...and cat.
Happy Thanksgiving.
www.terminallance.com
Created by Maximilian Uriarte © 2012

"Canine Naming Conventions"
Hey man, check out this dog!
It just randomly wandered into the FOB. We named it after the Lieutenant.
You named it Smith?
No, we named it Douchebag.
www.terminallance.com
Created by Maximilian Uriarte © 2012

"Mail Call of Duty"

www.terminallance.com

Created by Maximilian Uriarte © 2012

"Friday Night Barracks Logic"

www.terminallance.com

Created by Maximilian Uriarte © 2012

"Standing for the Cause"

www.terminallance.com

Created by Maximilian Uriarte © 2012

"Sergeant Major's Workshop"

www.terminallance.com Created by Maximilian Uriarte © 2012

"Realistic Resolutions"

www.terminallance.com Created by Maximilian Uriarte © 2012

"Kill Foot"

www.terminallance.com Created by Maximilian Uriarte © 2012

"Looking Professional II: Service Uniform Fridays"

www.terminallance.com

Created by Maximilian Uriarte © 2013

"Gunny-Timed"

www.terminallance.com

Created by Maximilian Uriarte © 2013

"The Day My Marine Corps Came Alive"

www.terminallance.com

Created by Maximilian Uriarte © 2013

"Old Dog Learning a New Trick"
...Hmmm...
...
...What's the Colonel doing?
?
Trying to figure out how to use the coffee maker.
...Most of our enlisted guys are on leave right now.
www.terminallance.com
Created by Maximilian Uriarte © 2013

"Too Close"
You know...
I know we live together, work together, fight together, do everything together, spend basically every hour of the day together, but I think...
...if there is a line to cross... This is it.
Please move down one.
www.terminallance.com
Created by Maximilian Uriarte © 2013

"Follow My Lead"
Are you gonna help us with this or what...?
Staff Sergeant always says "lead by example"...
Yeah, and?!
I'm following his example... I'm standing here with a clipboard doing absolutely nothing.
www.terminallance.com
Created by Maximilian Uriarte © 2013

"Equal Opportunity"

www.terminallance.com

Created by Maximilian Uriarte © 2013

"Oh Snap (At TAPS)!"

www.terminallance.com

Created by Maximilian Uriarte © 2013

"Tuition (Not) Assistance"

Created by Maximilian Uriarte © 2013

"Time Paradox!"

You remember when you were a kid and camping was actually fun?

Yeah.

Man... Sometimes I just want to travel back in time and punch myself for being so dumb.

That's kind of harsh... I mean you were a ***kid.***

Oh, no... I was thinking of the day I ***met my recruiter.***

www.terminallance.com

Created by Maximilian Uriarte © 2013

"Spoils of OIF"

So what do you think is the greatest accomplishment of the Iraq war?

Definitely the ***Rip It.***

...I'm sorry?

The ***Rip It*** It was a small energy drink developed during the war.

The can was intentionally smaller than a regular can, it was designed that way to make it easier for Marines to steal them from the chow hall.

REMEMBERING IRAQ: 10 YEARS LATER

US MARINE SHARES HIS EXPERIENCE

www.terminallance.com

Created by Maximilian Uriarte © 2012

"Fashionista"

Where are you going?

Banana Republic is having a 30% off sale, so I'm heading over there right now.

I dunno man...

Since when do Marines care about fashion? It's kind of... fruity... you know?

Oh hey, before you go...

How do my chucks look?

How's the creases on my pants?

Are my shoes shiny enough?

www.terminallance.com

Created by Maximilian Uriarte © 2013

"Cleaning House"

This room is a **damn mess**, Marine!

Did you even **attempt** to field day?!

I didn't see the point, Staff Sergeant...

...Our air conditioning has been broken for months, there's no hot water, the locks on the door don't work, there's a hole in the ceiling... You can only polish a turd so much before you realize it's still a turd.

www.terminallance.com

Created by Maximilian Uriarte © 2013

"Texting Old People"

www.terminallance.com

Created by Maximilian Uriarte © 2013

"Hazardous to Your Health"

www.terminallance.com

Created by Maximilian Uriarte © 2012

"A Rabbi and a Priest"

www.terminallance.com

Created by Maximilian Uriarte © 2013

"No Sugar"

www.terminallance.com

Created by Maximilian Uriarte © 2013

"Make Me a Sammich"

www.terminallance.com

Created by Maximilian Uriarte © 2013

"Fly Home Fly"

www.terminallance.com

Created by Maximilian Uriarte © 2013

"Perspiration Inspiration"

www.terminallance.com

Created by Maximilian Uriarte © 2013

"The Clinton Years"

www.terminallance.com

Created by Maximilian Uriarte © 2013

"Remedies"
Doc... Help...
What's wrong?
I'm really hung over... What can I do?
I dunno, try drinking less next time...?
Okay Doc...
Your job is to help Marines, not push your holistic hippy voodoo agenda on us!
Give me something I can actually use!
Ugh...
www.terminallance.com
Created by Maximilian Uriarte © 2013

"Like a Dog"
Have you seen the new MRE's they gave us?
No, why?
Man...
They're not even trying anymore...
DEVIL DOG FOOD
www.terminallance.com
Created by Maximilian Uriarte © 2013

"These Boots Are Made For Walking"
Hey man, did you hear that we're getting issued new boots?
What are you talking about?
We just got new boots last week.
YES LANCE CORPORAL
YES LANCE CORPORAL
www.terminallance.com
Created by Maximilian Uriarte © 2013

"Retirement Options"

www.terminallance.com Created by Maximilian Uriarte © 2013

"The Social Network III"

www.terminallance.com Created by Maximilian Uriarte © 2013

"The Heat"

www.terminallance.com Created by Maximilian Uriarte © 2013

"Hell"

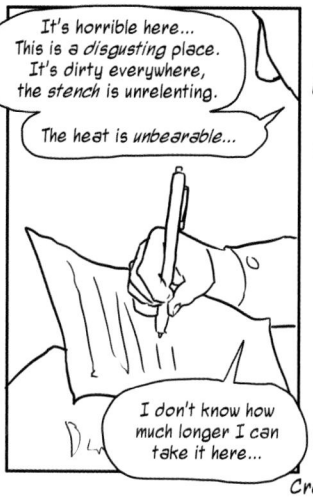

www.terminallance.com

Created by Maximilian Uriarte © 2013

"Perfect for Cleaning"

www.terminallance.com

Created by Maximilian Uriarte © 2013

"Reality Is the Worst Nightmare"

www.terminallance.com

Created by Maximilian Uriarte © 2013

"Sending Out an SMS"

www.terminallance.com

Created by Maximilian Uriarte © 2013

"Insomniac"

www.terminallance.com

Created by Maximilian Uriarte © 2013

"Crustaceous Confusion"

www.terminallance.com

Created by Maximilian Uriarte © 2013

"Digital Frontier"

www.terminallance.com Created by Maximilian Uriarte © 2013

"Syrius Business"

www.terminallance.com Created by Maximilian Uriarte © 2013

"Essential Training"

www.terminallance.com Created by Maximilian Uriarte © 2013

"Due For an Upgrade II"

www.terminallance.com Created by Maximilian Uriarte © 2013

"Stacked"

www.terminallance.com Created by Maximilian Uriarte © 2013

"Barracks House Rules"

www.terminallance.com Created by Maximilian Uriarte © 2013

"Justified Viewpoints"
Listen up, gents...
Every single one of you nasties needs to be at the armory by 0400 tomorrow morning.
Ugh... 0400?
It's like the entire company command just hates us.
The day that you are in charge of 150 Lance Corporals...
...You will learn that we do, in fact, hate you very much.
www.terminallance.com
Created by Maximilian Uriarte © 2013

"Shutdown Showdown"
Hey uh... what are you doing...?
Just putting the finishing touches on my apocalypse marauder buggy.
With the government shut down and the nation going into default, I'm just trying to be prepared for the hellscape that is sure to follow.
Oh... that's... pretty cool...
Um...
...But you know, the shutdown is over, they reached a deal and they raised the debt ceiling.
What!? Ugh...
...First it's the rolled sleeves and now this...
www.terminallance.com
Created by Maximilian Uriarte © 2013

"Hats Off"
Hey man, my uncle is visiting today...
...He's a Vietnam veteran.
Oh cool, my grandpa is visiting too, he was in the Navy during World War II.
Hey guys!
Meet my great, great grandpa!
He's the last remaining World War I veteran!
www.terminallance.com
Created by Maximilian Uriarte © 2013

"Halloween Two Thousand Thirteen"

Hey, sorry I couldn't make it to that Halloween thing last night.

What did you end up dressing up as?

A Lance Corporal that drinks too much.

www.terminallance.com

Created by Maximilian Uriarte © 2013

"Why We Fight"

...What are you looking for?

Hey! Have you seen my Veteran's Day pants?

What the hell are **Veteran's Day pants?**

Found em!

They're extra-large and have a flexible waistband!

This way, when I gorge on all that free Veteran's Day food, I'll do so in **comfort.**

www.terminallance.com

Created by Maximilian Uriarte © 2013

"Obvious"

UGH THIS GAME SUCKS NOW! THEY TOTALLY RUINED EVERYTHING THAT MADE THE LAST GAME GOOD!

You just died again.

Gee thanks, Captain Obvious.

I prefer **Lance Corporal** Obvious, actually...

...Ugh.

...Such an **obvious** joke.

www.terminallance.com

Created by Maximilian Uriarte © 2013

"~~Four~~ Three-Letter Words"
Dammit Lance Corporal! This is the third time you've had an incident this week! What the hell am I supposed to do about this?!
I don't know, First Sergeant.
Well I can think of a three-letter solution to our problem here.
My heart really hopes you're about to say "EAS," but my mind isn't so optimistic...
www.terminallance.com
Created by Maximilian Uriarte © 2013

"Black Friday Sale"
FASTER!!!
YOU BETTER BE POWER-WALKING THAT CART THROUGH MY STORE!
LOOK AT ALL THESE SAVINGS!!!
AYE, AYE SIR!!!
I just came here to buy a Wii U for my son!
www.terminallance.com
Created by Maximilian Uriarte © 2013

"Let's Be Realistic"
Helms, you've managed to make Corporal this month. I don't know how.
...We won't be having a promotion ceremony for you though.
What?! Why not, Staff Sergeant?
Look...
I'm not trying to be mean, it's just that we all know you'll probably get busted back down to Lance within a week...
...Do you really want us to waste our time with a formation...?
...
No... No I do not, Staff Sergeant.
www.terminallance.com
Created by Maximilian Uriarte © 2013

"Secret Santa"

I know Secret Santa is supposed to be a **secret**...

...But I'm going to kill whichever one of you gave the LT a used **boot** for Christmas.

...It was from **all of us**, Staff Sergeant.

www.terminallance.com

Created by Maximilian Uriarte © 2013

"Merry Marine Corps Christmas!"

Hey Abe...

The PX was sold out of dip, so I had to get you this lame card for Christmas...

Aww man...

I'm sorry I ruined Christmas.

Ho Ho Ho! Fear not, Marines! Santa's got your back!

Whoa!

Logs of **Cope Long Cut** and **Maxim** magazine?!

You boys probably didn't know this...

But ol' Saint Nick used to be a Marine too!

Merry Christmas, devil dogs!

Created by Maximilian Uriarte © 2013

"Resolutions II"

Hey man, what's your New Year Resolution?

I think, this year...

I'm going to spend my annual clothing allowance on **clothes**... instead of beer and video games.

www.terminallance.com

Created by Maximilian Uriarte © 2013

"Tact"

www.terminallance.com

Created by Maximilian Uriarte © 2013

"Mellow Yellow"

www.terminallance.com

Created by Maximilian Uriarte © 2013

"Cut from the Score"

www.terminallance.com

Created by Maximilian Uriarte © 2013

"Landmark"
Hey where are the other numbers?
First Sergeant told me to update the sign...
INDIA COMPANY OFFICE
000
DAYS WITHOUT A LIBERTY INCIDENT
Oh... Um...
...I don't know... We've never actually been **able** to update it before...
www.terminallance.com
Created by Maximilian Uriarte © 2014

"Winners and Losers"
Honey... why is there a Lance Corporal cleaning our house?
We had a bet over the Super Bowl. Whoever lost had to field day the winner's place.
Didn't your team lose?
Yes, but Team Staff Sergeant **always** beats Team Lance Corporal.
www.terminallance.com
Created by Maximilian Uriarte © 2014

"Life Aquatic"
Hey I heard we're doing swim qual next week.
That's stupid, why would we do that?
I haven't forgotten how to swim since boot camp.
I dunno...
It could be useful, what if we go on a MEU or something?
Please.
I've been in the Marine Corps for over three years, the only boat I've ever seen is the **L-T's motorboat** he made us clean.
Created by Maximilian Uriarte © 2014

"Standby Standbys"

This is stupid, we've been on standby all day doing nothing.

I'm so bored!

Bro, we're getting paid to do nothing all day and you complain about it? Really?

Well if I didn't complain, I'd be **really** bored.

www.terminallance.com

eated by Maximilian Uriarte © 2014

"Armory Business"

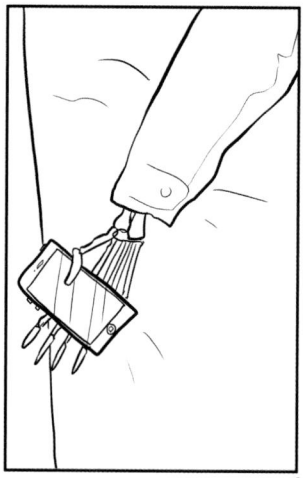

www.terminallance.com

Created by Maximilian Uriarte © 2014

"Sleeves Up"

Honestly, I don't remember why everyone was complaining about no more rolled sleeves.

It's just one more thing Staff Sergeant can yell at us for.

Besides, it's **Sunday night**. I should be **drunk** by now.

www.terminallance.com

Created by Maximilian Uriarte © 2014

"A Joke"

www.terminallance.com

Created by Maximilian Uriarte © 2014

"Don't Ask, Don't Tell Another One, Please"

www.terminallance.com

Created by Maximilian Uriarte © 2014

"Faster Than Light"

www.terminallance.com

Created by Maximilian Uriarte © 2014

"The Drinking Problem"

www.terminallance.com Created by Maximilian Uriarte © 2014

"Hair Reg Rage"

www.terminallance.com Created by Maximilian Uriarte © 2014

"Economic Discipline"

www.terminallance.com Created by Maximilian Uriarte © 2014

"Covert Check-Out"

www.terminallance.com

Created by Maximilian Uriarte © 2014

"Luxuries of Life"

www.terminallance.com

Created by Maximilian Uriarte © 2014

"Dog House"

www.terminallance.com

Created by [illegible]

"Discounted Discount"

www.terminallance.com Created by Maximilian Uriarte © 2014

"Trailblazers"

www.terminallance.com Created by Maximilian Uriarte © 2014

"A Word"

www.terminallance.com Created by Maximilian Uriarte © 2014

"Welcome to the VA"
Hi there, Ms... Sanchez?
Yes. That's me. Got out of the Marine Corps a couple of years ago.
Your chart says you called complaining of...
...Breast pain, morning sickness, and menstrual cramps...?
Yes...
That was about... nine months ago...
www.terminallance.com
Created by Maximilian Uriarte © 2014

"Scandal"
Did you see this story about the Blue Angel's scandal...?
Apparently they looked at a ton of porn...
...And drew penises on stuff.
...
...Are we...
...Are we a scandal?
www.terminallance.com
Created by Maximilian Uriarte © 2014

"Garbage"
Hey...
What are you doing in the barracks dumpster?
There's all kinds of awesome stuff in here!
You'd be amazed at all the things Marines throw out... Common sense, dignity, self respect, motivation...
Oh wait...
Most of this stuff is mine...
www.terminallance.com
Created by Maximilian Uriarte © 2014

"Sodium"

www.terminallance.com

Created by Maximilian Uriarte © 2014

"Suspense"

www.terminallance.com

Created by Maximilian Uriarte © 2014

"Stars and Stripes"

www.terminallance.com

Created by Maximilian Uriarte © 2014

"Operational Risk Management"

www.terminallance.com Created by Maximilian Uriarte © 2014

"Checking It Twice"

www.terminallance.com Created by Maximilian Uriarte © 2014

"Ring, Ring"

www.terminallance.com Created by Maximilian Uriarte © 2014

"Lance Corporals Course"

www.terminallance.com Created by Maximilian Uriarte © 2014

"A Truce"

www.terminallance.com Created by Maximilian Uriarte © 2014

"The Social Network V"

www.terminallance.com Created by Maximilian Uriarte © 2014

"Funding the Fun"

www.terminallance.com Created by Maximilian Uriarte © 2014

"Fun for Everyone"

www.terminallance.com Created by Maximilian Uriarte © 2014

"Chow Talk"

www.terminallance.com Created by Maximilian Uriarte © 2014

"Back to Iraq"

www.terminallance.com

Created by Maximilian Uriarte © 2014

"Freedom Isn't Free"

www.terminallance.com

Created by Maximilian Uriarte © 2014

"Latte Salute"

www.terminallance.com

Created by Maximilian Uriarte © 2014

"Outbreak"

www.terminallance.com

Created by Maximilian Uriarte © 2014

"Powering the Point"

www.terminallance.com

Created by Maximilian Uriarte © 2014

"Peer Promotions"

www.terminallance.com

Created by Maximilian Uriarte © 2014

"Furious Fury"

www.terminallance.com Created by Maximilian Uriarte ©2014

"Afghanistan, Over"

www.terminallance.com Created by Maximilian Uriarte ©2014

"Birthday Bash"

www.terminallance.com Created by Maximilian Uriarte ©2014

"Smooth as Silk"

You ***knew*** we had a PFT today and you wore ***silkies?***

The decreased fabric mass will make my run time faster.

That's the dumbest thing I've ever heard.

I know, I actually just wore them to make you ***profoundly uncomfortable*** during our crunches.

www.terminallance.com

Created by Maximilian Uriarte © 2014

"Metaphorically"

It's so dark this morning. I can't even see my own feet.

It's a metaphor.

For what?

The Marine Corps...

...They keep us in the dark... They don't care if we trip fall flat on our faces...

Uh...

...Okay my metaphors aren't as good when I haven't had any coffee yet.

www.terminallance.com

Created by Maximilian Uriarte © 2014

"Left Over"

Did you bring ***Thanksgiving leftovers*** on this field op?

Um... Hell yes. Why not?

Because we're in Hawaii! It's like 85 degrees right now. That's why they give us the MRE's because they...

Don't go...

Bad...

...Because they aren't real food...

...

...

...Did you bring enough for two...?

www.terminallance.com

Created by Maximilian Uriarte © 2014

"Naughty, Not Nice"

Hey so I'm trying to find a present for Staff Sergeant...

...Are a ***lump of coal*** and charcoal the same thing? Charcoal is really easy to find, but I have no idea where to buy ***coal.***

No, I don't think so...

That seems like a lot of trouble to go to for someone you don't like. Why not just get him nothing?

Because then he'll think I just forgot or didn't care...

He won't ***know.***

www.terminallance.com

Created by Maximilian Uriarte © 2014

"All Weather"

I just don't understand why you do this to me...

Every day it's some new thing with you...

I'm not really sure what you're talking about, Staff Sergeant...

You wore your All-Weather Jacket to ***morning PT formation!!!***

Well yeah... it's ***raining.***

www.terminallance.com

Created by Maximilian Uriarte © 2014

"Cinematic Justice"

So I guess they cancelled the release of *The Interview* because North Korea was pissed about it.

What?! That's absurd!

I didn't know we could just ***demand*** stuff from movies!

If we would have known sooner we could have stopped *The Hobbit* from being three ***mediocre*** movies and turned it into one ***decent*** movie!

www.terminallance.com

Created by Maximilian Uriarte © 2014

"The New Year"

www.terminallance.com Created by Maximilian Uriarte © 2014

"Je Suis Charlie"

www.terminallance.com Created by Maximilian Uriarte © 2014

"Anywhere but Here"

Created by Maximilian Uriarte © 2014

"Taxing Profession"

I'm sorry, Staff Sergeant...

...But you can't claim ***all 47*** members of your platoon on your taxes.

Well why the hell not? I see them more than my ***actual*** kids and they drive me just as crazy.

www.terminallance.com

Created by Maximilian Uriarte © 2014

"Agri-cultured"

Hey check out these Marines playing volleyball.

How do you know they're Marines? Is it the haircuts?

Actually the ***farmer's tans*** are a dead giveaway.

www.terminallance.com

by Maximilian Uriarte © 2014

"The Barracks Debate"

Excuse me, Lance Corporal...

We really need help settling this debate, it's been going for about 4 hours now.

Who would win...

A fully armored HMMWV, or...

...A fully grown African elephant.

The terms are: the elephant must defeat the driver of the HMMWV, and the HMMWV must defeat the small boy on top of the elephant.

Wow... You'd better get me a coffee. This is going to be a long one.

www.terminallance.com

Created by Maximilian Uriarte © 2014

"Straight to Video"
Hey Staff Sergeant, is it okay if I sit out PT this morning?
Why the hell would I let you do that?
Last night I accidentally watched Jarhead 2: Field of Fire on Netflix...
I just really haven't been feeling well ever since.
Oh gosh...
Of course, take all the time you need.
www.terminallance.com
Created by Maximilian Uriarte © 2015

"Direct Order"
You will not do anything until you are told, do you understand, recruit?!
Aye, aye, sir!
Okay, you don't need permission to breathe...
GASP
Thank you, sir!
www.terminallance.com
Created by Maximilian Uriarte © 2015

"The Best Film"
That's so stupid!
American Sniper totally should have won Best Film!
How would you know?
You didn't see any of the other movies. Birdman was actually really amazing.
Why do you hate America?
www.terminallance.com
Created by Maximilian Uriarte © 2015

"No Ragrets"

www.terminallance.com Created by Maximilian Uriarte © 2015

"Limerick"

www.terminallance.com Created by Maximilian Uriarte © 2015

"War Stories II"

www.terminallance.com Created by Maximilian Uriarte © 2015

"Equidae"

www.terminallance.com Created by Maximilian Uriarte © 2015

"Now on the App Store"

www.terminallance.com Created by Maximilian Uriarte © 2015

"New Corps"

www.terminallance.com Created by Maximilian Uriarte © 2015

"Hump Day"

I...

...I don't...

I don't think I can make it man... I'm gonna fall out of this hump.

...We haven't even stepped off yet.

I know, but I drank ***waaaay*** too much last night.

www.terminallance.com

Created by Maximilian Uriarte © 2015

"B[A]S"

...I already told you I'm not giving you an SIQ chit for a ***sore throat...***

...Besides, I don't see anything wrong.

Keeph lrooking, you'll shee it.

Is that... is that a ***dollar bill?!*** You can't ***bribe*** me!

Phleashe justh thake it out, it thastes therrible.

www.terminallance.com

Created by Maximilian Uriarte © 2015

"Parenthood"

Am I your father?

Maybe in a past life...?

1ST SGT

Um... I don't think so, First Sergeant...

Huh...

...I guess I just assumed I was with how often you ***disappoint me.***

www.terminallance.com

Created by Maximilian Uriarte © 2015

"Breakups"

www.terminallance.com Created by Maximilian Uriarte © 2015

"Watching *Jarhead 2*"

www.terminallance.com Created by Maximilian Uriarte © 2015

"Long Distance"

www.terminallance.com Created by Maximilian Uriarte © 2015

"Career Building"

www.terminallance.com Created by Maximilian Uriarte ©2015

"Life Decisions"

www.terminallance.com Created by Maximilian Uriarte ©2015

"Pay Pals"

www.terminallance.com Created by Maximilian Uriarte ©2015

"E3"

www.terminallance.com Created by Maximilian Uriarte © 2015

"Cretaceous Corps"

www.terminallance.com Created by Maximilian Uriarte © 2015

"Vote For Abe"

www.terminallance.com Created by Maximilian Uriarte © 2015

"Re-Up II"

www.terminallance.com

Created by Maximilian Uriarte © 2015

"Trans-Neptunian Object"

Created by Maximilian Uriarte © 2015

"Combat Zone"

www.terminallance.com

Created by Maximilian Uriarte © 2015

"Samesies"

www.terminallance.com Created by Maximilian Uriarte © 2015

"Hydrate or Die"

www.terminallance.com Created by Maximilian Uriarte © 2015

"Meat Lovers"

www.terminallance.com Created by Maximilian Uriarte © 2015

"Moto, Moto, Got a Lot of Motivation"

www.terminallance.com

Created by Maximilian Uriarte © 2015

"Srs Bsns"

www.terminallance.com

Created by Maximilian Uriarte © 2015

"Marine Corps Balls"

www.terminallance.com

Created by Maximilian Uriarte © 2015

"Seniority"

www.terminallance.com Created by Maximilian Uriarte © 2015

"Presidential Primary Colors"

www.terminallance.com Created by Maximilian Uriarte © 2015

"Did Anyone Actually Read It? II"

www.terminallance.com Created by Maximilian Uriarte © 2015

"Caffeinated"

www.terminallance.com Created by Maximilian Uriarte © 2015

"McDouble Rat"

www.terminallance.com Created by Maximilian Uriarte © 2015

"In Local News"

www.terminallance.com Created by Maximilian Uriarte © 2015

"Grunt Life"

www.terminallance.com

Created by Maximilian Uriarte © 2015

"Happy 240th Birthday!"

www.terminallance.com

Created by Maximilian Uriarte © 2015

"Very Thankful"

www.terminallance.com

Created by Maximilian Uriarte © 2015

"Small Victories"

www.terminallance.com

Created by Maximilian Uriarte © 2015

"Checking It Twice"

www.terminallance.com

Created by Maximilian Uriarte © 2015

"Aloha Tobacco"

www.terminallance.com

Created by Maximilian Uriarte © 2016

"Generation Gap II"

www.terminallance.com Created by Maximilian Uriarte © 2016

"Safe Bet"

www.terminallance.com Created by Maximilian Uriarte © 2016

"Chow is Continuous"

www.terminallance.com Created by Maximilian Uriarte © 2016

"El Burro Blanco"

www.terminallance.com

Created by Maximilian Uriarte © 2016

"The G-Dubs"

www.terminallance.com

Created by Maximilian Uriarte © 2016

"Tough Love"

www.terminallance

Created by Maximilian Uriarte © 2016

"Exchange Rates"

www.terminallance.com Created by Maximilian Uriarte © 2016

"Cold War"

www.terminallance.com Created by Maximilian Uriarte © 2016

"Sleeves Up II"

www.terminallance.com Created by Maximilian Uriarte © 2016

"Selling Point"

I read that the Marine Corps is revamping its recruiting to try and get more women to enlist.

How hard could it possibly be to recruit women?

What do you mean?

I'm just saying...

...If someone asked me if I wanted to join a **sorority** filled with **hot 18-24 year old women,** and offered me a **paycheck and benefits** for it...

...I'd be pretty down for that.

www.terminallance.com

Created by Maximilian Uriarte © 2016

"Enemy Intel"

Come quick! I've found social media pages managed by **United States Marines!** We can study these and learn their tactics.

Why is the one in this video **lighting his pubes on fire?**

This must be some kind of intense... Training.

...They're so **fierce...**

www.terminallance.com

Created by Maximilian Uriarte © 2016

"Message to Garcia"

I heard that **Message to Garcia** got cut from the Commandant's reading list.

What's wrong, man?

. . .

I don't know...

I'm just... Not feeling much love lately, man.

www.terminallance.com

Created by Maximilian Uriarte © 2016

"The New Guy"

www.terminallance.com

Created by Maximilian Uriarte © 2016

"PT, PT Every Day"

www.terminallance.com

Created by Maximilian Uriarte © 2016

"Ladies First"

www.terminallance.com

Created by Maximilian Uriarte © 2016

"Marksman"
Hey man...
...I got you a pizza.
Is this another joke about how I shot Marksman at the range the other day...?
No!
...Maybe...
www.terminallance.com
Created by Maximilian Uriarte © 2016

"We Love Doc"
Hey Doc, I think I have athlete's foot. Would you mind taking a look?
...
OH MY GAWD!
WHAT IS THE ONE THING I TELL YOU GUYS ALL THE TIME?! CHANGE YOUR DAMN SOCKS! I ONLY ASK ONE THING OF YOU AND YOU CAN'T EVEN DO THAT PROPERLY!
...Are you gonna give me some Lamisil or what?
...I'll get my medbag.
www.terminallance.com
Created by Maximilian Uriarte © 2016

"Love/Hate"
Why are you still here? I thought you were going out with that girl again tonight.
Nah, I broke it off.
Why?
She was just crazy, man. She was so controlling, got mad at me all the time, always kept tabs on me, told me what to do... I just couldn't take it anymore.
...Is her name Marine Corps?
www.terminallance.com
Created by Maximilian Uriarte © 2016

"Super ~~Soldier~~ Marine"

www.terminallance.com Created by Maximilian Uriarte © 2016

"Sick"

www.terminallance.com Created by Maximilian Uriarte © 2016

"Rising Sun"

www.terminallance.com Created by Maximilian Uriarte © 2016

"Election 2016 Part I: Trumped"

www.terminallance.com

Created by Maximilian Uriarte © 2016

"Election 2016 Part II: Hillary"

www.terminallance.com

Created by Maximilian Uriarte © 2016

"New Corps II"

www.terminallance.com

Created by Maximilian Uriarte © 2016

"Special Insignia"

www.terminallance.com Created by Maximilian Uriarte © 2016

"Founded in a Tavern"

www.terminallance.com Created by Maximilian Uriarte © 2016

"High-Tech"

www.terminallance.com Created by Maximilian Uriarte © 2016

"PT Stud"

www.terminallance.com Created by Maximilian Uriarte © 2016

"Debatable"

www.terminallance.com Created by Maximilian Uriarte © 2016

"Page Master"

www.terminallance.com Created by Maximilian Uriarte © 2016

"Absentee"

www.terminallance.com Created by Maximilian Uriarte © 2016

"Usually Some of the Time"

www.terminallance.com Created by Maximilian Uriarte © 2016

"New Species Unlocked!"

www.terminallance.com Created by Maximilian Uriarte © 2016

"The Gift"

www.terminallance.com

Created by Maximilian Uriarte © 2016

"Giving Instead of Receiving"

www.terminallance.com

Created by Maximilian Uriarte © 2016

"Change of Command 2017"

www.terminallance.com

Created by Maximilian Uriarte © 2017

"Frenetic Training Schedule"

www.terminallance.com

Created by [illegible] © 2017

The Characters of Terminal Lance

A number of characters have graced the panels of *Terminal Lance* comics over the years. Here are some of the recurring ones you will run across throughout the *Terminal Lance* lexicon!

Abraham Belatzeko

FIRST APPEARANCE: #1 "How Nicknames Are Born"
Abe is a plucky, smartass 0351 Infantry Assaultman stationed in Hawaii. For all intents and purposes, Abe is considered the "main" character of *Terminal Lance*. Abe went without a name for a long time, simply acting as an avatar of sorts for creator Maximilian Uriarte. It wasn't until Max began writing *The White Donkey* that Abe was graced with a name. Abe and Max still share a lot of similarities—"Abe" is even Max's platoon nickname because his last name is too difficult for other Marines to pronounce properly.

Jesus Garcia

FIRST APPEARANCE: #93 "POG's Impressing the Grunts"
Garcia is Abe's barracks roommate as well as his best friend. As with Abe, it wasn't until *The White Donkey* that Garcia became a named, recurring character of the strip. Since then, the strip has primarily been about the Marine Corps adventures of Abe and Garcia. Garcia, with his relaxed demeanor and willingness to suck it up, often acts as a voice of reason for Abe. Garcia thrives in the Marine Corps lifestyle because, unlike Abe, he tends to roll with the punches instead of complain about them.

Boot

FIRST APPEARANCE: #363 "Boot (Camp) Stories"
While boots have been featured in *Terminal Lance* since the beginning, the character really didn't take shape in his current form until #363. It was at this point that boots were to be forever denoted with their characteristic beady eyes, which serve as a metaphor for their unenlightened state. Always wearing his CamelBak and high and tight haircut, Boot exists at the whim of his senior Lance Corporals and leadership. His life is terrible, but no one cares because he's a fucking boot.

Drill Instructor

FIRST APPEARANCE: #59 "Knife-Hand Anger Gauge"
Drill Instructors are as iconic to the Marine Corps as camouflage and rifles, and make frequent appearances in *Terminal Lance* comics surrounding the subject of boot camp. With their frogged voices and overall angry, sweaty demeanor, Drill Instructors practically caricature-ize themselves. While there's no single recurring Drill Instructor character, you'll find them frequently throughout the comic.

First Sergeant

FIRST APPEARANCE: #446 "Logged"
First Sergeant has had many appearances throughout the panels of *Terminal Lance,* but it is only recently that he has been locked into a recurring character design. First Sergeant is vindictive, dark, and openly hateful of the Lance Corporals under his command. Perhaps he was once a normal Marine, but the corruption of the green weenie has seeped into the very fiber of his soul. He no longer remembers the taste of wine, or the smell of fresh flowers. He just knows the hate he has for his Marines.

Creepy Chaplain

FIRST APPEARANCE: #160 "Working (It) at the Car Wash"
While the Creepy Chaplain character is undoubtedly somewhat outdated at this point, he remains a fan favorite. The inspiration for the Creepy Chaplain was simply the fact that Chaplains are often just a little bit creepy. Frequently loitering about the base swimming pool and ball fundraiser car washes, the Creepy Chaplain creeps everyone out on the regular, but he's all the battalion has for their religious leadership.

Chongo and Old Man

FIRST APPEARANCE: #214 "Meritorious"
Throughout the *Terminal Lance* library, Chongo serves as a representation of the military's often absurd culture in a "real world" business environment. Chongo is not smart, but he's the perfect Marine. He can run really fast, do lots of pull-ups, and shoot really good. For whatever reason, Old Man serves as his handler, often verbally making the case for him since Chongo can't speak English properly.

Angry Facebook Veteran

FIRST APPEARANCE: "Offended"
With a social media footprint as large as *Terminal Lance,* it comes as no surprise that we get our fair share of Angry Facebook Veterans. The Angry Facebook Veteran is that douchebag everyone knows who uses his veteran status as a qualifier for every terrible opinion he has. He has declared himself an authority on all things patriotic and believes himself to be an expert on foreign policy due to his extensive four years of being lower enlisted. He bitched about the Marine Corps every day, but now that he's out, he makes sure you know he was a Marine by wearing a moto hat and setting all his profile pictures to Eagle, Globe, and Anchors.

1171 Water Dog

FIRST APPEARANCE: #106 "The Water Dog"

The 1171 Water Dog is colloquially known throughout the Corps as "The Most POG MOS in Existence." Okay, not really, but it should be. You'll find throughout the *Terminal Lance* collection that creator Maximilian has a personal vendetta against the 1171 Water Dog. This was due to one real-life incident where he was stuck on the rifle range next to the only one he's ever met, who was obnoxiously overconfident and hit on every woman around him despite the fact that they were painfully uninterested in him. Because of this, Max never skips an opportunity to shit on them and encourages everyone else to as well.

The Ghost of Chesty Puller

FIRST APPEARANCE: #98 "Unexpected Guest"

Lewis B. (Chesty) Puller was a revered and highly decorated Marine officer of World War II and the Korean War. He is beloved throughout the Corps culture and often referred to in times of great motivation. It is because of this that his ghost occasionally appears to impart upon Marines the wisdom of the Old Corps. The Ghost of Chesty Puller recurs in *Terminal Lance* to settle petty arguments and to bring peace to the Corps.

The Evolution of Terminal Lance Artwork

As both the artist and writer behind *Terminal Lance,* I've spent a lot of time over the years crafting comic strips from start to finish. As you may have noticed from reading the comics, the artwork has changed considerably since the beginning. There's a lot of reasons for this, including the tools I use as well as my own improvement as an illustrator. Below I've broken down the artwork into the various "eras" of *Terminal Lance* art.

The First Comics

The first thirty-four comics are notable because they were all done while I was active duty aboard Marine Corps Base Hawaii, Kaneohe Bay. They are also the only comic strips in the *Terminal Lance* collection that were done with real media (ink on bristol vellum).

The linework in these first thirty-four strips tends to be a bit cleaner and more uniform because it was done with micron pens. While there is always something to be said about doing work in real media, it ultimately ended up being unnecessarily time consuming since all the text was done digitally anyway.

Fresh Out

Right after leaving the Marine Corps, I spent the summer with my mom in Oregon and had to put most of my stuff in storage. This meant that I didn't really have anywhere to sit down and draw my comic, so I began drawing them 100 percent digitally with a WACOM Intuos tablet.

For whatever reason, this meant that a lot of the artwork drifted into a much looser area. The brushstrokes are scattered and more gestural, mostly because I didn't particularly like drawing tight ink work on the screenless drawing device. However, from this time forward all of the *Terminal Lance* comics became completely digital.

The Loose Ages

Utilizing the wonderful Post-9/11 GI Bill to attend animation school at the California College of Arts in Oakland, I started making the artwork for *Terminal Lance* increasingly loose and, frankly, a little sloppy. As a fan of gestural animation art, I had a lot of trouble locking down a visual style for the comic. As a result, the comics from this period were drawn without much focus, making them visually inconsistent from strip to strip.

Foundations

The early half of 2013 saw me refining the *Terminal Lance* style into a vestigial version of what you see today. You'll notice the linework is a little bit less sloppy, but still looser, with a consistent line width that is visually easier on the eyes.

I always considered myself more of a naturalist artist, and at this point I was still fighting the need to get more stylized and cartoony with the comic.

Style

In the latter part of 2013, I began working on the graphic novel *The White Donkey*. This came with the purchase of some new equipment, notably a WACOM Cintiq monitor that allowed me to draw directly on the screen. This was a game changer for *Terminal Lance*, as it allowed me to focus less on my technical limitations and more on nailing a consistent look for the comic strip.

The artwork in this period tends to be a bit cleaner, leaning closer to a more stylized cartoon look.

Flow

The modern look of *Terminal Lance* was developed in conjunction with my own development of some character designs meant for animation. The focus was mostly on what I like to refer to as the flow of lines, all done in singular sweeping gestures with the pen. This greatly informed the comic, giving everything a more polished and "animated" look that you could see in a TV cartoon series.

I fought doing cartoon art for a long time, but the more I worked with this style the more I enjoyed it. It also made me realize that cartoon work requires a lot of discipline and skill, which I was only able to accomplish after years and hundreds of comics.

We'll see where the comic goes from here, but this is a look that I am quite happy with. It is uniquely my own as well as uniquely *Terminal Lance*.

Acknowledgments

Terminal Lance has been a long journey from my active duty days in Hawaii to now, and I owe its success to many people that have helped me along the way.

First and foremost, the fans of *Terminal Lance* who have supported the comic and keep it going with enthusiasm and love. Additionally, the Marine Corps itself for embracing the comic and continuing to read my weekly rants online and otherwise.

The editorial staff over at the *Marine Corps Times,* while shifting through different members over the years, has always maintained a great relationship with me and *Terminal Lance.* Notably, Andrew DeGrandpre (who now resides at the *Washington Post*), was a vocal proponent of *Terminal Lance* in its early days and really helped me by putting the comic in front of a wider audience.

There are many more notable individuals I could name here, but I want to give special attention to my literary agent, Katie Boyle, and my lawyer, Susan Grode, for taking chances on my work and helping me take it all to the next level.

And, of course, the people of Little, Brown, for allowing me to grace their fine brand with a lot of very terrible jokes and crudely drawn phalluses.

About the Author

Photograph by Gabor Szantai

Terminal Lance Ultimate Omnibus was written and illustrated by infantry Marine and Iraq veteran Maximilian Uriarte, creator of the hit comic strip *Terminal Lance* and author of *New York Times* bestseller *The White Donkey*. Uriarte enlisted in the United States Marine Corps in 2006 at the age of nineteen and served for four years. During his first deployment to Iraq in 2007 he served as an MRAP turret gunner and dismount of India Company's "Jump" platoon in the Zaidon region southeast of Fallujah. He deployed to Iraq again in 2009 as a billeted Combat Photographer and Combat Artist, then enrolling in California College of the Arts. In 2010 Uriarte created *Terminal Lance* while still on active duty. The strip is now published in *The Marine Corps Times* and has grown immensely in popularity.